SPECIALIST

MICROSOFT®
EXCEL
2003

NITA RUTKOSKY

Pierce College at Puyallup
Puyallup, Washington

EMCParadigm
PUBLISHING

Project Editor	Sonja Brown
Developmental Editor	Courtney Kost
Senior Designer	Leslie Anderson
Technical Reviewer	Desiree Faulkner
Cover Designer	Jennifer Wreisner
Copyeditor	Susan Capecchi
Desktop Production Specialists	Erica Tava, Lisa Beller
Proofreader	Kathryn Savoie
Indexer	Nancy Fulton
Photo Researcher	Paul Spencer

Publishing Team—George Provol, Publisher; Janice Johnson, Director of Product Development and Instructional Design; Tony Galvin, Acquisitions Editor; Lori Landwer, Marketing Manager; Shelley Clubb, Electronic Design and Production Manager

Acknowledgments—The author and editors wish to thank the following instructors for their technical and academic contributions:

- Nancy Graviett, St. Charles Co. Community College, St. Peters, MO, for preparing the IG materials
- Susan Lynn Bowen, Valdosta Technical College, Valdosta, GA, for testing the exercises and assessing instruction
- Ann Lewis, Ivy Tech State College, Evansville, IN, for creating the Chapter Challenge case studies
- Denise Seguin, Fanshawe College, London, Ontario, Canada, for writing the introductions to Word 2003, Excel 2003, Access 2003, and PowerPoint 2003

Photo Credits: S1, (top to bottom) Owaki – Kulla/CORBIS, CORBIS, Rob Lewine/CORBIS; S2, AFP/CORBIS; S3, Jose Luis Pelaez, Inc./CORBIS; S4, LWA-JDC/CORBIS

Library of Congress Cataloging-in-Publication Data

Rutkosky, Nita Hewitt.
    Microsoft Excel 2003. Specialist / Nita Rutkosky.
      p. cm. -- (Benchmark series)
    Includes index.
    ISBN 0-7638-2047-4 (text)
1. Microsoft Excel (Computer file) 2. Business--Computer programs. 3. Electronic spreadsheets. I. Title. II. Benchmark series (Saint Paul, Minn.)

HF5548.4.M523R887 2004
005.54--dc22

2003060317

Care has been taken to verify the accuracy of information presented in this book. However, the author, editors, and publisher cannot accept any responsibility for Web, e-mail, newsgroup, or chat room subject matter or content, or for consequences from application of the information in this book, and make no warranty, expressed or implied, with respect to its content.

Trademarks: Some of the product names and company names included in this book have been used for identification purposes only and may be trademarks or registered trademarks of their respective manufacturers and sellers. The author, editors, and publisher disclaim any affiliation, association, or connection with, or sponsorship or endorsement by, such owners.

Microsoft and the Microsoft Office Logo are trademarks or registered trademarks of Microsoft Corporation in the United States and/or other countries, and the Microsoft Office Specialist Logo is used under license from owner.

EMC/Paradigm Publishing is independent from Microsoft Corporation, and not affiliated with Microsoft in any manner. This publication may be used in assisting students to prepare for a Microsoft Office Specialist Exam. Neither Microsoft, its designated program administrator or courseware reviewer, nor EMC/Paradigm Publishing warrants that use of this publication will ensure passing the relevant exam.

Text: ISBN 0-7638-2047-4
Product Number 05617

© 2004 by Paradigm Publishing, Inc.
    Published by EMCParadigm
    875 Montreal Way
    St. Paul, MN 55102

    (800) 535-6865
    E-mail: educate@emcp.com
    Web site: www.emcp.com

Printed in the United States of America
10 9 8 7 6 5

CONTENTS

EXCEL

WELCOME

You are about to begin working with a textbook that is part of the Benchmark Office 2003 Series. The word *Benchmark* in the title holds a special significance in terms of *what* you will learn and *how* you will learn. *Benchmark*, according to *Webster's Dictionary*, means "something that serves as a standard by which others may be measured or judged." In this text, you will learn the Microsoft Office Specialist skills required for certification on the Specialist and/or Expert level of one or more major applications within the Office 2003 suite. These skills are benchmarks by which you will be evaluated, should you choose to take one or more certification exams.

The design and teaching approach of this textbook also serve as a benchmark for instructional materials on software programs. Features and commands are presented in a clear, straightforward way, and each short section of instruction is followed by an exercise that lets you practice using the new feature. Gradually, as you move through each chapter, you will build your skills to the point of mastery. At the end of a chapter, you are offered the opportunity to demonstrate your newly acquired competencies—to prove you have met the benchmarks for using the Office suite or an individual program. At the completion of the text, you are well on your way to becoming a successful computer user.

EMC/Paradigm's Office 2003 Benchmark Series includes textbooks on Office 2003, Word 2003, Excel 2003, Access 2003 and PowerPoint 2003. Each book includes a Student CD, which contains documents and files required for completing the exercises. A CD icon and folder name displayed on the opening page of each chapter indicates that you need to copy a folder of files from the CD before beginning the chapter exercises. *(See the inside back cover for instructions on copying a folder.)*

Introducing Microsoft Office 2003

Microsoft Office 2003 is a suite of programs designed to improve productivity and efficiency in workplace, school, and home settings. A suite is a group of programs that are sold as a package and are designed to be used together, making it possible to exchange files among the programs. The major applications included in Office are Word, a word processing program; Excel, a spreadsheet program; Access, a database management program; and PowerPoint, a slide presentation program.

Using the Office suite offers significant advantages over working with individual programs developed by different software vendors. The programs in the Office suite use similar toolbars, buttons, icons, and menus, which means that once you learn the basic features of one program, you can use those same features in the other programs. This easy transfer of knowledge decreases the learning time and allows you to concentrate on the unique commands and options within each program. The compatibility of the programs creates seamless integration of data within and between programs and lets the operator use the program most appropriate for the required tasks.

New Features in Office 2003

Users of previous editions of Office will find that the essential features that have made Office popular still form the heart of the suite. New enhancements include improved templates for both business and personal use. The Smart Tags introduced in Office XP also have been enhanced in Office 2003 with special customization options. One of the most far-reaching changes is the introduction of XML (eXtensible Markup Language) capabilities. Some elements of this technology were essentially hidden behind the scenes in Office XP. Now XML has been brought to the forefront. XML enables data to be used more flexibly and stored regardless of the computer platform. It can be used between different languages, countries, and across the Internet. XML heralds a revolution in data exchange. At the same time, it makes efficient and effective use of internal data within a business.

Structure of the Benchmark Textbooks

Users of the Specialist Certification texts and the complete application textbooks may begin their course with an overview of computer hardware and software, offered in the *Getting Started* section at the beginning of the book. Your instructor may also ask you to complete the *Windows XP* and the *Internet Explorer* sections so you become familiar with the computer's operating system and the essential tools for using the Internet.

Instruction on the major programs within the Office suite is presented in units of four chapters each. Both the Specialist and Expert levels contain two units, which culminate with performance assessments to check your knowledge and skills. Each chapter contains the following sections:

- performance objectives that identify specifically what you are expected to learn
- instructional text that introduces and explains new concepts and features
- step-by-step, hands-on exercises following each section of instruction
- a chapter summary
- a knowledge self-check called Concepts Check
- skill assessment exercises called Skills Check
- a case study exercise called Chapter Challenge

Exercises offered at the end of units provide writing and research opportunities that will strengthen your performance in other college courses as well as on the job. The final activities simulate interesting projects you could encounter in the workplace.

Benchmark Series Ancillaries

The Benchmark Series includes some important resources that will help you succeed in your computer applications courses:

Snap Training and Assessment

A Web-based program designed to optimize skill-based learning for all of the programs of Microsoft Office 2003, Snap is comprised of:

- a learning management system that creates a virtual classroom on the Web, allowing the instructor to schedule tutorials and tests and to employ an electronic gradebook;
- over 200 interactive, multimedia tutorials, aligned to textbook chapters, that can be used for direct instruction or remediation;
- a test bank of over 1,800 performance skill items that simulate the operation of Microsoft Office and allow the instructor to assign pretests, to administer chapter posttests, and to create practice tests to help students prepare for Microsoft Office Specialist certification exams; and
- over 6,000 concept items that can be used in combined concepts/application courses to monitor student understanding of technical and computer literacy knowledge.

Online Resource Center

Internet Resource Centers hosted by EMC/Paradigm provide additional material for students and instructors using the Benchmark books. Online you will find Web links, updates to textbooks, study tips, quizzes and assignments, and supplementary projects.

Class Connection

Available for both WebCT and Blackboard, EMC/Paradigm's Class Connection is a course management tool for traditional and distance learning.

What does this logo mean?

It means this courseware has been approved by the Microsoft® Office Specialist program to be among the finest available for learning Microsoft Excel 2003. It also means that upon completion of this courseware, you may be prepared to take an exam for Microsoft Office Specialist qualification.

What is a Microsoft Office Specialist?

A Microsoft Office Specialist is an individual who has passed exams for certifying his or her skills in one or more of the Microsoft Office desktop applications such as Microsoft Word, Microsoft Excel, Microsoft PowerPoint, Microsoft Outlook, Microsoft Access, or Microsoft Project. The Microsoft Office Specialist Program typically offers certification exams at the Specialist and Expert skill levels. The Microsoft Office Specialist Program is the only program in the world approved by Microsoft for testing proficiency in Microsoft Office desktop applications and Microsoft Project. This testing program can be a valuable asset in any job search or career advancement.

More Information

- To learn more about becoming a Microsoft Office Specialist, visit www.microsoft.com/officespecialist
- To learn about other Microsoft Office Specialist approved courseware from EMC/Paradigm Publishing, visit www.emcp.com

Tom Tidwell

OFFICE **2003**

GETTING STARTED IN OFFICE 2003

In this textbook, you will learn to operate several microcomputer application programs that combine to make an application "suite." This suite of programs is called Microsoft Office 2003. The programs you will learn to operate are the **software**, which include instructions telling the computer what to do. Some of the software programs in the suite include a word processing program called *Word*, a spreadsheet program called *Excel*, a presentation program called *PowerPoint*, and a database program called *Access*.

Identifying Computer Hardware

The computer equipment you will use to operate the suite of programs is referred to as **hardware**. You will need access to a microcomputer system that should consist of the CPU, monitor, keyboard, printer, disk drives, and mouse. If you are not sure what equipment you will be operating, check with your instructor. The computer system displayed in Figure G.1 consists of six components. Each component is discussed separately in the material that follows.

FIGURE

G.1 *Microcomputer System*

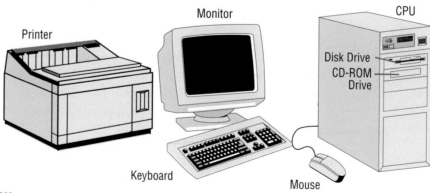

CPU

CPU stands for Central Processing Unit and it is the intelligence of the computer. All the processing occurs in the CPU. Silicon chips, which contain miniaturized circuitry, are placed on boards that are plugged into slots within the CPU. Whenever an instruction is given to the computer, that instruction is processed through circuitry in the CPU.

Monitor

The monitor is a piece of equipment that looks like a television screen. It displays the information of a program and the text being input at the keyboard. The quality of display for monitors varies depending on the type of monitor and the level of resolution. Monitors can also vary in size—generally from 14-inch size up to 21-inch size or larger.

Keyboard

The keyboard is used to input information into the computer. Keyboards for microcomputers vary in the number and location of the keys. Microcomputers have the alphabetic and numeric keys in the same location as the keys on a typewriter. The symbol keys, however, may be placed in a variety of locations, depending on the manufacturer. In addition to letters, numbers, and symbols, most microcomputer keyboards contain function keys, arrow keys, and a numeric keypad. Figure G.2 shows an enhanced keyboard.

FIGURE

G.2 **Microcomputer Enhanced Keyboard**

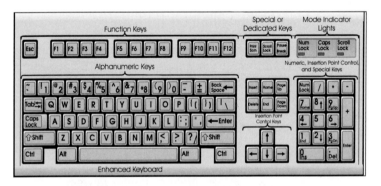

The 12 keys at the top of the enhanced keyboard, labeled with the letter F followed by a number, are called *function keys*. These keys can be used to perform functions within each of the suite programs. To the right of the regular keys is a group of *special* or *dedicated keys*. These keys are labeled with specific functions that will be performed when you press the key. Below the special keys are arrow keys. These keys are used to move the insertion point in the document screen.

In the upper right corner of the keyboard are three mode indicator lights. When certain modes have been selected, a light appears on the keyboard. For example, if you press the Caps Lock key, which disables the lowercase alphabet, a light appears next to Caps Lock. Similarly, pressing the Num Lock key will disable the special functions on the numeric keypad, which is located at the right side of the keyboard.

Disk Drives

Depending on the computer system you are using, Microsoft Office 2003 is installed on a hard drive or as part of a network system. Whether you are using

Office on a hard drive or network system, you will need to have available a CD drive and a floppy disk drive or other storage media. You will insert the CD (compact disk) that accompanies this textbook in the CD drive and then copy folders from the CD to a disk in the floppy disk drive. You will also save documents you complete at the computer to folders on your disk in the floppy drive.

Printer

When you create a document in Word, it is considered **soft copy**. If you want a **hard copy** of a document, you need to print it. To print documents you will need to access a printer, which will probably be either a laser printer or an ink-jet printer. A laser printer uses a laser beam combined with heat and pressure to print documents, while an ink-jet printer prints a document by spraying a fine mist of ink on the page.

Mouse

Many functions in the suite of programs are designed to operate more efficiently with a **mouse**. A mouse is an input device that sits on a flat surface next to the computer. A mouse can be operated with the left or the right hand. Moving the mouse on the flat surface causes a corresponding mouse pointer to move on the screen. Figure G.1 shows an illustration of a mouse.

Using the Mouse

The programs in the Microsoft Office suite can be operated using a keyboard or they can be operated with the keyboard and a mouse. The mouse may have two or three buttons on top, which are tapped to execute specific functions and commands. To use the mouse, rest it on a flat surface or a mouse pad. Put your hand over it with your palm resting on top of the mouse and your wrist resting on the table surface. As you move the mouse on the flat surface, a corresponding pointer moves on the screen.

When using the mouse, there are four terms you should understand—point, click, double-click, and drag. When operating the mouse, you may need to **point** to a specific command, button, or icon. Point means to position the mouse pointer on the desired item. With the mouse pointer positioned on the desired item, you may need to **click** a button on the mouse. Click means quickly tapping a button on the mouse once. To complete two steps at one time, such as choosing and then executing a function, **double-click** a mouse button. Double-click means to tap the left mouse button twice in quick succession. The term **drag** means to press and hold the left mouse button, move the mouse pointer to a specific location, and then release the button.

Using the Mouse Pointer

The mouse pointer will change appearance depending on the function being performed or where the pointer is positioned. The mouse pointer may appear as one of the following images:

The mouse pointer appears as an I-beam (called the **I-beam pointer**) in the document screen and can be used to move the insertion point or select text.

The mouse pointer appears as an arrow pointing up and to the left (called the **arrow pointer**) when it is moved to the Title bar, Menu bar, or one of the toolbars at the top of the screen or when a dialog box is displayed. For example, to open a new document with the mouse, you would move the I-beam pointer to the File option on the Menu bar. When the I-beam pointer is moved to the Menu bar, it turns into an arrow pointer. To make a selection, position the tip of the arrow pointer on the File option, and then click the left mouse button. At the drop-down menu that displays, make selections by positioning the arrow pointer on the desired option and then clicking the left mouse button.

The mouse pointer becomes a double-headed arrow (either pointing left and right, pointing up and down, or pointing diagonally) when performing certain functions such as changing the size of an object.

In certain situations, such as moving an object or image, the mouse pointer becomes a four-headed arrow. The four-headed arrow means that you can move the object left, right, up, or down.

When a request is being processed or when a program is being loaded, the mouse pointer may appear with an hourglass beside it. The hourglass image means "please wait." When the process is completed, the hourglass image is removed.

The mouse pointer displays as a hand with a pointing index finger in certain functions such as Help and indicates that more information is available about the item.

Choosing Commands

Once a program is open, several methods can be used in the program to choose commands. A command is an instruction that tells the program to do something. You can choose a command with one of the following methods:

- Click a toolbar button with the mouse
- Choose a command from a menu
- Use shortcut keys
- Use a shortcut menu

Choosing Commands on Toolbars

When a program such as Word or PowerPoint is open, several toolbars containing buttons for common tasks are available. In many of the suite programs, two toolbars are visible on the screen. One toolbar is called the Standard toolbar; the other is referred to as the Formatting toolbar. To choose a command from a toolbar, position the tip of the arrow pointer on a button, and then click the left mouse button. For example, to print the file currently displayed in the screen, position the tip of the arrow pointer on the Print button on the Standard toolbar, and then click the left mouse button.

Choosing Commands on the Menu Bar

Each of the suite programs contains a Menu bar that displays toward the top of the screen. This Menu bar contains a variety of options you can use to perform functions and commands on data. Functions are grouped logically into options, which display on the Menu bar. For example, features to work with files are grouped in the File option. Either the mouse or the keyboard can be used to make choices from the Menu bar or make a choice at a dialog box.

To use the mouse to make a choice from the Menu bar, move the I-beam pointer to the Menu bar. This causes the I-beam pointer to display as an arrow pointer. Position the tip of the arrow pointer on the desired option, and then click the left mouse button.

To use the keyboard, press the Alt key to make the Menu bar active. Options on the Menu bar display with an underline below one of the letters. To choose an option from the Menu bar, type the underlined letter of the desired option, or move the insertion point with the Left or Right Arrow keys to the option desired, and then press Enter. This causes a drop-down menu to display.

For example, to display the File drop-down menu in Word as shown in Figure G.3 using the mouse, position the arrow pointer on File on the Menu bar, and then click the left mouse button. To display the File drop-down menu with the keyboard, press the Alt key, and then type the letter F for File.

FIGURE

G.3 | *Word File Drop-Down Menu*

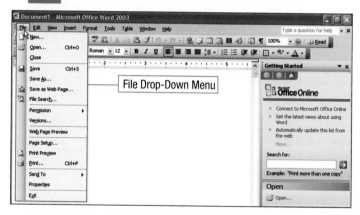

File Drop-Down Menu

Choosing Commands from Drop-Down Menus

To choose a command from a drop-down menu with the mouse, position the arrow pointer on the desired option, and then click the left mouse button. At the drop-down menu that displays, move the arrow pointer down the menu to the desired option, and then click the left mouse button.

To make a selection from the drop-down menu with the keyboard, type the underlined letter of the desired option. Once the drop-down menu displays, you do not need to hold down the Alt key with the underlined letter. If you want to close a drop-down menu without making a choice, click in the screen outside the drop-down menu, or press the Esc key twice.

If an option can be accessed by clicking a button on a toolbar, the button is displayed preceding the option in the drop-down menu. For example, buttons display before the New, Open, Save, Save as Web Page, File Search, Print Preview, and Print options at the File drop-down menu (see Figure G.3).

Some menu options may be gray shaded (dimmed). When an option is dimmed, that option is currently not available. For example, if you choose the Table option on the Menu bar, the Table drop-down menu displays with dimmed options including Merge Cells, Split Cells, and Split Table.

Some menu options are preceded by a check mark. The check mark indicates that the option is currently active. To make an option inactive (turn it off) using the mouse, position the arrow pointer on the option, and then click the left mouse button. To make an option inactive with the keyboard, type the underlined letter of the option.

If an option from a drop-down menu displays followed by an ellipsis (...), a dialog box will display when that option is chosen. A dialog box provides a variety of options to let you specify how a command is to be carried out. For example, if you choose File and then Print from the PowerPoint Menu bar, the Print dialog box displays as shown in Figure G.4.

FIGURE

G.4 *PowerPoint Print Dialog Box*

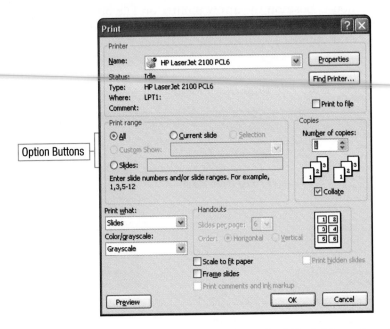

Or, if you choose Format and then Font from the Word Menu bar, the Font dialog box displays as shown in Figure G.5.

FIGURE

G.5 *Word Font Dialog Box*

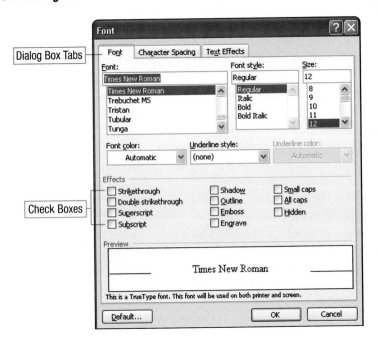

Some dialog boxes provide a set of options. These options are contained on separate tabs. For example, the Font dialog box shown in Figure G.5 contains a tab at the top of the dialog box with the word Font on it. Two other tabs display to the right of the Font tab—Character Spacing and Text Effects. The tab that displays in the front is the active tab. To make a tab active using the mouse, position the arrow pointer on the desired tab, and then click the left mouse button. If you are using the keyboard, press Ctrl + Tab or press Alt + the underlined letter on the desired tab. For example, to change the tab to Character Spacing in the Font dialog box, click Character Spacing, or press Ctrl + Tab, or press Alt + R.

To choose options from a dialog box with the mouse, position the arrow pointer on the desired option, and then click the left mouse button. If you are using the keyboard, press the Tab key to move the insertion point forward from option to option. Press Shift + Tab to move the insertion point backward from option to option. You can also hold down the Alt key and then press the underlined letter of the desired option. When an option is selected, it displays either in reverse video (white letters on a dark background) or surrounded by a dashed box called a *marquee*.

A dialog box contains one or more of the following elements: text boxes, list boxes, check boxes, option buttons, spin boxes, and command buttons.

Text Boxes

Some options in a dialog box require text to be entered. For example, the boxes below the *Find what* and *Replace with* options at the Excel Find and Replace dialog box shown in Figure G.6 are text boxes. In a text box, you type text or edit existing text. Edit text in a text box in the same manner as normal text. Use the Left and Right Arrow keys on the keyboard to move the insertion point without deleting text and use the Delete key or Backspace key to delete text.

FIGURE

G.6 **Excel Find and Replace Dialog Box**

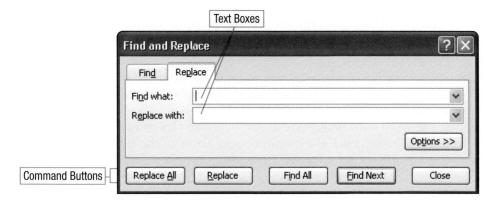

List Boxes

Some dialog boxes such as the Access Open dialog box shown in Figure G.7 may contain a list box. The list of files below the *Look in* option is contained in a list box. To make a selection from a list box with the mouse, move the arrow pointer to the desired option, and then click the left mouse button.

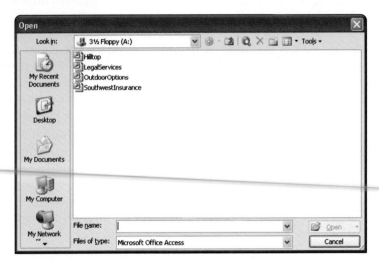

Some list boxes may contain a scroll bar. This scroll bar will display at the right side of the list box (a vertical scroll bar) or at the bottom of the list box (a horizontal scroll bar). Either a vertical scroll bar or a horizontal scroll bar can be used to move through the list if the list is longer than the box. To move down through a list on a vertical scroll bar, position the arrow pointer on the down scroll triangle and hold down the left mouse button. To scroll up through the list in a vertical scroll bar, position the arrow pointer on the up-pointing arrow and hold down the left mouse button. You can also move the arrow pointer above the scroll box and click the left mouse button to scroll up the list or move the arrow pointer below the scroll box and click the left mouse button to move down the list. To move through a list with a horizontal scroll bar, click the left-pointing arrow to scroll to the left of the list or click the right-pointing arrow to scroll to the right of the list.

To make a selection from a list using the keyboard, move the insertion point into the box by holding down the Alt key and pressing the underlined letter of the desired option. Press the Up and/or Down Arrow keys on the keyboard to move through the list.

In some dialog boxes where enough room is not available for a list box, lists of options are inserted in a drop-down list box. Options that contain a drop-down list box display with a down-pointing arrow. For example, the *Underline style* option at the Word Font dialog box shown in Figure G.5 contains a drop-down list. To display the list, click the down-pointing arrow to the right of the *Underline style* option box. If you are using the keyboard, press Alt + U.

Check Boxes

Some dialog boxes contain options preceded by a box. A check mark may or may not appear in the box. The Word Font dialog box shown in Figure G.5 displays a variety of check boxes within the *Effects* section. If a check mark appears in the box, the option is active (turned on). If there is no check mark in the check box, the option is inactive (turned off).

Any number of check boxes can be active. For example, in the Word Font dialog box, you can insert a check mark in any or all of the boxes in the *Effects* section and these options will be active.

To make a check box active or inactive with the mouse, position the tip of the arrow pointer in the check box, and then click the left mouse button. If you are using the keyboard, press Alt + the underlined letter of the desired option.

Option Buttons

In the PowerPoint Print dialog box shown in Figure G.4, the options in the *Print range* section are preceded by option buttons. Only one option button can be selected at any time. When an option button is selected, a green circle displays in the button.

To select an option button with the mouse, position the tip of the arrow pointer inside the option button, and then click the left mouse button. To make a selection with the keyboard, hold down the Alt key, and then press the underlined letter of the desired option.

Spin Boxes

Some options in a dialog box contain measurements or numbers that can be increased or decreased. These options are generally located in a spin box. For example, the Word Paragraph dialog box shown in Figure G.8 contains spin boxes located after the *Left*, *Right*, *Before*, and *After* options. To increase a number in a spin box, position the tip of the arrow pointer on the up-pointing arrow to the right of the desired option, and then click the left mouse button. To decrease the number, click the down-pointing arrow. If you are using the keyboard, press Alt + the underlined letter of the desired option, and then press the Up Arrow key to increase the number or the Down Arrow key to decrease the number.

FIGURE

G.8 **Word Paragraph Dialog Box**

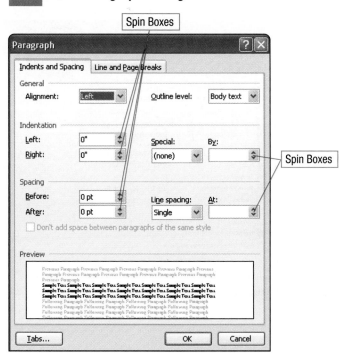

Command Buttons

In the Excel Find and Replace dialog box shown in Figure G.6, the boxes along the bottom of the dialog box are called *command buttons*. A command button is used to execute or cancel a command. Some command buttons display with an ellipsis (...). A command button that displays with an ellipsis will open another dialog box. To choose a command button with the mouse, position the arrow pointer on the desired button, and then click the left mouse button. To choose a command button with the keyboard, press the Tab key until the desired command button contains the marquee, and then press the Enter key.

Choosing Commands with Shortcut Keys

At the left side of a drop-down menu is a list of options. At the right side, shortcut keys for specific options may display. For example, the shortcut keys to save a document are Ctrl + S and are displayed to the right of the Save option at the File drop-down menu shown in Figure G.3. To use shortcut keys to choose a command, hold down the Ctrl key, type the letter for the command, and then release the Ctrl key.

Choosing Commands with Shortcut Menus

The software programs in the suite include menus that contain commands related to the item with which you are working. A shortcut menu appears right where you are working in the document. To display a shortcut menu, click the *right* mouse button or press Shift + F10.

For example, if the insertion point is positioned in a paragraph of text in a Word document, clicking the *right* mouse button or pressing Shift + F10 will cause the shortcut menu shown in Figure G.9 to display in the document screen.

FIGURE

G.9 **Word Shortcut Menu**

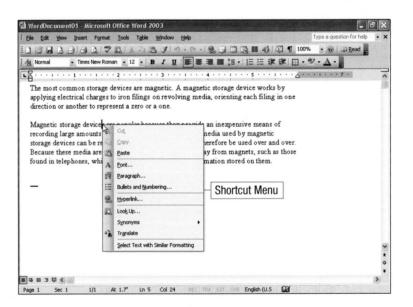

Getting Started

To select an option from a shortcut menu with the mouse, click the desired option. If you are using the keyboard, press the Up or Down Arrow key until the desired option is selected, and then press the Enter key. To close a shortcut menu without choosing an option, click anywhere outside the shortcut menu or press the Esc key.

Working with Multiple Programs

As you learn the various programs in the Microsoft Office suite, you will notice how executing commands in each is very similar. For example, the steps to save, close, and print are virtually the same whether you are working in Word, Excel, or PowerPoint. This consistency between programs greatly enhances a user's ability to easily transfer knowledge learned in one program to another within the suite.

Another appeal of Microsoft Office is the ability to have more than one program open at the same time. For example, you can open Word, create a document, and then open Excel, create a spreadsheet, and copy the spreadsheet into Word.

When a program is open, the name of the program, followed by the file name, displays in a button on the Taskbar. When another program is opened, the program name and file name display in a button that is positioned to the right of the first program button. Figure G.10 shows the Taskbar with Word, Excel, and PowerPoint open. To move from one program to another, all you need to do is click the button on the Taskbar representing the desired program file.

FIGURE

| G.10 | *Taskbar with Word, Excel, and PowerPoint Open* |

Completing Computer Exercises

Some computer exercises in this textbook require that you open an existing file. Exercise files are saved on the Student CD that accompanies this textbook. The files you need for each chapter are saved in individual folders. Before beginning a chapter, copy the necessary folder from the CD to a preformatted data disk. After completing exercises in a chapter, delete the chapter folder before copying the next chapter folder. (Check with your instructor before deleting a folder.)

The Student CD also contains model answers in PDF format for the exercises *within* (but not at the end of) each chapter so you can check your work. To access the PDF files, you will need to have Adobe Acrobat Reader installed on your computer's hard drive. The program and installation instructions are included on the Student CD in the AdobeAcrobatReader folder.

Copying a Folder

As you begin working in a chapter, copy the chapter folder from the CD to your disk. (Not every chapter contains a folder on the CD. For example, when completing exercises in the Access chapters, you will copy individual database files rather than individual chapter folders. Copy the chapter folder from the CD to your disk using the My Computer window by completing the following steps:

1. Insert the CD that accompanies this textbook in the CD drive.
2. Insert a formatted 3.5-inch disk in the disk drive.
3. At the Windows XP desktop, open the My Computer window by clicking the Start button and then clicking My Computer at the Start menu.
4. Double-click the CD drive in the contents pane (probably displays as *OFFICE2003_BENCH* followed by the drive letter).
5. Double-click the desired program folder name in the contents pane. (For example, if you are copying a folder for a Specialist Word chapter, double-click the *Word2003Specialist* folder.)
6. Click once on the desired chapter subfolder name to select it.
7. Click the Copy this folder hyperlink in the *File and Folder Tasks* section of the task pane.
8. At the Copy Items dialog box, click *3½ Floppy (A:)* in the list box and then click the Copy button.
9. After the folder is copied to your disk, close the My Computer window by clicking the Close button (white X on red background) that displays in the upper right corner of the window.

Deleting a Folder

Before copying a chapter folder onto your disk, delete any previous chapter folders. Do this in the My Computer window by completing the following steps:

1. Insert your disk in the disk drive.
2. At the Windows XP desktop, open the My Computer window by clicking the Start button and then clicking My Computer at the Start menu.
3. Double-click *3½ Floppy (A:)* in the contents pane.
4. Click the chapter folder in the list box.
5. Click the Delete this folder hyperlink in the *File and Folder Tasks* section of the task pane.
6. At the message asking if you want to remove the folder and all its contents, click the Yes button.
7. If a message displays asking if you want to delete a read-only file, click the Yes to All button.
8. Close the My Computer window by clicking the Close button (white X on red background) that displays in the upper right corner of the window.

Viewing or Printing the Exercise Model Answers

If you want to access the PDF model answer files, first make sure that Adobe Acrobat Reader is installed on your hard drive. (If it is not, installation instructions and the program file are available within the AdobeAcrobatReader folder on the Student CD.) Double-click the ExerciseModelAnswers(PDF) folder, double-click the desired chapter subfolder name, and double-click the appropriate file name to open the file. You can view and/or print the file to compare it with your own completed exercise file.

USING WINDOWS XP

A computer requires an operating system to provide necessary instructions on a multitude of processes including loading programs, managing data, directing the flow of information to peripheral equipment, and displaying information. Windows XP Professional is an operating system that provides functions of this type (along with much more) in a graphical environment. Windows is referred to as a ***graphical user interface*** (GUI—pronounced *gooey*) that provides a visual display of information with features such as icons (pictures) and buttons. In this introduction you will learn the basic features of Windows XP.

Historically, Microsoft has produced two editions of Windows—one edition for individual users (on desktop and laptop computers) and another edition for servers (on computers that provide service over networks). Windows XP is an upgrade and a merging of these two Windows editions and is available in two versions. The Windows XP Home Edition is designed for home use and Windows XP Professional is designed for small office and workstation use. Whether you are using Windows XP Home Edition or Windows XP Professional, you will be able to complete the steps in the exercises in this introduction.

Before using one of the software programs in the Microsoft Office suite, you will need to start the Windows XP operating system. To do this, turn on the computer. Depending on your computer equipment configuration, you may also need to turn on the monitor and printer. If you are using a computer that is part of a network system or if your computer is set up for multiple users, a screen will display showing the user accounts defined for your computer system. At this screen, click your user account name and, if necessary, type your password and then press the Enter key. The Windows XP operating system will start and, after a few moments, the desktop will display as shown in Figure W.1. (Your desktop may vary from what you see in Figure W.1.)

W.1 *Windows XP Desktop*

Exploring the Desktop

When Windows XP is loaded, the main portion of the screen is called the *desktop*. Think of the desktop in Windows as the top of a desk in an office. A business person places necessary tools—such as pencils, pens, paper, files, calculator—on the desktop to perform functions. Like the tools that are located on a desk, the desktop contains tools for operating the computer. These tools are logically grouped and placed in dialog boxes or panels that can be displayed using icons on the desktop. The desktop contains a variety of features for using your computer and software programs installed on the computer. The features available on the desktop are represented by icons and buttons.

Using Icons

Icons are visual symbols that represent programs, files, or folders. Figure W.1 identifies the *Recycle Bin* icon located on the Windows XP desktop. The Windows XP desktop on your computer may contain additional icons. Programs that have been installed on your computer may be represented by an icon on the desktop. Also, icons may display on your desktop representing files or folders. Double-click an icon and the program, file, or folder it represents opens on the desktop.

Using the Taskbar

The bar that displays at the bottom of the desktop (see Figure W.1) is called the *Taskbar*. The Taskbar, shown in Figure W.2, contains the Start button, a section that displays task buttons representing open programs, and the notification area.

W.2 *Windows XP Taskbar*

Start Button   Task Button Area   Notification Area

Click the Start button, located at the left side of the Taskbar, and the Start menu displays as shown in Figure W.3 (your Start menu may vary). You can also display the Start menu by pressing the Windows key on your keyboard or by pressing Ctrl + Esc. The left column of the Start menu contains pinned programs, which are programs that always appear in that particular location on the Start menu, and links to the most recently and frequently used programs. The right column contains links to folders, the Control Panel, online help, and the search feature.

F I G U R E

W.3 *Start Menu*

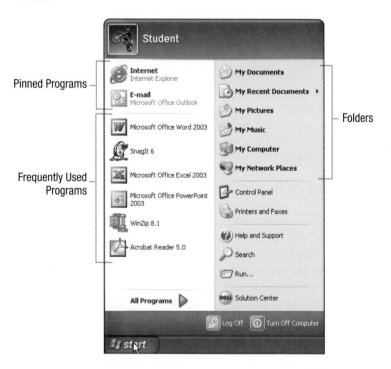

To choose an option from the Start menu, drag the arrow pointer to the desired option (referred to as *pointing*), and then click the left mouse button. Pointing to options at the Start menu followed by a right-pointing arrow will cause a side menu to display with additional options. When a program is open, a task button representing the program appears on the Taskbar. If multiple programs are open, each program will appear as a task button on the Taskbar (a few specialized tools may not).

exercise 1

1. Open Windows XP. (To do this, turn on the computer and, if necessary, turn on the monitor and/or printer. If you are using a computer that is part of a network system or if your computer is set up for multiple users, you may need to click your user account name and, if necessary, type your password and then press the Enter key. Check with your instructor to determine if you need to complete any additional steps.)

2. When the Windows XP desktop displays, open Microsoft Word by completing the following steps:

   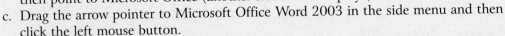

   Step 2d

   a. Position the arrow pointer on the Start button on the Taskbar and then click the left mouse button.
   b. At the Start menu, point to All Programs (a side menu displays) and then point to Microsoft Office (another side menu displays).
   c. Drag the arrow pointer to Microsoft Office Word 2003 in the side menu and then click the left mouse button.
   d. When the Microsoft Word program is open, notice that a task button representing Word displays on the Taskbar.

3. Open Microsoft Excel by completing the following steps:
   a. Position the arrow pointer on the Start button on the Taskbar and then click the left mouse button.
   b. At the Start menu, point to All Programs and then point to Microsoft Office.
   c. Drag the arrow pointer to Microsoft Office Excel 2003 in the side menu and then click the left mouse button.
   d. When the Microsoft Excel program is open, notice that a task button representing Excel displays on the Taskbar to the right of the task button representing Word.

   Step 4

4. Switch to the Word program by clicking the task button on the Taskbar representing Word.

5. Switch to the Excel program by clicking the task button on the Taskbar representing Excel.

6. Exit Excel by clicking the Close button that displays in the upper right corner of the Excel window. (The Close button contains a white *X* on a red background.)

   Step 6

   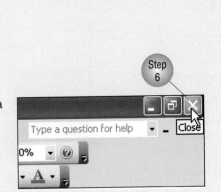

7. Exit Word by clicking the Close button that displays in the upper right corner of the Word window.

Exploring the Notification Area

The notification area is located at the right side of the Taskbar and contains the system clock along with small icons representing specialized programs that run in the background. Position the arrow pointer over the current time in the notification area of the Taskbar and today's date displays in a small yellow box above the time. Double-click the current time displayed on the Taskbar and the Date and Time Properties dialog box displays as shown in Figure W.4.

FIGURE

W.4   *Date and Time Properties Dialog Box*

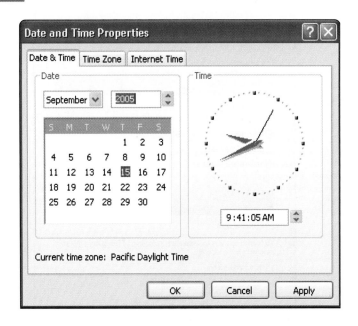

Change the date with options in the *Date* section of the dialog box. For example, to change the month, click the down-pointing arrow at the right side of the option box containing the current month and then click the desired month at the drop-down list. Change the year by clicking the up- or down-pointing arrow at the right side of the option box containing the current year until the desired year displays. To change the day, click the desired day in the monthly calendar that displays in the dialog box. To change the time, double-click either the hour, minute, or seconds and then type the appropriate time or use the up- and down-pointing arrows to adjust the time.

Some programs, when installed, will add an icon to the notification area of the Taskbar. Display the name of the icon by positioning the mouse pointer on the icon and, after approximately one second, the icon label displays in a small yellow box. Some icons may display information in the yellow box rather than the icon label. If more icons have been inserted in the notification area than can be viewed at one time, a left-pointing arrow button displays at the left side of the notification area. Click this left-pointing arrow button and the remaining icons display.

Setting Taskbar Properties

By default, the Taskbar is locked in its current position and size. You can change this default setting, along with other default settings, with options at the Taskbar and Start Menu Properties dialog box, shown in Figure W.5. To display this dialog box, position the arrow pointer on any empty spot on the Taskbar, and then click the *right* mouse button. At the shortcut menu that displays, click Properties.

FIGURE

W.5 **Taskbar and Start Menu Properties Dialog Box**

Each property is controlled by a check box. Property options containing a check mark are active. Click the option to remove the check mark and make the option inactive. If an option is inactive, clicking the option will insert a check mark in the check box and turn on the option (make it active).

exercise 2

CHANGING TASKBAR PROPERTIES

1. Make sure Windows XP is open and the desktop displays.
2. Hide the Taskbar and remove the display of the clock by completing the following steps:
   a. Position the arrow pointer on any empty area on the Taskbar and then click the *right* mouse button.
   b. At the shortcut menu that displays, click Properties.
   c. At the Taskbar and Start Menu Properties dialog box, click *Auto-hide the taskbar*. (This inserts a check mark in the check box.)
   d. Click *Show the clock*. (This removes the check mark from the check box.)

e. Click the Apply button.

f. Click OK to close the dialog box.

3. Display the Taskbar by positioning the mouse pointer at the bottom of the screen. When the Taskbar displays, notice that the time no longer displays at the right side of the Taskbar.

4. Return to the default settings for the Taskbar by completing the following steps:

a. With the Taskbar displayed (if it does not display, position the mouse pointer at the bottom of the desktop), position the arrow pointer on any empty area on the Taskbar and then click the *right* mouse button.

b. At the shortcut menu that displays, click Properties.

c. At the Taskbar and Start Menu Properties dialog box, click *Auto-hide the taskbar*. (This removes the check mark from the check box.)

d. Click *Show the clock*. (This inserts a check mark in the check box.)

e. Click the Apply button.

f. Click OK to close the dialog box.

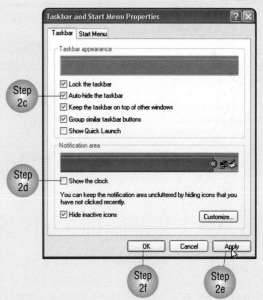

Turning Off the Computer

When you are finished working with your computer, you can choose to shut down the computer completely, shut down and then restart the computer, put the computer on standby, or tell the computer to hibernate. Do not turn off your computer until your screen goes blank. Important data is stored in memory while Windows XP is running and this data needs to be written to the hard drive before turning off the computer.

To shut down your computer, click the Start button on the Taskbar and then click *Turn Off Computer* at the Start menu. At the Turn off computer window, shown in Figure W.6, click the *Stand By* option and the computer switches to a low power state causing some devices such as the monitor and hard disks to turn off. With these devices off, the computer uses less power. Stand By is particularly useful for saving battery power for portable computers. Tell the computer to "hibernate" by holding down the Shift key while clicking the *Stand By* option. In hibernate mode, the computer saves everything in memory on disk, turns off the monitor and hard disk, and then turns off the computer. Click the *Turn Off* option if you want to shut down Windows XP and turn off all power to the computer. Click the *Restart* option if you want to restart the computer and restore the desktop exactly as you left it. You can generally restore your desktop from either standby or hibernate by pressing once on the computer's power button. Usually, bringing a computer out of hibernation takes a little longer than bringing a computer out of standby.

W.6 *Turn Off Computer Window*

Managing Files and Folders

As you begin working with programs in Windows XP, you will create files in which data (information) is saved. A file might contain a Word document, an Excel workbook, or a PowerPoint presentation. As you begin creating files, consider creating folders into which those files will be stored. File management tasks such as creating a folder and copying and moving files and folders can be completed at the My Computer window. To display the My Computer window shown in Figure W.7, click the Start button on the Taskbar and then click My Computer. The various components of the My Computer window are identified in Figure W.7.

W.7 *My Computer Window*

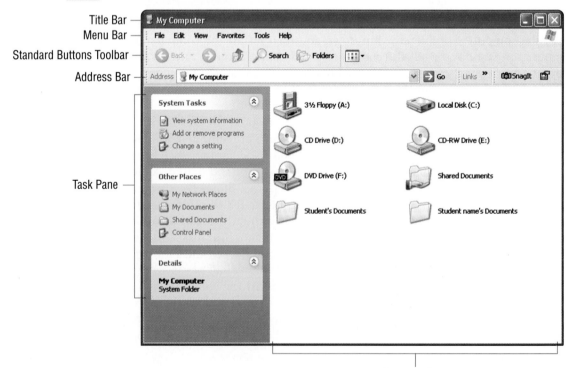

Copying, Moving, and Deleting Files/Folders

File and folder management activities might include copying and moving files or folders from a folder or drive to another or deleting files or folders. The My Computer window offers a variety of methods for copying, moving, and deleting files/folders. You can use options in the task pane, drop-down menu options, or shortcut menu options. This section will provide you with the steps for copying, moving, and deleting files/folders using options in the task pane.

To copy a file/folder to another folder or drive, first display the file in the contents pane by identifying the location of the file. If the file is located in the My Documents folder, click the My Documents hyperlink in the *Other Places* section of the task pane. If the file is located on the hard drive, double-click the desired drive in the contents pane and if the file is located on a floppy disk or CD, double-click the desired drive letter or CD letter. Next, click the folder or file name in the contents pane that you want to copy. This changes the options in the task pane to include management options such as renaming, moving, copying, and deleting folders or files. Click the Copy this folder (or Copy this file) hyperlink in the task pane and the Copy Items dialog box displays as shown in Figure W.8. At the Copy Items dialog box, click the desired folder or drive and then click the Copy button.

F I G U R E

| W.8 | *Copy Items Dialog Box*

To move a file or folder to another folder or drive, select the file or folder and then click the Move this folder (or Move this file) hyperlink. At the Move Items dialog box, specify the location, and then click the Move button. Copying a file or folder leaves the file or folder in the original location and saves a copy at the new location, while moving removes the file or folder from the original location and moves it to the new location.

You can easily remove (delete) a file or folder from the My Computer window. To delete a file or folder, click the file or folder in the contents pane, and then click the <u>Delete this folder</u> (or <u>Delete this file</u>) hyperlink in the task pane. At the dialog box asking you to confirm the deletion, click Yes. A deleted file or folder is sent to the Recycle Bin. You will learn more about the Recycle Bin in the next section.

In Exercise 3, you will insert the CD that accompanies this book into the CD drive. When the CD is inserted, the drive may automatically activate and a dialog box may display on the screen telling you that the disk or device contains more than one type of content and asking what you want Windows to do. If this dialog box displays, click Cancel to remove the dialog box.

exercise 3

COPYING A FILE AND FOLDER AND DELETING A FILE

1. At the Windows XP desktop, insert the CD that accompanies this textbook into the CD drive. If a dialog box displays telling you that the disk or device contains more than one type of content and asking what you want Windows to do, click Cancel.
2. At the Windows XP desktop, open the My Computer window by clicking the Start button on the Taskbar and then clicking My Computer at the Start menu.
3. Copy a file from the CD that accompanies this textbook to a disk in drive A by completing the following steps:
   a. Insert a formatted 3.5-inch disk in drive A.
   b. In the contents pane, double-click the name of the drive containing the CD (probably displays as OFFICE2003_BENCH followed by a drive letter). (Make sure you double-click because you want the contents of the CD to display in the contents pane.)
   c. Double-click the *Windows* folder in the contents pane.
   d. Click *WordDocument01* in the contents pane to select it.
   e. Click the <u>Copy this file</u> hyperlink located in the *File and Folder Tasks* section of the task pane.
   f. At the Copy Items dialog box, click *3½ Floppy (A:)* in the dialog box list box.
   g. Click the Copy button.
4. Delete **WordDocument01** from drive A by completing the following steps:
   a. Click the <u>My Computer</u> hyperlink located in the *Other Places* section of the task pane.
   b. Double-click *3½ Floppy (A:)* in the contents pane.

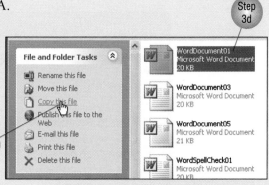

Step 3d

Step 3e

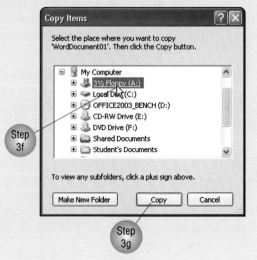

Step 3f

Step 3g

7. At the Recycle Bin window, restore **WordSpellCheck01** through **WordSpellCheck04** to the My Documents folder by completing the following steps:
   a. Select **WordSpellCheck01** through **WordSpellCheck04** in the contents pane of the Recycle Bin window. (If these files are not visible, you will need to scroll down the list of files.)
   b. With the files selected, click the <u>Restore the selected items</u> hyperlink in the *Recycle Bin Tasks* section of the task pane.

8. Close the Recycle Bin window by clicking the Close button located in the upper right corner of the window.
9. Display the My Computer window.
10. Click the <u>My Documents</u> hyperlink in the *Other Places* section of the task pane.
11. Delete the files you restored by completing the following steps:
    a. Select **WordSpellCheck01** through **WordSpellCheck04** in the contents pane. (If these files are not visible, you will need to scroll down the list of files. These are the files you recovered from the Recycle Bin.)
    b. Click the <u>Delete the selected items</u> hyperlink in the *File and Folder Tasks* section of the task pane.
    c. At the message asking you to confirm the deletion, click Yes.
12. Close the window.

Emptying the Recycle Bin

Just like a wastepaper basket, the Recycle Bin can get full. To empty the Recycle Bin, position the arrow pointer on the *Recycle Bin* icon on the desktop and then click the *right* mouse button. At the shortcut menu that displays, click Empty Recycle Bin. At the message asking you to confirm the deletion, click Yes. You can also empty the Recycle Bin by double-clicking the *Recycle Bin* icon. At the Recycle Bin window, click the <u>Empty the Recycle Bin</u> hyperlink in the *Recycle Bin Tasks* section of the task pane. At the message asking you to confirm the deletion, click Yes. (You can also empty the Recycle Bin by clicking File on the Menu bar and then clicking Empty Recycle Bin at the drop-down menu.)

Emptying the Recycle Bin deletes all files/folders. You can delete a specific file/folder from the Recycle Bin (rather than all files/folders). To do this, double-click the *Recycle Bin* icon on the desktop. At the Recycle Bin window, select the file/folder or files/folders you want to delete. Click File on the Menu bar and then click Delete at the drop-down menu. (You can also right-click a selected file/folder and then click Delete at the shortcut menu.) At the message asking you to confirm the deletion, click Yes.

exercise 7

(Before completing this exercise, check with your instructor to determine if you can delete files/folders from the Recycle Bin.)

1. At the Windows XP desktop, double-click the Recycle Bin icon.
2. At the Recycle Bin window, empty the contents of the Recycle Bin by completing the following steps:
   a. Click the Empty the Recycle Bin hyperlink in the *Recycle Bin Tasks* section of the task pane.
   b. At the message asking you to confirm the deletion, click Yes.
3. Close the Recycle Bin window by clicking the Close button located in the upper right corner of the window.

When the Recycle Bin is emptied, the files cannot be recovered by the Recycle Bin or by Windows XP. If you have to recover a file, you will need to use a file recovery program such as Norton Utilities. These utilities are separate programs, but might be worth their cost if you ever need them.

Creating a Shortcut

If you use a file or program on a consistent basis, consider creating a shortcut to the file or program. A shortcut is a specialized icon that represents very small files that point the operating system to the actual item, whether it is a file, a folder, or an application. For example, in Figure W.10, the *Shortcut to PracticeDocument* icon represents a path to a specific file in the Word 2003 program. The icon is not the actual file but a path to the file. Double-click the shortcut icon and Windows XP opens the Word 2003 program and also opens the file named PracticeDocument.

FIGURE

W.10 *PracticeDocument Shortcut Icon*

One method for creating a shortcut is to display the My Computer window and then display the drive or folder where the file is located. Right-click the desired file, point to Send To, and then click Desktop (create shortcut). You can easily delete a shortcut icon from the desktop by dragging the shortcut icon to the *Recycle Bin* icon. This deletes the shortcut icon but does not delete the file to which the shortcut pointed.

exercise 8

1. At the Windows XP desktop, display the My Computer window.
2. Make sure your disk is inserted in drive A.
3. Double-click *3½ Floppy (A:)* in the contents pane.
4. Double-click the *Windows* folder in the contents pane.
5. Change the display of files to a list by clicking the Views button on the Standard Buttons toolbar and then clicking *List* at the drop-down list.
6. Create a shortcut to the file named **WordLetter01** by right-clicking on *WordLetter01*, pointing to Send To, and then clicking Desktop (create shortcut).

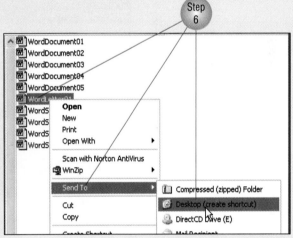

7. Close the My Computer window by clicking the Close button located in the upper right corner of the window.
8. Open Word 2003 and the file named **WordLetter01** by double-clicking the **WordLetter01** shortcut icon on the desktop.
9. After viewing the file in Word, exit Word by clicking the Close button that displays in the upper right corner of the window.
10. Delete the **WordLetter01** shortcut icon by completing the following steps:
    a. At the desktop, position the mouse pointer on the **WordLetter01** shortcut icon.
    b. Hold down the left mouse button, drag the icon on top of the *Recycle Bin* icon, and then release the mouse button.

Customizing the Desktop

You can customize the Windows XP desktop to fit your particular needs and preferences. For example, you can choose a different theme, change the desktop background, add a screen saver, and apply a different appearance to windows, dialog boxes, and menus. To customize the desktop, position the arrow pointer on any empty location on the desktop and then click the *right* mouse button. At the shortcut menu that displays, click Properties. This displays the Display Properties dialog box with the Themes tab selected as shown in Figure W.11.

FIGURE

W.11 | *Display Properties Dialog Box with Themes Tab Selected*

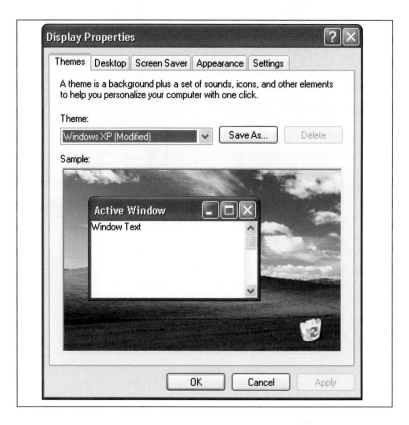

Changing the Theme

A Windows XP theme specifies a variety of formatting such as fonts, sounds, icons, colors, mouse pointers, background, and screen saver. Windows XP contains two themes—Windows XP (the default) and Windows Classic (which appears like earlier versions of Windows). Other themes are available as downloads from the Microsoft Web site. Change the theme with the *Theme* option at the Display Properties dialog box with the Themes tab selected.

Changing the Desktop

With options at the Display Properties dialog box with the Desktop tab selected, as shown in Figure W.12, you can choose a different desktop background and customize the desktop. Click any option in the *Background* list box and preview the results in the preview screen. With the *Position* option, you can specify that the background image is centered, tiled, or stretched on the desktop. Use the *Color* option to change the background color and click the Browse button to choose a background image from another location or Web site.

F I G U R E

W.12 *Display Properties Dialog Box with Desktop Tab Selected*

Adding a Screen Saver

If your computer sits idle for periods of time, consider adding a screen saver. A screen saver is a pattern that changes constantly, thus eliminating the problem of an image staying on the screen too long. To add a screen saver, display the Display Properties dialog box and then click the Screen Saver tab. This displays the dialog box as shown in Figure W.13.

W.13 *Display Properties Dialog Box with Screen Saver Tab Selected*

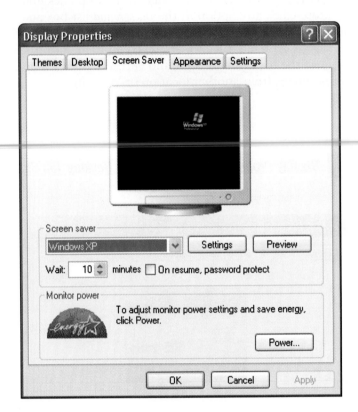

Click the down-pointing arrow at the right side of the *Screen saver* option box to display a list of installed screen savers. Click a screen saver and a preview displays in the monitor located toward the top of the dialog box. Click the Preview button and the dialog box is hidden and the screen saver displays on your monitor. Move the mouse or click a button on the mouse and the dialog box will reappear.

If your computer's hardware is Energy Star compatible, the *Monitor power* section is enabled. Click the Power button and a dialog box displays with options for choosing a power scheme appropriate to the way you use your computer. The dialog box also includes options for specifying how long the computer can be left unused before the monitor and hard disk are turned off and the system goes to standby or hibernate mode.

Changing Colors

Click the Appearance tab at the Display Properties dialog box and the dialog box displays as shown in Figure W.14. At this dialog box, you can change the desktop scheme. Schemes are predefined collections of colors used in windows, menus, title bars, and system fonts. Windows XP loads with the Windows XP style color scheme. Choose a different scheme with the *Windows and buttons* option and choose a specific color with the *Color scheme* option.

W.14 *Display Properties Dialog Box with Appearance Tab Selected*

Changing Settings

Click the Settings tab at the Display Properties dialog box and the dialog box displays as shown in Figure W.15. At this dialog box, you can set color and screen resolution.

W.15 *Display Properties Dialog Box with Settings Tab Selected*

The *Color quality* option determines how many colors your monitor displays. The more colors that are shown, the more realistic the images will appear. However, a lot of computer memory is required to show thousands of colors. Your exact choice is determined by the specific hardware you are using. The *Screen resolution* slide bar sets the screen's resolution. The higher the number, the more you can fit onto your screen. Again, your actual values depend on your particular hardware.

exercise 9

(Before completing this exercise, check with your instructor to determine if you can customize the desktop.)

1. At the Windows XP desktop, display the Display Properties dialog box by positioning the arrow pointer on an empty location on the desktop, clicking the *right* mouse button, and then clicking Properties at the shortcut menu.

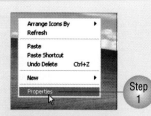

2. At the Display Properties dialog box, change the desktop background by completing the following steps:
   a. Click the Desktop tab.
   b. If a background is selected in the *Background* list box (other than the *(None)* option), make a note of this background name.
   c. Click *Blue Lace 16* in the *Background* list box. (If this option is not available, choose another background.)
   d. Make sure *Tile* is selected in the *Position* list box.
   e. Click OK to close the dialog box.

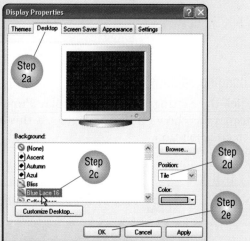

3. After viewing the desktop with the Blue Lace 16 background, remove the background image and change the background color by completing the following steps:
   a. Display the Display Properties dialog box.
   b. At the Display Properties dialog box, click the Desktop tab.
   c. Click *(None)* in the *Background* list box.
   d. Click the down-pointing arrow at the right side of the *Color* option and then click the dark red option at the color palette.
   e. Click OK to close the Display Properties dialog box.

4. After viewing the desktop with the dark red background color, add a screen saver and change the wait time by completing the following steps:
   a. Display the Display Properties dialog box.

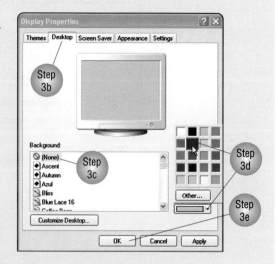

    b. At the Display Properties dialog box, click the Screen Saver tab. (If a screen saver is already selected in the *Screen saver* option box, make a note of this screen saver name.)

    c. Click the down-pointing arrow at the right side of the *Screen saver* option box.

    d. At the drop-down list that displays, click a screen saver that interests you. (A preview of the screen saver displays in the screen located toward the top of the dialog box.)

    e. Click a few other screen savers to see how they will display on the monitor.

    f. Click OK to close the Display Properties dialog box. (At the desktop the screen saver will display, by default, after the monitor has sat idle for one minute.)

5. Return all settings back to the default by completing the following steps:

    a. Display the Display Properties dialog box.

    b. Click the Desktop tab.

    c. If a background and color were selected when you began this exercise, click that background name in the *Background* list box and change the color back to the original color.

    d. Click the Screen Saver tab.

    e. At the Display Properties dialog box with the Screen Saver tab selected, click the down-pointing arrow at the right side of the *Screen saver* option box, and then click *(None)*. (If a screen saver was selected before completing this exercise, return to that screen saver.)

    f. Click OK to close the Display Properties dialog box.

Exploring Windows XP Help and Support

Windows XP includes an on-screen reference guide providing information, explanations, and interactive help on learning Windows features. The on-screen reference guide contains complex files with hypertext used to access additional information by clicking a word or phrase.

Using the Help and Support Center Window

Display the Help and Support Center window shown in Figure W.16 by clicking the Start button on the Taskbar and then clicking Help and Support at the Start menu. The appearance of your Help and Support Center window may vary slightly from what you see in Figure W.16.

If you want to learn about a topic listed in the *Pick a Help topic* section of the window, click the desired topic and information about the topic displays in the window. Use the other options in the Help and Support Center window to get assistance or support from a remote computer or Windows XP newsgroups, pick a specific task, or learn about the additional help features. If you want help on a specific topic and do not see that topic listed in the *Pick a Help topic* section of the window, click inside the *Search* text box (generally located toward the top of the window), type the desired topic, and then press Enter or click the Start searching button (white arrow on a green background).

W.16 *Help and Support Center Window*

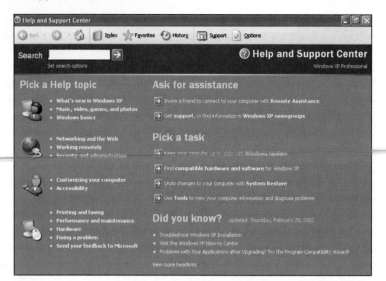

exercise 10

CUSTOMIZING THE DESKTOP

1. At the Windows XP desktop, use the Help and Support feature to learn about new Windows XP features by completing the following steps:
   a. Click the Start button on the Taskbar and then click Help and Support at the Start menu.
   b. At the Help and Support Center window, click the <u>What's new in Windows XP</u> hyperlink located in the *Pick a Help topic* section of the window.
   c. Click the <u>What's new topics</u> hyperlink located in the *What's new in Windows XP* section of the window. (This displays a list of Help options at the right side of the window.)
   d. Click the <u>What's new in Windows XP</u> hyperlink located at the right side of the window below the subheading *Overviews, Articles, and Tutorials*.
   e. Read the information about Windows XP that displays at the right side of the window.
   f. Print the information by completing the following steps:
      1) Click the Print button located on the toolbar that displays above the information titled *What's new in Windows XP Professional*.
      2) At the Print dialog box, make sure the correct printer is selected and then click the Print button.
2. Return to the opening Help and Support Center window by clicking the Home button located on the Help and Support Center toolbar.
3. Use the *Search* text box to search for information on deleting files by completing the following steps:

Step 1b

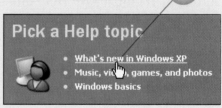

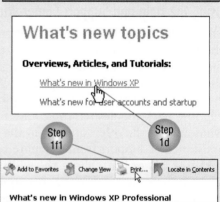

a. Click in the *Search* text box located toward the top of the Help and Support Center window.

b. Type **deleting files** and then press Enter.

c. Click the <u>Delete a file or folder</u> hyperlink that displays in the *Search Results* section of the window (below the *Pick a task* subheading).

d. Read the information about deleting a file or folder that displays at the right side of the window and then print the information by clicking the Print button on the toolbar and then clicking the Print button at the Print dialog box.

e. Click the <u>Delete or restore files in the Recycle Bin</u> hyperlink that displays in the *Search Results* section of the window.

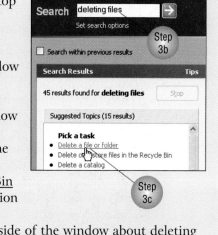

f. Read the information that displays at the right side of the window about deleting and restoring files in the Recycle Bin and then print the information.

4. Close the Help and Support Center window by clicking the Close button located in the upper right corner of the window.

Displaying an Index of Help and Support Topics

Display a list of help topics available by clicking the Index button on the Help and Support Center window toolbar. This displays an index of help topics at the left side of the window as shown in Figure W.17. Scroll through this list until the desired topic displays and then double-click the topic. Information about the selected topic displays at the right side of the window. If you are looking for a specific topic or keyword, click in the *Type in the keyword to find* text box, type the desired topic or keyword, and then press Enter.

FIGURE

W.17 | ***Help and Support Center Window with Index Displayed***

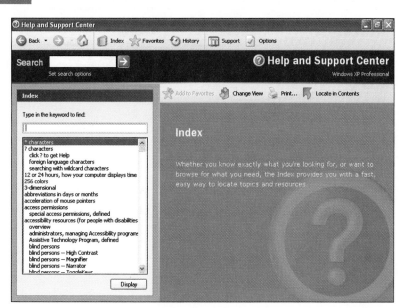

exercise 11

1. At the Windows XP desktop, use the Index to display information on accessing programs by completing the following steps:
   a. Click the Start button on the Taskbar and then click Help and Support at the Start menu.
   b. Click the Index button on the Help and Support Center window toolbar.
   c. Scroll down the list of Index topics until *accessing programs* is visible and then double-click the subheading *overview* that displays below *accessing programs*.
   d. Read the information that displays at the right side of the window and then print the information.

2. Find information on adding a shortcut to the desktop by completing the following steps:
   a. Select and delete the text *overview* that displays in the *Type in the keyword to find* text box and then type shortcuts.
   b. Double-click the subheading *for specific programs* that displays below the *shortcuts* heading.
   c. Read the information that displays at the right side of the window and then print the information.

3. Close the Help and Support Center window by clicking the Close button located in the upper right corner of the window.

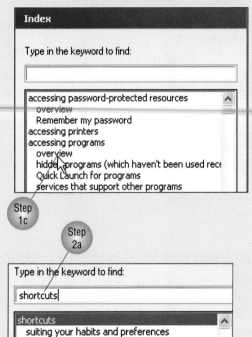

Step 1c

Step 2a

Step 2b

OFFICE 2003

BROWSING THE INTERNET USING INTERNET EXPLORER

Microsoft Internet Explorer is a Web browser program with options and features for displaying sites as well as navigating and searching for information on the Internet. The *Internet* is a network of computers connected around the world. Users access the Internet for several purposes: to communicate using e-mail, to subscribe to news groups, to transfer files, to socialize with other users around the globe in "chat" rooms, and largely to access virtually any kind of information imaginable.

Using the Internet, people can access a phenomenal amount of information for private or public use. To use the Internet, three things are generally required: an Internet Service Provider (ISP), a program to browse the Web (called a *Web browser*), and a *search engine*. In this section, you will learn how to use the Internet Explorer Web browser to browse Web sites, search for specific sites, and download a Web page and image.

Browsing the Internet

You will use the Microsoft Internet Explorer Web browser to locate information on the Internet. Uniform Resource Locators, referred to as URLs, are the method used to identify locations on the Internet. The steps for browsing the Internet vary but generally include: opening Internet Explorer, typing the URL for the desired site, navigating the various pages of the site, printing Web pages, and then closing Internet Explorer.

To launch Internet Explorer, double-click the *Internet Explorer* icon on the Windows desktop. Figure IE.1 identifies the elements of the Internet Explorer, version 6, window. The Web page that displays in your Internet Explorer window may vary from what you see in Figure IE.1.

IE.1 *Internet Explorer Window*

Title Bar
Menu Bar
Toolbar
Address Bar

Vertical Scroll Bar

If you know the URL for the desired Web site, click in the Address bar, type the URL, and then press Enter. In a few moments, the Web site opening page displays in the Internet Explorer window. URLs (Uniform Resource Locators) are the method used to identify locations on the Internet. The format of a URL is *http://server-name.path.* The first part of the URL, *http*, stands for HyperText Transfer Protocol, which is the protocol or language used to transfer data within the World Wide Web. The colon and slashes separate the protocol from the server name. The server name is the second component of the URL. For example, in the URL http://www.microsoft.com, the server name is *microsoft.* The last part of the URL specifies the domain to which the server belongs. For example, *.com* refers to "commercial" and establishes that the URL is a commercial company. Other examples of domains include *.edu* for "educational," *.gov* for "government," and *.mil* for "military."

exercise 1

BROWSING THE INTERNET WITH INTERNET EXPLORER

1. Make sure you are connected to the Internet through an Internet Service Provider and that the Windows desktop displays. (Check with your instructor to determine if you need to complete steps for accessing the Internet.)
2. Launch Microsoft Internet Explorer by double-clicking the *Internet Explorer* icon located on the Windows desktop.
3. At the Internet Explorer window, explore the Web site for Yosemite National Park by completing the following steps:
    a. Click in the Address bar, type **www.nps.gov/yose** and then press Enter.

Step 3a

b. Scroll down the Web site home page for Yosemite National Park by clicking the down-pointing arrow on the vertical scroll bar located at the right side of the Internet Explorer window.

c. Print the Web site home page by clicking the Print button located on the Internet Explorer toolbar.

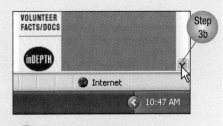

4. Explore the Web site for Glacier National Park by completing the following steps:

a. Click in the Address bar, type **www.nps.gov/glac** and then press Enter.

b. Print the Web site home page by clicking the Print button located on the Internet Explorer toolbar.

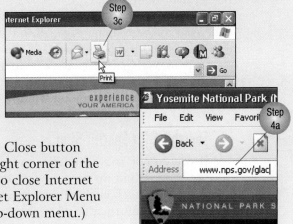

5. Close Internet Explorer by clicking the Close button (contains an *X*) located in the upper right corner of the Internet Explorer window. (You can also close Internet Explorer by clicking File on the Internet Explorer Menu bar and then clicking Close at the drop-down menu.)

Navigating Using Hyperlinks

Most Web pages contain "hyperlinks" that you click to connect to another page within the Web site or to another site on the Internet. Hyperlinks may display in a Web page as underlined text in a specific color or as images or icons. To use a hyperlink, position the mouse pointer on the desired hyperlink until the mouse pointer turns into a hand, and then click the left mouse button. Use hyperlinks to navigate within and between sites on the Internet. The Internet Explorer toolbar contains a Back button that, when clicked, will take you back to the previous Web page. If you click the Back button and then want to go back to the previous page, click the Forward button. By clicking the Back button, you can back your way out of hyperlinks and return to the Web site home page.

exercise 2

VISITING WEB SITES AND NAVIGATING USING HYPERLINKS

1. Make sure you are connected to the Internet and then double-click the *Internet Explorer* icon on the Windows desktop.

2. At the Internet Explorer window, display the White House Web page and navigate in the page by completing the following steps:

a. Click in the Address bar, type whitehouse.gov and then press Enter.

b. At the White House home Web page, position the mouse pointer on a hyperlink that interests you until the pointer turns into a hand, and then click the left mouse button.

c. At the Web page, click the Back button. (This returns you to the White House home page.)

d. At the White House home Web page, click the Forward button to return to the previous Web page.

e. Print the Web page by clicking the Print button on the Internet Explorer toolbar.

3. Display the Amazon.com Web site and navigate in the site by completing the following steps:

a. Click in the Address bar, type www.amazon.com and then press Enter.

b. At the Amazon.com home page, click a hyperlink related to books.

c. When a book Web page displays, click the Print button on the Internet Explorer toolbar.

4. Close Internet Explorer by clicking the Close button (contains an *X*) located in the upper right corner of the Internet Explorer window.

Searching for Specific Sites

If you do not know the URL for a specific site or you want to find information on the Internet but do not know what site to visit, complete a search with a search engine. A search engine is a software program created to search quickly and easily for desired information. A variety of search engines are available on the Internet, each offering the opportunity to search for specific information. One method for searching for information is to click the Search button on the Internet Explorer toolbar. This displays a Search Companion task pane, as shown in figure IE.2 (your task pane may vary) with options for completing a search. Another method for completing a search is to visit the Web site home page for a search engine and use options at the site.

FIGURE

IE.2 *Internet Explorer Search Companion Task Pane*

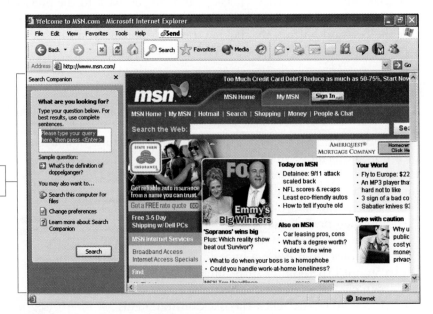

Search Companion Task Pane

exercise 3

1. Make sure you are connected to the Internet and then double-click the *Internet Explorer* icon on the Windows desktop.
2. At the Internet Explorer window, search for sites on bluegrass music by completing the following steps:
   a. Click the Search button on the Internet Explorer toolbar. (This displays the Search Companion task pane at the left side of the window.)
   b. Type **Bluegrass music** in the *What are you looking for?* text box and then press Enter.
   c. When a list of sites displays in the Search Companion task pane, click a site that interests you.
   d. When the Web site home page displays, click the Print button.

   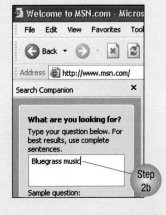

3. Click the Search button on the Internet Explorer toolbar to remove the Search Companion task pane.
4. Use the Yahoo search engine to find sites on bluegrass music by completing the following steps:
   a. Click in the Address bar, type www.yahoo.com and then press Enter.

   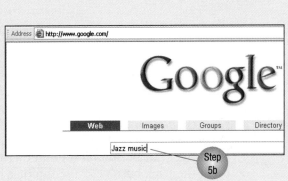

   b. At the Yahoo Web site, click in the search text box, type **Bluegrass music** and then press Enter. (Notice that the sites displayed vary from the sites displayed in the earlier search.)
   c. Click hyperlinks until a Web site displays that interests you.
   d. When the site displays, click the Print button on the Internet Explorer toolbar.
5. Use the Google search engine to find sites on jazz music by completing the following steps:
   a. Click in the Address bar, type www.Google.com and then press Enter.
   b. When the Google Web site home page displays, click in the search text box, type **Jazz music** and then press Enter.
   c. Click a site that interests you.
   d. When the Web site home page displays, click the Print button on the Internet Explorer toolbar.
6. Close Internet Explorer.

Completing Advanced Searches for Specific Sites

The Internet contains a phenomenal amount of information. Depending on what you are searching for on the Internet and the search engine you use, some searches can result in several thousand "hits" (sites). Wading through a large number of sites can be very time-consuming and counterproductive. Narrowing a search to very specific criteria can greatly reduce the number of hits for a search. To narrow a search, use the advanced search options offered by the search engine.

exercise 4

1. Make sure you are connected to the Internet and then double-click the *Internet Explorer* icon on the Windows desktop.
2. Search for sites on skydiving in Oregon by completing the following steps:
   a. Click in the Address bar and then type www.yahoo.com.
   b. At the Yahoo Web site home page, click an advanced search hyperlink (this hyperlink may display as Advanced or Advanced search).
   c. At the advanced search page, click in the search text box specifying that you want all words you type to appear in the Web page (this text box may display as "all of these words").
   d. Type skydiving Oregon tandem static line. (This limits the search to Web pages containing all of the words typed in the search text box.)

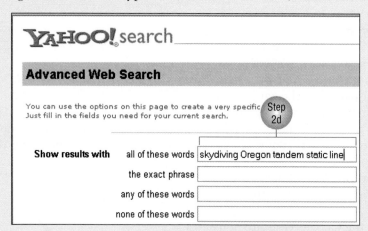

e. Choose any other options at the advanced search Web page that will narrow your search.
   f. Click the Search button.
   g. When the list of Web sites displays, click a hyperlink that interests you.
   h. Click the Print button on the Internet Explorer toolbar to print the Web page.
   i. Click the Back button on the Internet Explorer toolbar until the Yahoo Search Options page displays.
3. Close Internet Explorer.

Downloading Images, Text, and Web Pages from the Internet

The image(s) and/or text that display when you open a Web page as well as the Web page itself can be saved as a separate file. This separate file can be viewed, printed, or inserted in another file. The information you want to save in a separate file is downloaded from the Internet by Internet Explorer and saved in a folder of your choosing with the name you specify. Copyright laws protect much of the information on the Internet. Before using information downloaded from the Internet, check the site for restrictions. If you do use information, make sure you properly cite the source.

exercise 5

1. Make sure you are connected to the Internet and then double-click the *Internet Explorer* icon on the Windows desktop.
2. Download a Web page and image from Banff National Park by completing the following steps:
   a. Use a search engine of your choosing to search for the Banff National Park Web site.
   b. From the list of sites that displays, choose a site that contains information about Banff National Park and at least one image of the park.
   c. Insert a formatted disk in drive A. (Check with your instructor to determine if you should save the Web page on a disk or save it into a folder on the hard drive or network.)
   d. Save the Web page as a separate file by clicking File on the Internet Explorer Menu bar and then clicking Save As at the drop-down menu.
   e. At the Save Web Page dialog box, click the down-pointing arrow at the right side of the *Save in* option and then click *3¹/₂ Floppy (A:)* at the drop-down list. (This step may vary depending on where your instructor wants you to save the Web page.)
   f. Click in the *File name* text box (this selects the text inside the box), type BanffWebPage and then press Enter.
3. Save the image as a separate file by completing the following steps:
   a. Right-click the image of the park. (The image that displays may vary from what you see to the right.)
   b. At the shortcut menu that displays, click Save Picture As.

c. At the Save Picture dialog box, change the *Save in* option to drive A (or the location specified by your instructor).

d. Click in the *File name* text box, type BanffImage and then press Enter.

4. Close Internet Explorer.

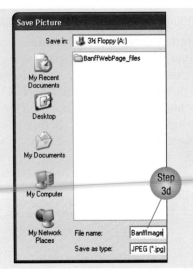

OPTIONAL exercise

OPENING THE SAVED WEB PAGE AND IMAGE IN A WORD DOCUMENT

1. Open Microsoft Word by clicking the Start button on the Taskbar, pointing to *All Programs*, pointing to *Microsoft Office*, and then clicking *Microsoft Office Word 2003*.

2. With Microsoft Word open, insert the image in a document by completing the following steps:

a. Click Insert on the Menu bar, point to Picture, and then click From File.

b. At the Insert Picture dialog box, change the *Look in* option to drive A (or the location where you saved the Banff image) and then double-click ***BanffImage***.

c. When the image displays in the Word document, print the document by clicking the Print button on the Word Standard toolbar.

d. Close the document by clicking File on the Menu bar and then clicking Close at the drop-down menu. At the message asking if you want to save the changes, click No.

3. Open the ***BanffWebPage*** file by completing the following steps:

a. Click File on the Menu bar and then click Open at the drop-down menu.

b. At the Open dialog box, change the *Look in* option to drive A (or the location where you saved the Web page), and then double-click ***BanffWebPage***.

c. Print the Web page by clicking the Print button on the Word Standard toolbar.

d. Close the ***BanffWebPage*** file by clicking File and then Close.

4. Close Word by clicking the Close button (contains an *X*) that displays in the upper right corner of the screen.

MICROSOFT® EXCEL

Tracking and analyzing numerical data is a large component of the daily activity in today's workplace. Microsoft Excel 2003 is a popular choice among individuals and companies for organizing, analyzing, and presenting numerical information.

Organizing Information

Numbers are the foundation of every business transaction. Think about all of the various numbers that a person needs to organize for a typical purchase: account numbers, stock numbers, quantities, sale price, cost price, taxes, total due, amount received—just to name a few. Now consider a different scenario in which you want to track the egg production of a chicken farm. You might want to factor in the volume of feed, the number of eggs produced each day by each hen, the total production by day, by week, by month, and so on. These are just two examples of the type of information for which you could find a use for Excel.

Spreadsheet software organizes data in columns and rows—an electronic version of an accountant's ledger—only with a lot more power and versatility. In Microsoft Excel, information is organized by creating column and row headings called

Making EXCEL Work for YOU!

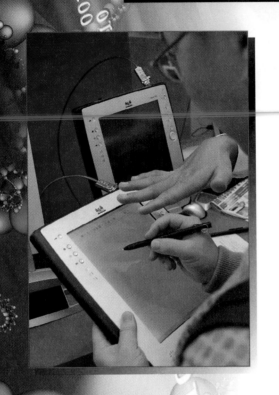

labels. Numbers, called *values,* are entered below and beside the headings and then formulas are created to perform calculations. The completed document is referred to as a *worksheet.*

The potential uses for an application like Excel are only limited by your imagination—any type of document that can be set up in the column/row format is a candidate for an Excel worksheet.

Not sure how to set up the information you want to track? Go to Office Online and browse the templates at the Microsoft Web site. Several templates are available that already contain labels and formulas, so all you have to do is fill in the data. You can preview a template before downloading it to make sure it will meet your needs. The templates site is continually updated, so keep checking for new additions.

Analyzing Information

The true power of Excel lies in its ability to analyze information at the click of a mouse. Once a worksheet has been created you can play the *what-if* game. For example, suppose you have used Excel to set up a personal budget. You can use its calculating and projecting features to answer questions: What if I receive an increase in wages? What if I spend less on groceries? What if I put more money down on the house I want to buy? Whenever you change a value in a worksheet, Excel automatically recalculates other values that are

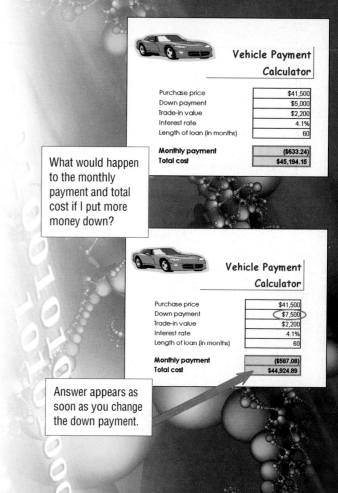

Vehicle Payment Calculator

Purchase price	$41,500
Down payment	$5,000
Trade-in value	$2,200
Interest rate	4.1%
Length of loan (in months)	60
Monthly payment	($633.24)
Total cost	$45,194.15

What would happen to the monthly payment and total cost if I put more money down?

Vehicle Payment Calculator

Purchase price	$41,500
Down payment	$7,500
Trade-in value	$2,200
Interest rate	4.1%
Length of loan (in months)	60
Monthly payment	($587.08)
Total cost	$44,924.89

Answer appears as soon as you change the down payment.

dependent on the number you changed. In an instant you have your answer.

Excel includes several predefined formulas, called *functions* that make the task of constructing complex worksheets easier to manage. So math is not your favorite subject? Not a problem with Excel's Insert Function dialog box, which helps you build a formula by prompting you with explanations for each parameter.

Use the Sort and Filter features in Excel to help you analyze the data in various arrangements. With the click of a button on the toolbar you can rearrange the order of the worksheet to sort in ascending or descending order by a single column or by multiple columns. Use the Filter by Selection or Filter by Form commands to reduce the data you are viewing by temporarily hiding rows that do not meet your criteria. For

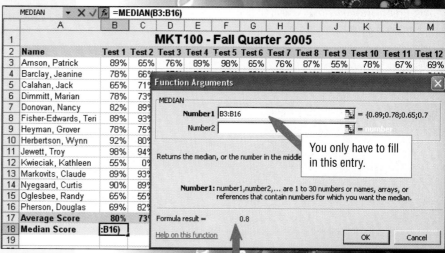

MEDIAN   =MEDIAN(B3:B16)

	A	B	C	D	E	F	G	H	I	J	K	L	M
1					**MKT100 - Fall Quarter 2005**								
2	**Name**	Test 1	Test 2	Test 3	Test 4	Test 5	Test 6	Test 7	Test 8	Test 9	Test 10	Test 11	Test 12
3	Arnson, Patrick	89%	65%	76%	89%	98%	65%	76%	87%	55%	78%	67%	69%
4	Barclay, Jeanine	78%	66%										
5	Calahan, Jack	65%	71%										
6	Dimmitt, Marian	78%	73%										
7	Donovan, Nancy	82%	89%										
8	Fisher-Edwards, Teri	89%	93%										
9	Heyman, Grover	78%	75%										
10	Herbertson, Wynn	92%	80%										
11	Jewett, Troy	98%	94%										
12	Kwieciak, Kathleen	55%	0%										
13	Markovits, Claude	89%	93%										
14	Nyegaard, Curtis	90%	89%										
15	Oglesbee, Randy	65%	55%										
16	Pherson, Douglas	69%	82%										
17	**Average Score**	80%	73%										
18	**Median Score**	:B16)											
19													

Function Arguments

MEDIAN
Number1 B3:B16   = {0.89;0.78;0.65;0.7
Number2   = number

You only have to fill in this entry.

Returns the median, or the number in the middle

Number1: number1,number2,... are 1 to 30 numbers or names, arrays, or references that contain numbers for which you want the median.

Formula result =   0.8

Help on this function   OK   Cancel

The dialog box provides assistance with building complex formulae by providing explanations of each requirement. As you fill in the dialog box, Excel creates the corresponding formula including all required syntax.

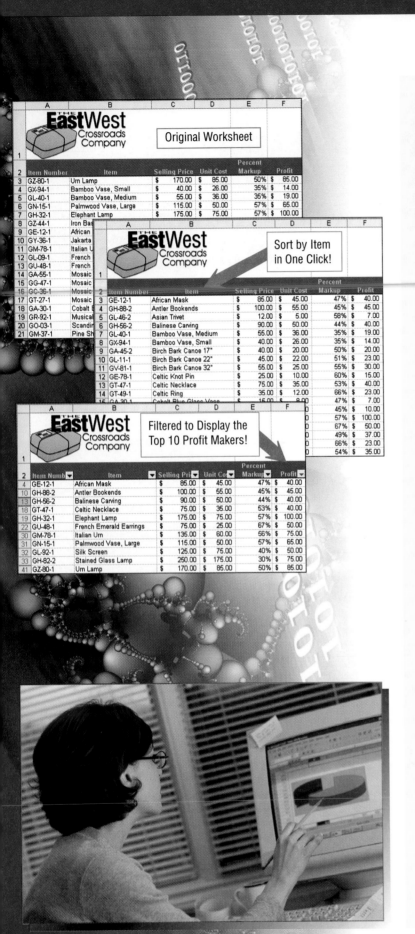

example, in a workplace scenario, you might want to view only the top ten sales amounts to identify the star performers in your organization.

Presenting Information

With information already structured in columns and rows, the task of interpreting the results is already simplified. Add some color and other rich text enhancements to draw the reader's attention to important titles, totals, or other results and you have just made the process even easier! Add clip art, photographs, or other media to a worksheet using the ClipArt task pane.

It is said that a picture is worth a thousand words. Why not use Excel's charting capabilities to turn those numbers into a chart—a pictorial representation that enables a reader to more easily distinguish the impact of the differences between columns of numbers? Excel can render both two-dimensional and three-dimensional charts in several chart types, a sampling of which are: column, bar, line, pie, area, radar, doughnut, and scatter.

Knowing how to use Excel is a prerequisite for many jobs in our information-driven economy. Creating worksheets in Microsoft Excel 2003 is as simple as one, two, three:

1. Set up the column and row headings.
2. Enter the data.
3. Create the formulas.

Within a short period of time, you will *excel* at creating, editing, and formatting worksheets!

MICROSOFT® EXCEL

UNIT 1: Preparing and Formatting a Worksheet

➤ Preparing an Excel Worksheet

➤ Formatting an Excel Worksheet

➤ Inserting Formulas in a Worksheet

➤ Enhancing a Worksheet

BENCHMARK MICROSOFT® EXCEL 2003

MICROSOFT OFFICE SPECIALIST SKILLS—UNIT 1

Reference No.	Skill	Pages
XL03S-1	**Creating Data and Content**	
XL03S-1-1	Enter and Edit Cell Contents	
	Enter data (text and symbols) in a cell	S10-S20
	Automatically enter data (AutoComplete, AutoCorrect, AutoFill)	S17-S20
	Edit data in a cell	S15-S17
	Enter and edit numbers in cells	S42-S47
	Clear data in cells	S54-S55
XL03S-2	**Analyzing Data**	
XL03S-2-1	Filter lists using AutoFilter	S127-S129
XL03S-2-2	Sort lists	S122-S126
XL03S-2-3	Insert and modify formulas	
	Use AutoSum button to insert formula	S69-S71
	Write formulas with mathematical operators and edit formulas	S71-S76
	Insert formulas with the Insert Function button and edit formulas	S76-S89
	Use absolute and mixed cell references in formulas	S89-S91
XL03S-3	**Formatting Data and Content**	
XL03S-3-1	Apply and modify cell formats	
	Format cells with AutoFormat	S23-S25
	Apply formatting with buttons on the Formatting toolbar	S35-S37
	Format data in cells	S42-S51
	Apply borders and shading to cells	S55-S61
XL03S-3-3	Modify row and column formats	
	Change column width and row heights	S37-S42
	Insert rows and columns	S51-S54
	Align, indent, and rotate data in cells	S47-S49
	Hide and unhide columns and rows	S111-S113
XL03S-5	**Managing Workbooks**	
XL03S-5-2	Insert, delete, and move cells	
	Insert and delete cells, rows, and columns	S51-S55
XL03S-5-5	Preview data in other views	
	Preview a worksheet	S33-S34
	Display worksheet in Page Break view	S106-S108
XL03S-5-7	Setup pages for printing	
	Print specific area of a worksheet	S113-S114
	Change worksheet orientation	S98-S101
	Insert headers and footers in a worksheet	S99-S103
	Change worksheet margins	S103-S105
	Center a worksheet horizontally and vertically	S105-S106
	Print column and row titles on multiple pages	S108-S110
	Print gridlines and row and column headings	S110-S111
XL03S-5-8	Print data	
	Print a workbook	S12
	Set up, customize, and print worksheets and selected data	S97-S116

PREPARING AN EXCEL WORKSHEET

PERFORMANCE OBJECTIVES

Upon successful completion of Chapter 1, you will be able to:

➤ **Identify the various elements of an Excel worksheet**
➤ **Create, save, and print a worksheet**
➤ **Enter data in a worksheet**
➤ **Edit data in a worksheet**
➤ **Apply an AutoFormat to cells in a worksheet**
➤ **Use the Help feature**

Many companies use a spreadsheet for numerical and financial data and to analyze and evaluate information. An Excel spreadsheet can be used for such activities as creating financial statements, preparing budgets, managing inventory, and analyzing cash flow. In addition, numbers and values can be easily manipulated to create "what if" situations. For example, using a spreadsheet, a person in a company can ask questions such as "What if the value in this category is decreased? How would that change affect the department budget?" Questions like these can be easily answered in an Excel spreadsheet. Change the value in a category and Excel will recalculate formulas for the other values. In this way, a spreadsheet can be used not only for creating financial statements or budgets, but also as a planning tool.

Creating a Worksheet

Open Excel by clicking the Start button at the left side of the Taskbar, pointing to All Programs, pointing to Microsoft Office, and then clicking Microsoft Office Excel 2003. (Depending on your operating system, these steps may vary.) When Excel is open, you are presented with a blank worksheet like the one shown in Figure 1.1. The elements of a blank Excel worksheet are described in Table 1.1.

On your screen, the Standard and Formatting toolbars may display side by side with only a portion of the buttons visible. If this is the case, move the Formatting toolbar below the Standard toolbar by completing the following steps:

1. Click Tools and then Customize.

2. At the Customize dialog box, click the Options tab.

3. Click the *Show Standard and Formatting toolbars on two rows* option to insert a check mark in the check box.

4. Click the Close button to close the dialog box.

The display of the Standard and Formatting toolbars (as well as other toolbars) can be turned on or off. To do this, position the mouse pointer anywhere on a toolbar, and then click the *right* mouse button. At the drop-down menu that displays, click the toolbar name you want turned on or off. You can also turn on or off the display of a toolbar by clicking View on the Menu bar, pointing to Toolbars, and then clicking the toolbar name.

FIGURE

1.1 *Blank Excel Worksheet*

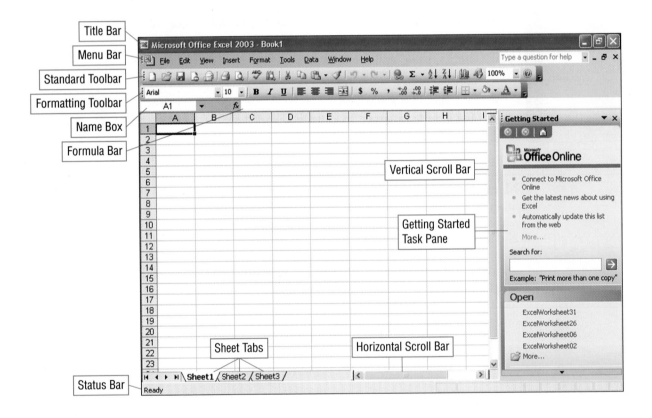

Title bar	The Title bar displays the name of the program along with the name of a workbook. The buttons at the far right side of the Title bar can be used to minimize, restore, or close Excel.
Menu bar	Excel commands are grouped into related functions and placed on the Menu bar. For example, options for formatting cells, rows, or columns are grouped in the Format option on the Menu bar.
Standard toolbar	Icons for the most common commands in Excel are placed on the Standard toolbar.
Formatting toolbar	Options that are used to format elements of a worksheet are placed on buttons on the Formatting toolbar.
Name box	The cell address, also called the cell reference, displays in the Name box and includes the column letter and row number.
Formula bar	The Formula bar provides information about the active cell. Formulas can be entered and edited in the Formula bar.
Scroll bars	A vertical scroll bar displays toward the right side of the worksheet (immediately left of the task pane) and a horizontal scroll bar displays at the bottom of the worksheet. These scroll bars are used to navigate within a worksheet.
Task pane	The task pane presents features to help the user easily identify and use more of the program. The name of the task pane and the features contained in the task pane change depending on the actions being performed by the user.
Sheet tabs	Sheet tabs identify the current worksheet. The tab for the active worksheet displays with a white background while the inactive worksheets display with a gray background (the background color may vary depending on the Windows color scheme).
Status bar	The Status bar is located below the horizontal scroll bar and displays information about the worksheet and the currently active cell.
Worksheet area	The worksheet area is a collection of cells where information such as labels, values, or formulas is entered. (A cell is an intersection between a row and a column.)

A document created in Excel is referred to as a **workbook**. An Excel workbook consists of individual worksheets (or **sheets**) like the sheets of paper in a notebook. Notice the tabs located toward the bottom of the Excel window that are named *Sheet1*, *Sheet2*, and so on. The area containing the gridlines in the Excel window is called the **worksheet area**. Figure 1.2 identifies the elements of the worksheet area. Create a worksheet in the worksheet area that will be saved as part of a workbook. Columns in a worksheet are labeled with letters of the alphabet and rows are numbered.

F I G U R E

| 1.2 | *Elements of a Worksheet Area*

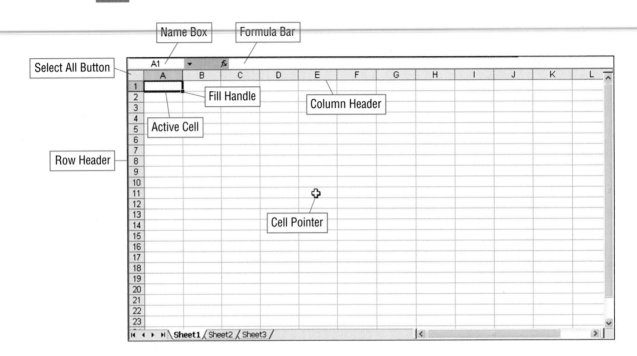

The gray horizontal and vertical lines that define the cells in the worksheet area are called **gridlines**. When the insertion point (which displays as a thick white plus sign) is positioned in a cell, the **cell address**, also called the **cell reference**, displays at the left side of the Formula bar in what is called the **Name box**. The cell reference includes the column letter and row number. For example, if the insertion point is positioned in the first cell of the worksheet, the cell reference *A1* displays in the Name box located at the left side of the Formula bar. In a worksheet, the cell containing the insertion point is considered the **active cell** and a thick black border surrounds the active cell.

HINT
To make a cell active, position the cell pointer in the cell and then click the left mouse button.

Entering Data in a Cell

Enter data such as a heading, number, or value in a cell. To enter data in a cell, make the desired cell active, and then type the data. To move the insertion point to the next cell in the worksheet, press the Tab key. Other commands for moving the insertion point within a worksheet are displayed in Table 1.2.

1.2 Commands for Moving Insertion Point in a Worksheet

To move the insertion point here	Press
Down to the next cell	Enter
Up to the next cell	Shift + Enter
Next cell	Tab
Previous cell	Shift + Tab
Cell at beginning of row	Home
Next cell in the direction of the arrow	Up, Down, Left, or Right Arrow key
Last cell in worksheet	Ctrl + End
First cell in worksheet	Ctrl + Home
Cell in next window (approximately 16-24 rows)	Page Down
Cell in previous window (approximately 16-24 rows)	Page Up
Cell in window to right (approximately 8-11 columns)	Alt + Page Down
Cell in window to left (approximately 8-11 columns)	Alt + Page Up

Another method for moving the insertion point to a specific cell is to use the Go To feature. To use this feature, click Edit and then Go To. At the Go To dialog box, type the cell reference in the *Reference* text box, and then click OK.

> **HINT**
> Ctrl + G is the keyboard command to display the Go To dialog box.

When you are ready to type data into the active cell, check the Status bar. The word *Ready* should display at the left side. As data is being typed in the cell, the word *Ready* changes to *Enter*. Data being typed in a cell displays in the cell as well as in the Formula bar. If the data being typed is longer than the cell can accommodate, the data overlaps the next cell to the right (it does not become a part of the next cell—it simply overlaps it). You will learn how to change column widths to accommodate data later in this chapter.

If the data you enter in a cell consists of text and the text does not fit into the cell, it overlaps the next cell. If, however, you enter a number in a cell, specify it as a number (rather than text) and the number is too long to fit in the cell, Excel changes the display of the number to number symbols *(###)*. This is because Excel does not want you to be misled by a number when you see only a portion of it in the cell.

In addition to moving the insertion point with the keyboard, you can also move it using the mouse. To make a specific cell active with the mouse, position the mouse pointer, which displays as a white plus sign (called the ***cell pointer***), on the desired cell, and then click the left mouse button. The cell pointer displays as a white plus sign when positioned in a cell in the worksheet and displays as an arrow pointer when positioned on other elements of the Excel window such as toolbars or scroll bars.

Scroll through a worksheet using the horizontal and/or vertical scroll bars. Scrolling shifts the display of cells in the worksheet area, but does not change the active cell. Scroll through a worksheet until the desired cell is visible and then click the desired cell.

Save

Save a Workbook
1. Click Save button.
2. Type workbook name.
3. Press Enter.

Saving a Workbook

Save an Excel workbook, which may consist of a worksheet or several worksheets, by clicking the Save button on the Standard toolbar, clicking File and then Save, or by pressing Ctrl + S. At the Save As dialog box, type a name for the workbook in the *File name* text box, and then press Enter or click Save. A workbook file name can contain up to 255 characters, including drive letter and any folder names, and can include spaces. Some symbols cannot be used in a file name, such as:

forward slash (/)	question mark (?)
backslash (\)	quotation mark (")
greater than sign (>)	colon (:)
less than sign (<)	semicolon (;)
asterisk (*)	pipe symbol (|)

To save an Excel workbook in the ExcelChapter01S folder on your disk, display the Save As dialog box and then click the down-pointing arrow at the right side of the *Save in* option box. Click *3½ Floppy (A:)* that displays in the drop-down list and then double-click *ExcelChapter01S* in the list box. Note that you cannot give a workbook the same name in first uppercase and then lowercase letters.

Open

Open a Workbook
1. Click Open button.
2. Display desired folder.
3. Double-click workbook name.

Opening a Workbook

Open an Excel workbook by displaying the Open dialog box and then double-clicking the desired workbook name. Display the Open dialog box by clicking the Open button on the Standard toolbar or by clicking File and then Open, or by pressing Ctrl + O.

Print

Print a Workbook
Click Print button.
OR
1. Click File, Print.
2. Click OK.

Printing a Workbook

Click the Print button on the Standard toolbar to print the active worksheet. You can also print a worksheet by clicking File and then Print, or by pressing Ctrl + P. At the Print dialog box that displays, click the OK button.

Closing a Workbook and Exiting Excel

To close an Excel workbook, click the Close button that displays at the right side of the Menu bar (the second Close button from the top) or click File and then Close. To exit Excel, click the Close button that displays at the right side of the Title bar (the first Close button from the top) or click File and then Exit. You can also exit Excel by double-clicking the *Excel* icon that displays at the left side of the Menu bar.

Close   Excel

Close a Workbook
Click Close button.
OR
Click File, Close.

Expanding Drop-Down Menus

Microsoft Excel personalizes menus and toolbars as you work. When you click an option on the Menu bar, only the most popular options display (considered first-rank options). A drop-down menu that displays first-rank options is referred to as an **adaptive menu**. To expand a drop-down menu and display the full set of options (first-rank options as well as second-rank options), click the down-pointing arrows that display at the bottom of the drop-down menu. A drop-down menu will also expand if you click an option on the Menu bar and then pause on the menu for a few seconds. Second-rank options on the expanded drop-down menu display in a light gray color. If you choose a second-rank option, it is promoted and becomes a first-rank option the next time the drop-down menu is displayed.

If you want all menu options displayed when you click an option, you would complete the following steps:

1. Click Tools, expand the drop-down menu by clicking the down-pointing arrows that display at the bottom of the menu, and then click Customize.
2. At the Customize dialog box, click the Options tab.
3. At the Customize dialog box with the Options tab selected, click in the *Always show full menus* check box to insert a check mark.
4. Click the Close button to close the dialog box.

Display Full Drop-Down Menus
1. Click Tools, Customize.
2. Click Options tab.
3. Click *Always show full menus* option.
4. Click Close button.

In this textbook, you will not be instructed to expand the drop-down menu. If you do not see a specified option, click the down-pointing arrows that display at the bottom of the menu to expand it. Or, consider following the steps above to show full menus.

Completing Computer Exercises

At the end of sections within chapters and at the end of chapters, you will be completing hands-on exercises at the computer. These exercises will provide you with the opportunity to practice the presented functions and commands. The skill assessment exercises at the end of each chapter include general directions. If you do not remember how to perform a particular function, refer to the text in the chapter.

Copying Data Workbooks

In several exercises in each chapter, you will be opening workbooks provided with this textbook. Before beginning each chapter, copy the chapter folder from the CD that accompanies this textbook to a floppy disk (or other folder). For this chapter, copy to your disk or directory the ExcelChapter01S subfolder from the Excel2003Specialist folder on the CD that accompanies this textbook. Steps on how to copy a folder from the CD to your floppy disk are printed on the inside of the back cover of this textbook.

Changing the Default Folder

At the end of this and the remaining chapters in the textbook, you will be saving workbooks. More than likely, you will want to save workbooks onto a disk. You will also be opening workbooks that have been saved on your disk. To save workbooks in and open workbooks from the chapter folder on your disk, you will need to specify the drive where your disk is located as the default folder. Once you specify the chapter folder on your disk, Excel uses this as the default folder until you exit the Excel program. The next time you open Excel, you will again need to specify the drive where your disk is located.

Change the default folder at the Open dialog box or the Save As dialog box. To change the folder to the ExcelChapter01S folder on the disk in drive A at the Open dialog box, you would complete the following steps:

1. Click the Open button on the Standard toolbar (the second button from the left), or click File and then Open.
2. At the Open dialog box, click the down-pointing arrow at the right side of the *Look in* option box.
3. From the drop-down list that displays, click *3½ Floppy (A:)*.
4. Double-click *ExcelChapter01S* that displays in the list box.
5. Click the Cancel button in the lower right corner of the dialog box.

Change Default Folder
1. Click Tools, Options.
2. Click General tab.
3. Type desired folder in *Default file location* text box.
4. Click OK.

If you want to change the default folder permanently, make the change at the Options dialog box with the General tab selected, as shown in Figure 1.3. To permanently change the default folder to drive A, you would complete these steps:

1. Click Tools and then Options.
2. At the Options dialog box, click the General tab.
3. Select the text that displays in the *Default file location* text box and then type A:\.
4. Click the OK button.

1.3 *Options Dialog Box with General Tab Selected*

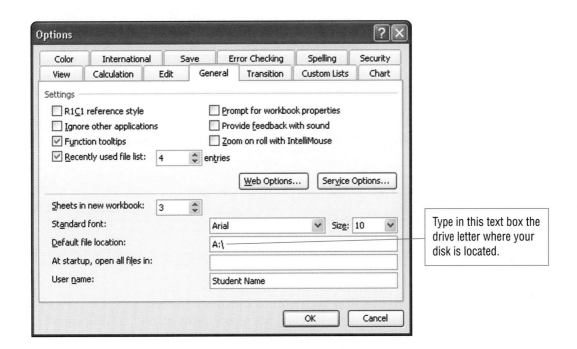

Type in this text box the drive letter where your disk is located.

Editing Data in a Cell

Edit data being typed in a cell by pressing the Backspace key to delete the character left of the insertion point or pressing the Delete key to delete the character to the right of the insertion point. To change the data in a cell, click the cell once to make it active, and then type the new data. When a cell containing data is active, anything typed will take the place of the existing data. If you want to edit only a portion of the data in a cell, double-click the cell. This makes the cell active, moves the insertion point inside the cell, and displays the word *Edit* at the left side of the Status bar. Move the insertion point using the arrow keys or the mouse and then make the needed corrections. If you are using the keyboard, you can press the Home key to move the insertion point to the first character in the cell or Formula bar, or press the End key to move the insertion point to the last character.

When you are done editing the data in the cell, be sure to change out of the Edit mode. To do this, make another cell active. You can do this by pressing Enter, Tab, or Shift + Tab. You can also change out of the Edit mode and return to the Ready mode by clicking another cell or clicking the Enter button on the Formula bar.

If the active cell does not contain data, the Formula bar displays only the cell reference (by column letter and row number). As data is being typed in a cell, the two buttons shown in Figure 1.4 display on the Formula bar to the right of the Name box. Click the Cancel button to delete the current cell entry. You can also delete the cell entry by pressing the Esc key. Click the Enter button to indicate that you are done typing or editing the cell entry. When you click the Enter button on the Formula bar, the word *Enter* (or *Edit*) located at the left side of the Status bar changes to *Ready*.

Cancel   Enter

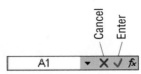

1.4   *Buttons on the Formula Bar*

(Before completing computer exercises, copy to your disk the ExcelChapter01S subfolder from the Excel2003Specialist folder on the CD that accompanies this textbook. Steps on how to copy a folder are presented on the inside of the back cover of this textbook. Do this every time you start exercises in a chapter.)

exercise 1

CREATING AND EDITING A WORKSHEET

1. Open Excel by completing the following steps:
   a. At the Windows desktop, click the Start button that displays at the left side of the Taskbar.
   b. At the pop-up menu that displays, point to All Programs.
   c. At the side menu that displays, point to Microsoft Office.
   d. At the side menu that displays, click Microsoft Office Excel 2003. (Depending on your operating system, these steps may vary.)
2. At the Excel worksheet that displays, create the worksheet shown in Figure 1.5 by completing the following steps:
   a. With cell A1 the active cell (displays with a thick black border), type Name.
   b. Press the Tab key. (This makes cell B1 the active cell.)
   c. Type Hours and then press the Tab key. (This makes cell C1 the active cell.)
   d. Type Rate and then press Enter to move the insertion point to cell A2.
   e. With A2 the active cell, type the name Avery.
   f. Continue typing the data shown in Figure 1.5. Type the dollar signs as shown in the figure. Use the Tab key to move to the next cell in the row, press Shift + Tab to move to the previous cell in the row, or press the Enter key to move down a row to the cell at the left margin. (For other commands for moving the insertion point, refer to Table 1.2.)
3. After typing the data shown in the cells in Figure 1.5, save the worksheet by completing the following steps:
   a. Click the Save button on the Standard toolbar.
   b. At the Save As dialog box, click the down-pointing arrow to the right of the *Save in* option.
   c. From the drop-down list that displays, click *3½ Floppy (A:)* (this may vary depending on your system).
   d. Double-click the *ExcelChapter01S* folder that displays in the list box.
   e. Select the text in the *File name* text box and then type sec1x01.
   f. Press Enter or click the Save button.

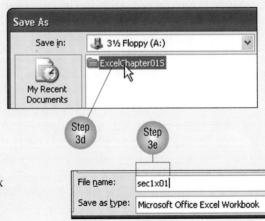

EXCEL

4. Print **sec1x01** by clicking the Print button on the Standard toolbar. (The gridlines will not print.)
5. With the worksheet still open, make the following edits:
    a. Double-click cell A6 (contains *Mikulich*).
    b. Move the insertion point immediately left of the *k* and then type **c**. (This changes the spelling to *Mickulich*.)
    c. Click once in cell A3 (contains *Connors*) and then type **Bryant**. (Clicking only once allows you to type over the existing data.)
    d. Click once in cell B4 (contains *24*), type **30**, and then press Enter.
    e. Edit cell C7 by completing the following steps:
        1) Click Edit and then Go To.
        2) At the Go To dialog box, type **C7** in the *Reference* text box, and then click OK.
        3) Type **$14.25** (over *$10.00*).
    f. Click once in any other cell.
6. Click the Save button on the Standard toolbar to save the worksheet again.
7. Click the Print button on the Standard toolbar to print the worksheet again.
8. Close the worksheet by clicking File on the Menu bar and then clicking Close at the drop-down menu.

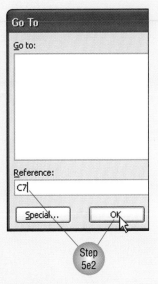

Step 5e2

FIGURE

1.5   **Exercise 1**

	A	B	C	D
1	Name	Hours	Rate	
2	Avery	45	$19.50	
3	Connors	35	$18.75	
4	Estrada	24	$15.00	
5	Juergens	24	$17.50	
6	Mikulich	20	$15.25	
7	Talbot	15	$10.00	
8				

Using Automatic Entering Features

Excel contains several features that help you enter data into cells quickly and efficiently. These features include *AutoComplete*, which automatically inserts data in a cell that begins the same as a previous entry; *AutoCorrect*, which automatically corrects many common typographical errors; and *AutoFill*, which will automatically insert words, numbers, or formulas in a series.

The AutoComplete feature will automatically insert data in a cell that begins the same as a previous entry. If the data inserted by AutoComplete is the data you want in the cell, press Enter. If it is not the desired data, simply continue typing the correct data. This feature can be very useful in a worksheet that contains repetitive data entries. For example, consider a worksheet that repeats the word *Payroll*. The second and subsequent times this word is to be inserted in a cell, simply typing the letter *P* will cause AutoComplete to insert the entire word.

The AutoCorrect feature automatically corrects many common typing errors. To see what symbols and words are in the AutoCorrect feature, click Tools and then AutoCorrect Options. This displays the AutoCorrect dialog box with the AutoCorrect tab selected as shown in Figure 1.6 with a list box containing the replacement data.

1.6 *AutoCorrect Dialog Box with AutoCorrect Tab Selected*

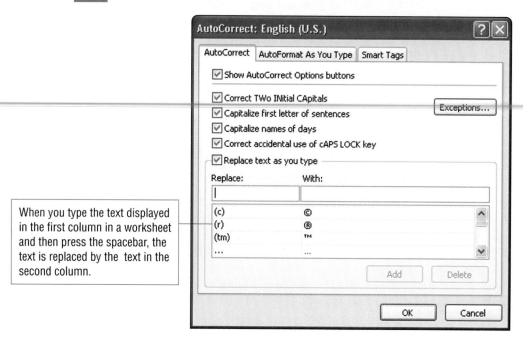

When you type the text displayed in the first column in a worksheet and then press the spacebar, the text is replaced by the text in the second column.

At the AutoCorrect dialog box, type the text shown in the first column in the list box and the text in the second column is inserted in the cell. Along with symbols, the AutoCorrect dialog box contains commonly misspelled words and common typographical errors. The AutoCorrect feature is a helpful tool when entering text in cells.

exercise 2

INSERTING DATA IN CELLS WITH AUTOCOMPLETE

1. Create the worksheet shown in Figure 1.7. To begin, display a clear worksheet window. (If a blank screen displays, click the New button on the Standard toolbar [first button from the left].)
2. Type the text in cell A1 and insert the ® symbol by typing (r). AutoCorrect will change (r) to ® when you press the Enter key.
3. Type the remaining text in the cells. AutoCorrect will correct the spelling of *Benifits*. When you type the W in *West* in cell B5, the AutoComplete feature will insert *West*. Accept this by pressing the Tab key. (Pressing the Tab key accepts *West* and also makes the next cell in the row active.) Use the AutoComplete feature to enter *West* in B6 and B8 and *North* in cell B7. Use AutoComplete to enter the second and subsequent occurrences of *No* and *Yes*.
4. Save the worksheet and name it **sec1x02**.
5. Print **sec1x02**.
6. Close **sec1x02**.

1.7 **Exercise 2**

	A	B	C	D
1	Team Net®			
2	Employee	Location	Benefits	
3	Abbot	West	No	
4	Blalock	North	No	
5	Calhoun	West	Yes	
6	Davis	West	Yes	
7	Hogan	North	Yes	
8	Mikelson	West	No	
9				

When a cell is active, a thick black border surrounds it and a small black square displays in the bottom right side of the border. This black square is called the AutoFill *fill handle* (see Figure 1.2). With the fill handle, you can quickly fill a range of cells with the same data or with consecutive data. For example, suppose you need to insert the year 2005 in consecutive cells. To do this quickly, type 2005 in the first cell, position the mouse pointer on the fill handle, hold down the left mouse button, drag across the cells where you want the year inserted, and then release the mouse button.

You can also use the fill handle to insert a series in consecutive cells. For example, suppose you are creating a worksheet with data for all of the months in the year. Type January in the first cell, position the mouse pointer on the fill handle, hold down the left mouse button, drag down or across to 11 more cells, and then release the mouse button. Excel automatically inserts the other 11 months in the year in the proper order. When using the fill handle, the cells must be adjacent. Table 1.3 identifies the sequence inserted in cells by Excel when specific data is entered.

1.3 **AutoFill Fill Handle Series**

Enter this data (Commas represent data in separate cells.)	And the fill handle will insert this sequence in adjacent cells
January	February, March, April, and so on…
Jan	Feb, Mar, Apr, and so on…
Jan 04, Jan 05	Jan-04, Jan-05, Jan-06, Jan-07, and so on…
Monday	Tuesday, Wednesday, Thursday, and so on…
Product 1	Product 2, Product 3, Product 4, and so on…
Qtr 1	Qtr 2, Qtr 3, Qtr 4
2, 4	6, 8, 10, and so on…

Certain sequences, such as *2, 4* and *Jan 04, Jan 05,* require that both cells be selected before using the fill handle. If only the cell containing *2* is active, the fill handle will insert *2*s in the selected cells. The list in Table 1.3 is only a sampling of what the fill handle can do. You may find a variety of other sequences that can be inserted in a worksheet using the fill handle.

An Auto Fill Options button displays when you fill cells with the fill handle. Click this button and a list of options displays for filling the cells. By default, data and formatting are filled in each cell. You can choose to fill only the formatting in the cells or fill only the data without the formatting.

Turning On/Off and Maneuvering in the Task Pane

When you first open Microsoft Excel, the Getting Started task pane displays at the right side of the screen. With options in the Getting Started task pane, you can open a specific worksheet, create a new worksheet, or search for specific information about Office. Depending on the actions you are performing, the task pane may be removed from the screen. For example, if you click the New button on the Standard toolbar, a clear worksheet window displays and the task pane is removed. You can control whether the display of the task pane is on or off by clicking View and then Task Pane. You can also close the task pane by clicking the Close button (contains an *X*) located in the upper right corner of the task pane.

As you learn more features in Excel, the options in the task pane as well as the task pane name may change. Maneuver within various task panes with buttons on the task pane toolbar. Click the Back button (contains a left arrow) on the toolbar to display the previous task pane or click the Forward button (contains a right arrow) to display the next task pane. Click the Home button to return to the Getting Started task pane. You can also maneuver within various task panes by clicking the Other Task Panes button (contains the name of the task pane and a down arrow) and then clicking the desired task pane at the drop-down list.

The task pane can be docked and undocked. By default, the task pane is docked at the right side of the screen. Undock (move) the task pane by positioning the mouse pointer to the right of the task pane toolbar, holding down the left mouse button (mouse pointer turns into a four-headed arrow), and then dragging the task pane to the desired location. If you undock the task pane, you can dock it back at the right side of the screen by double-clicking to the right of the task pane toolbar.

exercise 3

INSERTING DATA IN CELLS WITH THE FILL HANDLE

1. Create the worksheet shown in Figure 1.8. To begin, display a clear worksheet window. (If a blank screen displays, click the New button on the Standard toolbar [first button from the left].)
2. Type **January** in cell B1.

3. Position the mouse pointer on the fill handle for cell B1, hold down the left mouse button, drag across to cell G1, and then release the mouse button.

Step 3

4. Type the years (2002, 2003, and so on) in cells A2 through A5.
5. Make cell B2 active and then type **100**.
6. Drag the fill handle for cell B2 to cell E2. (This inserts *100* in cells C2, D2, and E2.)

Step 6

7. Type the text in the remaining cells as shown in Figure 1.8. Use the fill handle to fill adjacent cells.
8. Save the worksheet and name it **sec1x03**.
9. Print and then close **sec1x03**.

F I G U R E

1.8 **Exercise 3**

	A	B	C	D	E	F	G	H
1		January	February	March	April	May	June	
2	2002	100	100	100	100	125	125	
3	2003	150	150	150	150	175	175	
4	2004	200	200	200	150	150	150	
5	2005	250	250	250	250	250	250	
6								

Selecting Cells

Cells within a worksheet can be formatted in a variety of ways. For example, the alignment of data in cells or rows can be changed or character formatting can be added. To identify the cells that are to be affected by the formatting, select the specific cells.

Selecting Cells Using the Mouse

Select specific cells in a worksheet using the mouse or select columns or rows. Methods for selecting cells using the mouse display in Table 1.4.

1.4   *Selecting with the Mouse*

To select this	Do this
Column	Position the cell pointer on the column header (a letter) and then click the left mouse button.
Row	Position the cell pointer on the row header (a number) and then click the left mouse button.
Adjacent cells	Drag with mouse to select specific cells.
Nonadjacent cells	Hold down the Ctrl key while clicking column header, row header, or specific cells.
All cells in worksheet	Click Select All button (refer to Figure 1.2).

HINT

Select nonadjacent columns or rows by holding down the Ctrl key while selecting cells.

Selected cells, except the active cell, display with a light blue background (this may vary) rather than a white background. The active cell is the first cell in the selection block and displays in the normal manner (white background with black data). Selected cells remain selected until you click a cell with the mouse or press an arrow key on the keyboard.

HINT

The first cell in a range displays with a white background and is the active cell.

Selecting Cells Using the Keyboard

The keyboard can be used to select specific cells within a worksheet. Table 1.5 displays the commands for selecting specific cells.

1.5   *Selecting Cells Using the Keyboard*

To select	Press
Cells in direction of arrow key	Shift + arrow key
To beginning of row	Shift + Home
To beginning of worksheet	Shift + Ctrl + Home
To last cell in worksheet containing data	Shift + Ctrl + End
An entire column	Ctrl + spacebar
An entire row	Shift + spacebar
An entire worksheet	Ctrl + A or Ctrl + Shift + spacebar

exercise 7

1. At a clear document screen, display information on entering data in a worksheet. To begin, click the Microsoft Office Excel Help button on the Standard toolbar. (This displays the Excel Help task pane.)

2. Type **How do I enter data in a cell?** in the *Search* text box and then press Enter.

3. Click the <u>Enter data in worksheet cells</u> hyperlink in the results list box. (This displays the Microsoft Office Excel Help window.)

4. Click the <u>Show All</u> hyperlink that displays in the upper right corner of the window.

5. Read the information about entering data in cells. (You will need to scroll down the window to display all of the information.)

6. Click the Close button to close the Microsoft Office Excel Help window.

7. Close the Search Results task pane.

Step 2

Excel Help

Assistance

Search for:
How do I enter data in a cell?

Table of Contents

Office Online

Step 3

Search Results

30 results from Office Online

Enter data in worksheet cells
Help > Entering and Editing Data

Enter data in a cell from a list you specify
Help > Validating Cell Entries

CHAPTER summary

➤ Use an Excel spreadsheet to create financial statements, prepare budgets, manage inventory, and analyze cash flow. Numbers and values can be easily manipulated in an Excel spreadsheet to answer "what if" questions.

➤ A document created in Excel is called a workbook. A workbook consists of individual worksheets. The intersections of columns and rows in a worksheet are referred to as cells.

➤ An Excel window contains the following elements: Title bar, Menu bar, Standard toolbar, Formatting toolbar, Formula bar, worksheet area, task pane, scroll bars, sheet tabs, and Status bar.

➤ The gray horizontal and vertical lines that define cells in the worksheet area are called gridlines.

➤ When the insertion point is positioned in a cell, the cell reference displays in the Name box located at the left side of the Formula bar. The cell reference includes the column letter and row number.

➤ To enter data in a cell, make the cell active, and then type the data. To move the insertion point to the next cell, press the Tab key. To move the insertion point to the previous cell, press Shift + Tab. For other insertion point movement commands, refer to Table 1.2.

- ➤ Data being entered in a cell displays in the cell as well as in the Formula bar.
- ➤ If data entered in a cell consists of text (letters) and the text does not fit into the cell, it overlaps the cell to the right. However, if the data being entered are numbers and do not fit in the cell, the numbers are changed to number symbols (###).
- ➤ To replace data in a cell, click the cell once, and then type the new data. To edit data within a cell, double-click the cell, and then make necessary changes.
- ➤ The AutoComplete feature will automatically insert a previous entry if the character or characters being typed in a cell match a previous entry.
- ➤ The AutoCorrect feature corrects many common typographical errors.
- ➤ Use the AutoFill fill handle to fill a range of cells with the same or consecutive data.
- ➤ The task pane presents features to help the user easily identify and use more of the program.
- ➤ Select all cells in a column by clicking the column header. Select all cells in a row by clicking the row header. Select all cells in a worksheet by clicking the Select All button located immediately to the left of the column headers.
- ➤ To select cells with the mouse, refer to Table 1.4; to select cells using the keyboard, refer to Table 1.5.
- ➤ Apply automatic formatting to selected cells in a worksheet with autoformats available at the AutoFormat dialog box.
- ➤ Get help by typing a question in the Ask a Question text box located at the right side of the Menu bar.
- ➤ Display the Excel Help task pane by clicking the Microsoft Office Excel Help button on the Standard toolbar or by clicking Help and then Microsoft Office Excel Help.

FEATURES summary

FEATURE	BUTTON	MENU	KEYBOARD
Save As dialog box		File, Save As	
Open dialog box	📂	File, Open	Ctrl + O
Print worksheet	🖨		
Print dialog box		File, Print	Ctrl + P
Close worksheet		File, Close	
AutoFormat dialog box		Format, AutoFormat	
Excel Help task pane	⊙	Help, Microsoft Office Excel Help	F1

CONCEPTS check

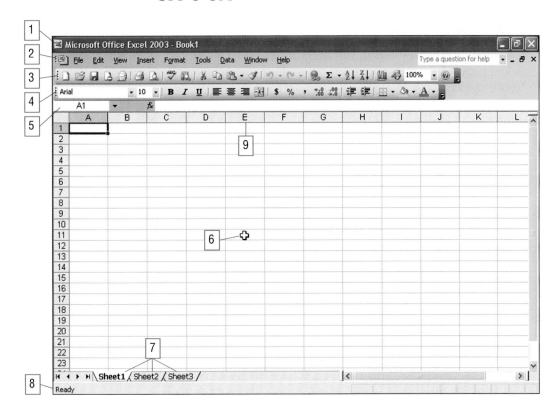

Identifying: Look at the Excel screen shown above. This screen contains numbers with lines pointing to specific items. On a blank sheet of paper, write the name of the item that corresponds with the number in the Excel screen.

Completion: On a blank sheet of paper, indicate the correct term, symbol, or command for each description.

1. Press this key on the keyboard to move the insertion point to the next cell.
2. Press these keys on the keyboard to move the insertion point to the previous cell.
3. Columns in a worksheet are labeled with this.
4. Rows in a worksheet are labeled with this.
5. Click this button in the worksheet area to select all cells in the table.
6. The gray horizontal and vertical lines that define the cells in a worksheet area are referred to as this.
7. If a number entered in a cell is too long to fit inside the cell, the number is changed to this.
8. Data being typed in a cell displays in the cell as well as here.
9. This is the name of the small black square that displays in the bottom right corner of the active cell.
10. To select nonadjacent columns using the mouse, hold down this key on the keyboard while clicking the column headers.
11. Automatically apply formatting to selected cells in a worksheet with formats available at this dialog box.

SKILLS check

Assessment 1

1. Create the worksheet shown in Figure 1.10.
2. Select cells A1 through C5 and then apply the *Accounting 1* AutoFormat.
3. Save the worksheet and name it **sec1sc01**.
4. Print and then close **sec1sc01**.

FIGURE

1.10 *Assessment 1*

	A	B	C	D
1	Expense	Original	Current	
2	Labor	97000	98500	
3	Material	129000	153000	
4	Permits	1200	1350	
5	Tax	1950	2145	
6				

Assessment 2

1. Create the worksheet shown in Figure 1.11. To create the © symbol in cell A1, type (c). Type the misspelled words as shown and let the AutoCorrect feature correct the spelling. Use the AutoComplete feature to insert the second occurrence of *Category*, *Available*, and *Balance*.
2. Select cells A1 through B7 and then apply the *Classic 2* AutoFormat.
3. Save the worksheet and name it **sec1sc02**.
4. Print and then close **sec1sc02**.

FIGURE

1.11 *Assessment 2*

	A	B	C
1	Premiere Plan©		
2	Plan A	Catagory	
3		Availalbe	
4		Balence	
5	Plan B	Category	
6		Available	
7		Balence	
8			

Assessment 3

1. Create the worksheet shown in Figure 1.12. Type Monday in cell B2 and then use the fill handle to fill in the remaining days of the week. Use the fill handle to enter other repetitive data.
2. Select cells A1 through F4 and then apply an autoformat of your choosing.
3. Save the worksheet and name it **sec1sc03**.
4. Print and then close **sec1sc03**.

FIGURE

1.12 *Assessment 3*

	A	B	C	D	E	F	G
1	CAPITAL INVESTMENTS						
2		Monday	Tuesday	Wednesday	Thursday	Friday	
3	Budget	350	350	350	350	350	
4	Actual	310	425	290	375	400	
5							

Assessment 4

1. Use the Help feature to learn more about how to scroll within an Excel worksheet.
2. Read and then print the information provided by Help.
3. Create a worksheet containing the information. Set this up as a worksheet with two columns (cells will contain only text—not numbers). Create a title for the worksheet.
4. Apply an autoformat to the cells in the table.
5. Save the completed worksheet and name it **sec1sc04**.
6. Print and then close **sec1sc04**.

CHAPTER challenge

You have been hired to manage a small business, Barry's Better Built Barns, which specializes in selling and building yard barns. Barry has asked you to prepare a sample budget based on last year's data. His operating income last year was $500,000. His expenses included: Salaries, $75,000; Building Materials, $122,000; Paint, $15,000; and Miscellaneous, $17,000. Create a worksheet showing this information. Apply an autoformat to the cells in the worksheet. Save the workbook.

Barry would like to know what his net income was for last year. This can be calculated by subtracting the total expenses from gross income. Use the Help feature to learn how to create simple formulas. Using the worksheet created in the first part of the Chapter Challenge, insert a formula that adds the total expenses and identify that amount appropriately. Also, insert a formula that subtracts total expenses from the net income. Again, identify the amount appropriately. Save and print the workbook.

 **INTEGRATED**

In Word, create a short memo to Barry that includes the information from the worksheet created in the first part of the Chapter Challenge. Copy the information into the memo. Explain how the net income was calculated. Also, provide an explanation of your recommendations for the upcoming year's budget based on last year's information. Save the memo and print it.

FORMATTING AN EXCEL WORKSHEET

PERFORMANCE OBJECTIVES

Upon successful completion of Chapter 2, you will be able to:

➤ Preview a worksheet
➤ Apply formatting to data in cells
➤ Change column widths
➤ Change row heights
➤ Format numbers in a worksheet
➤ Insert rows and columns in a worksheet
➤ Delete cells, rows, and columns in a worksheet
➤ Clear data in cells
➤ Add borders, shading, and patterns to cells in a worksheet
➤ Repeat the last action
➤ Automate formatting with Format Painter

The appearance of a worksheet on the screen and how it looks when printed is called the *format*. In the previous chapter, you learned how to apply formatting automatically with choices at the AutoFormat dialog box. You can also apply specific formatting to cells in a worksheet. For example, you can change column width and row height; apply character formatting such as bold, italics, and underlining; specify number formatting; insert and delete rows and columns; and apply borders, shading, and patterns to cells.

Preview a Worksheet
Click Print Preview button in Print dialog box.
OR
Click Print Preview button on Standard toolbar.
OR
Click File, Print Preview.

Print
Preview

Previewing a Worksheet

Before printing a worksheet, consider previewing it to see how it will appear when printed. To preview a worksheet, click the Preview button in the Print dialog box; click the Print Preview button on the Standard toolbar; or click File and then Print Preview. This causes the worksheet to display on the screen as it will appear when printed. Figure 2.1 displays the worksheet named ExcelWorksheet01 in Print Preview. Note that the gridlines in the worksheet will not print.

2.1 *Worksheet in Print Preview*

Print Preview
Toolbar

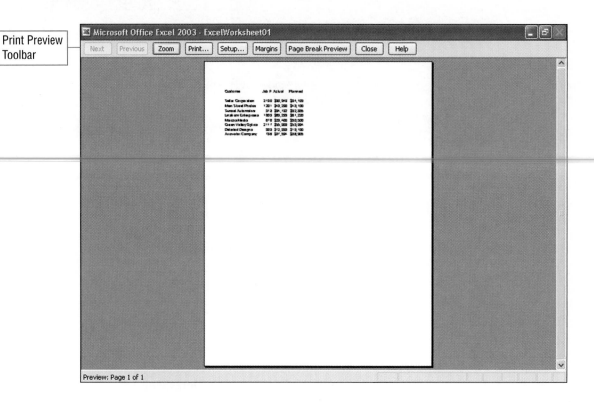

HINT

In Print Preview with the Margins button active, change worksheet margins by dragging margin borders.

To zoom in on the worksheet and make the display bigger, click the Zoom button on the Print Preview toolbar. This toolbar displays at the top of the screen immediately below the Title bar. Click the Print button on the Print Preview toolbar to send the worksheet to the printer. Click the Setup button and the Page Setup dialog box displays where you can specify the orientation of the page and the paper size. Clicking the Margins button causes margin boundary lines to display on the worksheet. Clicking this button again removes the margin boundary lines. After viewing the worksheet, click the Close button to remove Print Preview and return to the worksheet.

HINT

Click the *Selection* option at the Zoom drop-down list and the selected area fills the window.

```
100%  ▼
```

Zoom

Changing the Zoom Setting

In Print Preview, you can zoom in on the worksheet and make the display bigger. You can also change the size of the display at the worksheet (not in Print Preview) with the options on the Zoom button. To change the percentage of display, click the down arrow at the right side of the Zoom button on the Standard toolbar and then click the desired percentage at the drop-down list. You can also click the Zoom button to select the current percentage measurement, type a new percentage, and then press Enter.

Applying Formatting with Buttons on the Formatting Toolbar

A variety of formatting can be applied to cells in a worksheet using buttons on the Formatting toolbar. With buttons on the Formatting toolbar shown in Figure 2.2, you can change the font and font size and bold, italicize, and underline data in cells. To apply bold to a cell or selected cells, click the Bold button on the Formatting toolbar; click the Italic button to apply italics; and click the Underline button to apply underlining formatting.

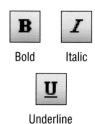

B Bold   **I** Italic

U Underline

FIGURE

2.2 **Formatting Toolbar**

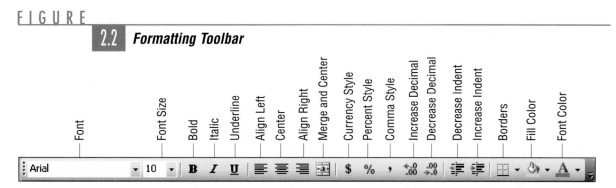

With other buttons on the Formatting toolbar, you can change the alignment of text within cells, increase or decrease the number of digits after a decimal point, increase or decrease indents, change the cell border, add fill color to a cell, and change text color.

(Note: Before completing computer exercises, delete the ExcelChapter01S folder on your disk. Next, copy the ExcelChapter02S subfolder from the Excel2003Specialist folder on the CD that accompanies this textbook to your disk and then make ExcelChapter02S the active folder.)

exercise 1

FORMATTING AND PREVIEWING A WORKSHEET

1. Open **ExcelWorksheet01**.
2. Save the worksheet with Save As and name it **sec2x01**.
3. Select and then bold and italicize the first row by completing the following steps:
   a. Position the cell pointer on the row 1 header (this is the number 1 that displays at the left side of the screen, immediately left of *Customer*) and then click the left mouse button.
   b. Click the Bold button and then click the Italic button on the Formatting toolbar.
4. Select and then bold the data in cells A3 through A10 by completing the following steps:

Step 3b

	Arial		10		**B** *I* <u>U</u>
	A1	▼		*fx*	Customer

	A	B	C
1	Customer	Job #	Actual
2			
3	Sellar Corporation	2130	$30,349
4	Main Street Photos	1201	$48,290
5	Sunset Automotive	318	$34,192

Step 3a

a. Position the cell pointer in cell A3, hold down the left mouse button, drag the cell pointer to cell A10, and then release the mouse button.

b. Click the Bold button on the Formatting toolbar.

5. Select and then italicize the data in cells B3 through D10 by completing the following steps:

a. Position the cell pointer in cell B3, hold down the left mouse button, drag the cell pointer to cell D10, and then release the mouse button.

b. Click the Italic button on the Formatting toolbar.

6. Click in cell A1. (This deselects the cells.)

7. Preview the worksheet by completing the following steps:

a. Click the Print Preview button on the Standard toolbar.

b. At the print preview screen, click the Zoom button. (This increases the display of the worksheet cells.)

c. After viewing the worksheet, click the Close button.

8. Change the zoom display by completing the following steps:

a. Click the down-pointing arrow at the right side of the Zoom button on the Standard toolbar and then click *200%* at the drop-down list.

b. After viewing the worksheet at 200% display, click the Zoom button (this selects *200%*), type 150, and then press Enter. (This changes the zoom percentage to 150%.)

c. Change the zoom back to 100% by clicking the down-pointing arrow at the right side of the Zoom button and then clicking *100%* at the drop-down list.

9. Save, print, and then close **sec2x01**. (The gridlines will not print.)

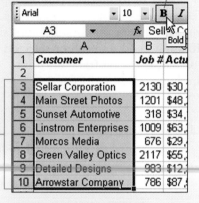

exercise 2

CHANGING THE FONT AND FONT COLOR FOR DATA IN A WORKSHEET

1. Open **ExcelWorksheet01**.

2. Save the worksheet with Save As and name it **sec2x02**.

3. Select the entire worksheet and then change the font and font color by completing the following steps:

a. Click the Select All button. (This is the gray button that displays immediately left of column header A and immediately above row header 1.)

b. Click the down-pointing arrow at the right side of the Font button on the Formatting toolbar.

c. At the drop-down list that displays, scroll down the list and then click *Garamond*. (If Garamond is not available, choose another serif typeface such as Century.)

d. Click the down-pointing arrow at the right side of the Font Size button on the Formatting toolbar and then click *11* at the drop-down list.

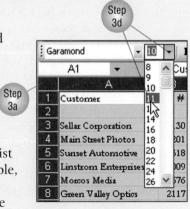

e. Click the down-pointing arrow at the right side of the Font Color button (this is the last button on the Formatting toolbar). At the palette of color choices, click the Blue color that is the sixth color from the left in the second row.

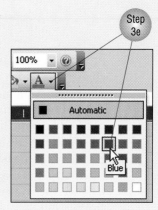

4. Click once in cell A6 and then change *Linstrom Enterprises* to *Jefferson, Inc.*

5. Double-click in cell A7 and then change *Morcos Media* to *Morcos Corp.* (Include the period after *Corp.*)

6. Click once in cell C6 and then change *$63,293* to *$59,578.*

7. Click once in any other cell.

8. Preview the worksheet by completing the following steps:

	A	B	C	D
1	Customer	Job #	Actual	Planned
2				
3	Sellar Corporation	2130	$30,349	$34,109
4	Main Street Photos	1201	$48,290	$48,100
5	Sunset Automotive	318	$34,192	$32,885
6	Jefferson, Inc.	1009	$59,578	$61,220
7	Morcos Corp.	676	$29,400	$30,500
8	Green Valley Optics	2117	$55,309	$58,394
9	Detailed Designs	983	$12,398	$13,100
10	Arrowstar Company	786	$87,534	$86,905

Step 4
Step 5
Step 6

a. Click the Print Preview button on the Standard toolbar.
b. At the print preview screen, increase the size of the display by clicking the Zoom button. (Skip this step if the size is already increased.)
c. After viewing the worksheet, click the Close button.

9. Save, print, and then close **sec2x02**. (The gridlines will not print. If you are not printing on a color printer, the data will print in black rather than blue.)

Changing Column Width

Columns in a worksheet are the same width by default. In some worksheets you may want to change column widths to accommodate more or less data. Changes to column widths can be made using the mouse on column boundaries or at a dialog box.

Changing Column Width Using Column Boundaries

The mouse can be used to change the width of a column or selected columns. For example, to change the width of column B, you would position the mouse pointer on the black boundary line between columns B and C in the column header until the mouse pointer turns into a double-headed arrow pointing left and right and then drag the boundary to the right to increase the size or to the left to decrease the size. The width of selected columns that are adjacent can be changed at the same time. To do this, select the columns and then drag one of the column boundaries within the selected columns. As the boundary is being dragged, the column width changes for all selected columns.

As a column boundary is being dragged, the column width displays in a yellow box above the mouse pointer. The column width number that displays represents the average number of characters in the standard font that can fit in a cell.

QUICK STEPS

Change Column Width
Drag column boundary line.
OR
Double-click column boundary.
OR
1. Click Format, Column, Width.
2. Type desired number.
3. Click OK.

exercise 3

1. At a blank Excel worksheet, create the worksheet shown in Figure 2.3. To begin, change the width of column A by completing the following steps:
   a. Position the mouse pointer on the column boundary in the column header between columns A and B until it turns into a double-headed arrow pointing left and right.
   b. Hold down the left mouse button, drag the column boundary to the right until *Width: 17.00 (124 pixels)* displays in the yellow box, and then release the mouse button.

2. Change the width of columns B, C, and D by completing the following steps:
   a. Select columns B, C, and D. To do this, position the cell pointer on the letter *B* in the column header, hold down the left mouse button, drag the cell pointer to the letter *D* in the column header, and then release the mouse button.
   b. Position the cell pointer on the column boundary between columns B and C until it turns into a double-headed arrow pointing left and right.
   c. Hold down the left mouse button, drag the column boundary to the right until *Width: 13.00 (96 pixels)* displays in the yellow box, and then release the mouse button.

3. Type the data in the cells as shown in Figure 2.3. Type the dollar signs and decimal points as shown. (Consider using the fill handle for the months. To do this, type October in cell B1, position the mouse pointer on the fill handle, hold down the left mouse button, drag to cell D1, and then release the mouse button.)

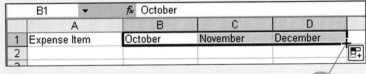

4. After typing the data in the cells, make the following formatting changes:
   a. Select the entire worksheet and then change the font to 12-point Tahoma (or a similar typeface).
   b. Select row 1 and then apply bold and italic formatting.

5. Click in cell A1. (This deselects the cells.)

6. Save the worksheet and name it **sec2x03**.

7. Preview the worksheet.

8. Print and then close **sec2x03**.

FIGURE

2.3 **Exercise 3**

	A	B	C	D	E
1	Expense Item	October	November	December	
2	Salaries	$25,450.50	$26,090.65	$26,445.00	
3	Lease	$5,650.00	$5,650.00	$5,650.00	
4	Insurance	$5,209.65	$5,335.55	$5,621.45	
5	Utilities	$2,100.50	$2,249.75	$2,441.35	
6	Maintenance	$1,430.00	$1,119.67	$1,450.50	
7					

EXCEL

A column width in an existing worksheet can be adjusted to fit the longest entry in the column. To automatically adjust a column width to the longest entry, position the cell pointer on the column boundary at the right side of the column and then double-click the left mouse button.

exercise 4

1. Open **ExcelWorksheet01**.
2. Save the worksheet with Save As and name it **sec2x04**.
3. Select the entire worksheet and then change the font to 14-point Times New Roman.
4. Adjust the width of the first column to accommodate the longest entry in the column by completing the following steps:
    a. Position the cell pointer on the column boundary between columns A and B until it turns into a double-headed arrow pointing left and right.
    b. Double-click the left mouse button.

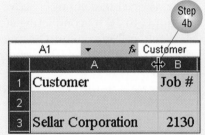

5. Select row 1 and then click the Bold button on the Formatting toolbar.
6. Click in cell A1. (This deselects the cells.)
7. Save, preview, print, and then close **sec2x04**.

Changing Column Width at the Column Width Dialog Box

At the Column Width dialog box shown in Figure 2.4, you can specify a column width number. The column width number represents the average number of characters in the standard font that will fit in a cell. Increase the column width number to make the column wider or decrease the column width number to make the column narrower.

To display the Column Width dialog box, click Format, point to Column, and then click Width. At the Column Width dialog box, type the number representing the average number of characters in the standard font that you want to fit in the column, and then press Enter or click OK.

FIGURE

2.4 *Column Width Dialog Box*

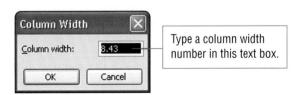

Type a column width number in this text box.

exercise 5

1. At a blank Excel worksheet, create the worksheet shown in Figure 2.5. To begin, change the width of column A by completing the following steps:
   a. Make sure any cell in column A is active.
   b. Click Format, point to Column, and then click Width.
   c. At the Column Width dialog box, type **10** in the *Column width* text box.
   d. Click OK to close the dialog box.

   Step 1c

   Column Width ☒

   Column width: [10]

   [OK]   [Cancel]

   Step 1d

2. Make any cell in column B active and then change the width of column B to *5* by completing steps similar to those in Step 1.
3. Make any cell in column C active and then change the width of column C to *10* by completing steps similar to those in Step 1.
4. Make any cell in column D active and then change the width of column D to *10* by completing steps similar to those in Step 1.
5. Type the data in the cells as shown in Figure 2.5. Use the fill handle to insert the months.

A2	▼	*fx* Ja
	A	B	C
1	Month	Emp	Actual
2	January		
3	February		
4	March		
5	April		
6	May		
7	June		
8			

6. After typing the data in the cells, make the following formatting changes:
   a. Select the entire worksheet and then change the font to 12-point Garamond (or a similar serif typeface).
   b. Select row 1 and then apply bold formatting.
7. Click in cell A1.
8. Save the worksheet and name it **sec2x05**.
9. Preview, print, and then close **sec2x05**.

   Step 5

FIGURE

2.5 *Exercise 5*

	A	B	C	D	E
1	Month	Emp	Actual	Budget	
2	January	320	$3,121.50	$3,005.60	
3	February	197	$3,450.78	$3,500.20	
4	March	763	$2,109.45	$2,229.67	
5	April	804	$4,312.50	$4,110.30	
6	May	334	$5,110.40	$4,995.00	
7	June	105	$1,894.35	$1,995.15	
8					

Change Row Height
Drag row boundary line.
OR
1. Click Format, Row, Height.
2. Type desired number.
3. Click OK.

Changing Row Height

Row height can be changed in much the same manner as column width. For example, you can change the row height using the mouse on a row boundary, or at the Row Height dialog box.

Changing Row Height Using Row Boundaries

Change row height using a row boundary in the same manner as you learned to change column width. To do this, position the cell pointer on the boundary between rows in the row header until it turns into a double-headed arrow pointing up and down, hold down the left mouse button, drag up or down until the row is the desired height, and then release the mouse button.

The height of selected rows that are adjacent can be changed at the same time. (The height of nonadjacent rows will not all change at the same time.) To do this, select the rows, and then drag one of the row boundaries within the selected rows. As the boundary is being dragged, the row height changes for all selected rows.

As a row boundary is being dragged, the row height displays in a yellow box above the mouse pointer. The row height number that displays represents a point measurement. A vertical inch contains approximately 72 points. Increase the point size to increase the row height; decrease the point size to decrease the row height.

exercise 6

CHANGING ROW HEIGHT USING A ROW BOUNDARY

1. Open **ExcelWorksheet05**.
2. Save the worksheet with Save As and name it **sec2x06**.
3. Change the font size of *January* to 14 by completing the following steps:
   a. Make cell A1 the active cell.
   b. Click the down-pointing arrow at the right of the Font Size button on the Formatting toolbar.
   c. From the drop-down list that displays, click *14*.
4. Change the height of row 1 by completing the following steps:
   a. Position the cell pointer in the row header on the row boundary between rows 1 and 2 until it turns into a double-headed arrow pointing up and down.
   b. Hold down the left mouse button, drag the row boundary down until *Height: 27.00 (36 pixels)* displays in the yellow box, and then release the mouse button.

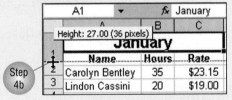

5. Change the height of rows 2 through 8 by completing the following steps:
   a. Select rows 2 through 8. To do this, position the cell pointer on the number 2 in the row header, hold down the left mouse button, drag the cell pointer to the number 8 in the row header, and then release the mouse button.
   b. Position the cell pointer on the row boundary between rows 2 and 3 until it turns into a double-headed arrow pointing up and down.
   c. Hold down the left mouse button, drag the row boundary down until *Height: 21.00 (28 pixels)* displays in the yellow box, and then release the mouse button.

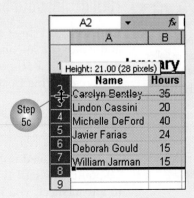

6. Click in cell A1.
7. Save, preview, print, and then close **sec2x06**.

Changing Row Height at the Row Height Dialog Box

At the Row Height dialog box shown in Figure 2.6, you can specify a row height number. To display the Row Height dialog box, click Format, point to Row, and then click Height.

F I G U R E

2.6 *Row Height Dialog Box*

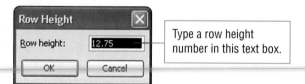

Type a row height number in this text box.

exercise 7

CHANGING ROW HEIGHT AT THE ROW HEIGHT DIALOG BOX

1. Open **ExcelWorksheet07**.
2. Save the worksheet with Save As and name it **sec2x07**.
3. Change the font size of *REAL PHOTOGRAPHY* to 14 points.
4. Change the height of row 1 by completing the following steps:
   a. With cell A1 active, click Format, point to Row, and then click Height.
   b. At the Row Height dialog box, type **30** in the *Row height* text box, and then click OK.
5. Change the height of rows 2 through 10 by completing the following steps:
   a. Select rows 2 through 10.
   b. Click Format, point to Row, and then click Height.
   c. At the Row Height dialog box, type **20** in the *Row height* text box, and then press Enter or click OK.
6. Click in cell A1.
7. Save, preview, print, and then close **sec2x07**.

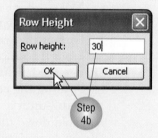

Step 4b

Formatting Data in Cells

An Excel worksheet contains default formatting. For example, by default, letters and words are aligned at the left of a cell, numbers are aligned at the right, and data is set in a 10-point sans serif typeface such as Arial. Depending on the data you are entering in cells, you may want to change some of these default settings.

Formatting Numbers

Numbers in a cell, by default, are aligned at the right and decimals and commas are not displayed unless they are typed in the cell. Also, numbers display in a 10-point sans serif typeface such as Arial. Depending on the type of numbers used in a worksheet, you may want to change these default settings. You can format numbers using a format symbol, or change number formatting with buttons on the Formatting toolbar or with options at the Format Cells dialog box.

EXCEL

Format symbols you can use to format numbers include a percent sign (%), a comma (,), and a dollar sign ($). For example, if you type the number *$45.50* in a cell, Excel automatically applies Currency formatting to the number. If you type *45%*, Excel automatically applies the Percent formatting to the number.

Five buttons on the Formatting toolbar can be used to format numbers in cells. The five buttons are shown and described in Table 2.1.

TABLE

2.1 ***Number Formatting Buttons on Formatting Toolbar***

Click this button	Named	To do this
$	Currency Style	Add a dollar sign, any necessary commas, and a decimal point followed by two decimal digits, if none are typed; right-align number in cell
%	Percent Style	Multiply cell value by 100 and display result with a percent symbol; right-align number in cell
,	Comma Style	Add any necessary commas and a decimal point followed by two decimal digits, if none are typed; right-align number in cell
←.0 .00	Increase Decimal	Increase number of decimal places displayed after decimal point in selected cells
.00 →.0	Decrease Decimal	Decrease number of decimal places displayed after decimal point in selected cells

Specify the formatting for numbers in cells in a worksheet before typing the numbers, or format existing numbers in a worksheet. The Increase Decimal and Decrease Decimal buttons on the Formatting toolbar will change decimal places for existing numbers only.

Increase Decimal

Decrease Decimal

1. Open **ExcelWorksheet08**.
2. Save the worksheet with Save As and name it **sec2x08**.
3. Change the width of column A to 13.00.
4. Select columns B, C, and D, and then change the column width to 10.00.
5. Change the width of column E to 8.00.
6. Make the following number formatting changes:
   a. Select cells B3 through D12.
   b. Click the Currency Style button on the Formatting toolbar.
   c. Click twice the Decrease Decimal button on the Formatting toolbar. (The numbers in the selected cells should not contain any decimal places.)

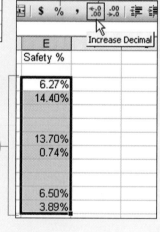

   d. Select cells E3 through E12.
   e. Click the Percent Style button on the Formatting toolbar.
   f. Click twice the Increase Decimal button on the Formatting toolbar. (There should now be two decimal places in the percent numbers in the selected cells.)
7. Select and then bold column A.
8. Select cells B1 through E1 and then click the Bold button.
9. Click in cell A1.
10. Save, print, and then close **sec2x08**.

HINT

Another method for displaying the Format Cells dialog box is to right-click a cell and then click Format Cells at the shortcut menu.

Numbers in cells can also be formatted with options at the Format Cells dialog box with the Number tab selected as shown in Figure 2.7. Display this dialog box by clicking Format and then Cells.

2.7 *Format Cells Dialog Box with Number Tab Selected*

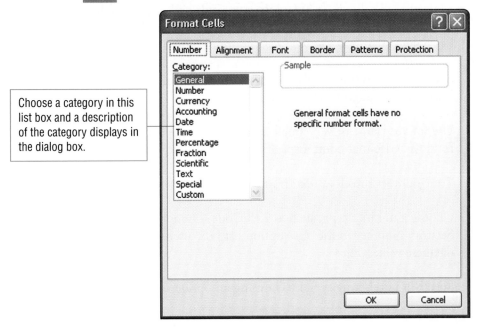

Choose a category in this list box and a description of the category displays in the dialog box.

The left side of the dialog box displays number categories. The default category is *General*. At this setting no specific formatting is applied to numbers except right-aligning numbers in cells. The other number categories are described in Table 2.2.

TABLE

2.2 *Number Categories at the Format Cells Dialog Box*

Click this category	To apply this number formatting
Number	Specify number of decimal places and whether or not a thousand separator should be used; choose the display of negative numbers; right-align numbers in cell
Currency	Apply general monetary values; dollar sign is added as well as commas and decimal points, if needed; right-align numbers in cell
Accounting	Line up the currency symbol and decimal points in a column; add dollar sign and two digits after a decimal point; right-align numbers in cell
Date	Display date as date value; specify the type of formatting desired by clicking an option in the *Type* list box; right-align date in cell
Time	Display time as time value; specify the type of formatting desired by clicking an option in the *Type* list box; right-align time in cell

Continued on next page

Click this category	To apply this number formatting
Percentage	Multiply cell value by 100 and display result with a percent symbol; add decimal point followed by two digits by default; number of digits can be changed with the *Decimal places* option; right-align number in cell
Fraction	Specify how fraction displays in cell by clicking an option in the *Type* list box; right-align fraction in cell
Scientific	Use for very large or very small numbers. Use the letter *E* to tell Excel to move a decimal point a specified number of positions
Text	Treat number in cell as text; number is displayed in cell exactly as typed
Special	Choose a number type, such as ZIP Code, Phone Number, or Social Security Number in the *Type* option list box; useful for tracking list and database values
Custom	Specify a numbering type by choosing an option in the *Type* list box

exercise 9

FORMATTING NUMBERS AT THE FORMAT CELLS DIALOG BOX

1. Open **ExcelWorksheet02**.
2. Save the worksheet with Save As and name it **sec2x09**.
3. Change the number formatting by completing the following steps:
   a. Select cells B2 through D8.
   b. Click Format and then Cells.
   c. At the Format Cells dialog box with the Number tab selected, click *Currency* in the *Category* list box.
   d. Click the down-pointing arrow at the right of the *Decimal places* option until *0* displays in the *Decimal places* text box.
   e. Click OK to close the dialog box.
4. Select and then bold and italicize row 1.
5. Save and then print **sec2x09**.
6. With **sec2x09** still open, change the display of negative numbers by completing the following steps:

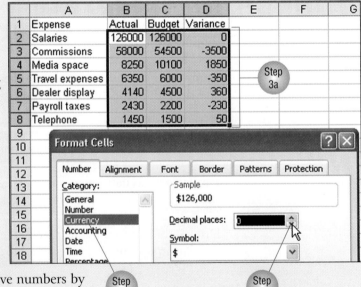

a. Select cells D2 through D8.
b. Click Format and then Cells.
c. At the Format Cells dialog box, click the fourth option displayed in the Negative numbers list box (displays as *($1,234)*).
d. Click OK to close the dialog box.
e. Click in cell A1.
7. Save, print, and then close **sec2x09**.

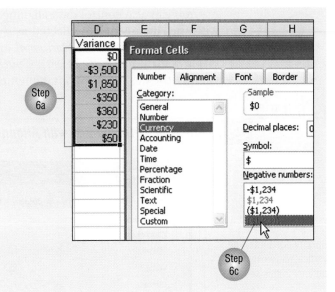

Aligning, Indenting, and Rotating Data in Cells

The alignment of data in cells depends on the type of data entered. For example, words or text combined with numbers entered in a cell are aligned at the left edge of the cell while numbers are aligned at the right. Alignment of data can be controlled with buttons on the Formatting toolbar or options at the Format Cells dialog box with the Alignment tab selected.

Four buttons on the Formatting toolbar, shown in Figure 2.8, can be used to control the alignment of data in a cell or selected cells. Click the Align Left button to align data at the left side of a cell, click the Center button to align data between the left and right side of a cell, and click Align Right to align data at the right side of a cell. Click the Merge and Center button to merge selected cells and center data within the merged cells. If you have merged cells and want to split them again, select the cells and then click the Merge and Center button.

Indent text within a cell or selected cells by clicking the Increase Indent button or the Decrease Indent button on the Formatting toolbar. These buttons are identified in Figure 2.8. The Increase Indent button will move text within the cell or selected cells to the right while the Decrease Indent button will move text to the left.

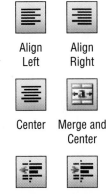

FIGURE

2.8 *Alignment and Indent Buttons on the Formatting Toolbar*

You can also control data aligning and indenting at the Format Cells dialog box with the Alignment tab selected as shown in Figure 2.9. Click the down-pointing arrow at the right of the *Horizontal* option box and a list of alignment options displays including *Left (Indent), Center, Right, Fill, Justify,* and *Center Across Selection.* Choose the desired horizontal alignment from this list.

FIGURE

2.9 *Format Cells Dialog Box with Alignment Tab Selected*

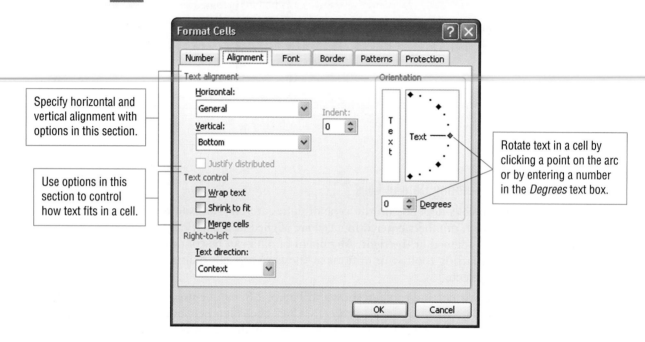

Specify horizontal and vertical alignment with options in this section.

Use options in this section to control how text fits in a cell.

Rotate text in a cell by clicking a point on the arc or by entering a number in the *Degrees* text box.

By default, data in a cell is aligned at the bottom of the cell. Change this alignment to top, center, or justify with choices from the *Vertical* drop-down list. To display this list, click the down-pointing arrow at the right side of the *Vertical* option. Use the *Indent* text box to indent cell contents from the left side of the cell. Each increment entered in the *Indent* text box is equivalent to the width of one character.

In the *Orientation* section, you can choose to rotate data. A portion of the *Orientation* section shows points on an arc. Click a point on the arc to rotate the text along that point. You can also type a rotation degree in the *Degrees* text box. Type a positive number to rotate selected text from the lower left to the upper right of the cell. Type a negative number to rotate selected text from the upper left to the lower right of the cell.

As you learned earlier, if data typed in a cell is longer than the cell, it overlaps the next cell to the right. If you want data to remain in a cell and wrap to the next line within the same cell, click the *Wrap text* option in the *Text control* section of the dialog box. Click the *Shrink to fit* option to reduce the size of the text font so all selected data fits within the column. Use the *Merge cells* option to combine two or more selected cells into a single cell.

If you want to enter data on more than one line within a cell, enter the data on the first line and then press Alt + Enter. Pressing Alt + Enter moves the insertion point to the next line within the same cell.

1. Open **ExcelWorksheet01**.
2. Save the worksheet with Save As and name it **sec2x10**.
3. Select the entire worksheet and then change the font to 12-point Tahoma (or a similar sans serif typeface).
4. Automatically increase the width of column A by positioning the cell pointer on the boundary between columns A and B and then double-clicking the left mouse button.
5. Select row 1, click the Bold button, and then click the Center button on the Formatting toolbar.
6. Select cells B3 through B10 and then click the Center button on the Formatting toolbar.
7. Change the orientation of data in cells by completing the following steps:
    a. Select cells B1 through D1.
    b. Click Format and then Cells.
    c. At the Format Cells dialog box, click the Alignment tab.
    d. Select *0* in the *Degrees* text box and then type 45.
    e. Click OK to close the dialog box.

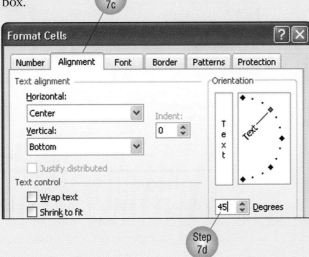

8. Merge and center data in a cell by completing the following steps:
    a. Select cells A12 through D12.
    b. Click the Merge and Center button on the Formatting toolbar.
    c. Double-click in the newly merged cell.
    d. Turn on bold, type YEARLY JOB REPORT, and then press Enter.

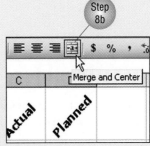

9. Enter text on a separate line in cell A1 by completing the following steps:
    a. Double-click cell A1.
    b. Move the insertion point to the end of *Customer*.
    c. Press Alt + Enter.
    d. Type Products Dept.
10. Save, print, and then close **sec2x10**.

HINT
Use the Format Painter button on the Standard toolbar to copy formatting from one range of cells to another.

Changing the Font at the Format Cells Dialog Box

As you learned earlier in this chapter, the font for data can be changed with the Font button on the Formatting toolbar and the font size can be changed with the Font Size button. The font for data in selected cells can also be changed at the Format Cells dialog box with the Font tab selected as shown in Figure 2.10.

FIGURE

2.10 *Format Cells Dialog Box with Font Tab Selected*

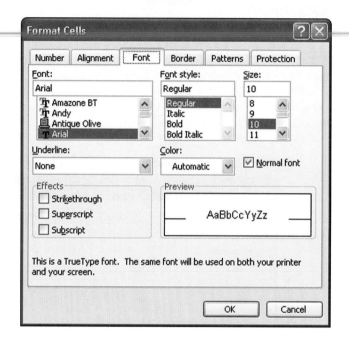

At the Format Cells dialog box with the Font tab selected, you can change the font, font style, font size, and font color. You can also change the underlining method and add effects such as superscript and subscript.

exercise 11

CHANGING THE FONT AND FONT COLOR OF DATA IN CELLS

1. Open **ExcelWorksheet02**.
2. Save the worksheet with Save As and name it **sec2x11**.
3. Change the font and font color by completing the following steps:
   a. Select the entire worksheet.
   b. Click Format and then Cells.
   c. At the Format Cells dialog box, click the Font tab.

d. At the Format Cells dialog box with the Font tab selected, click *Garamond* in the *Font* list box (you will need to scroll down the list to make this font visible).

e. Click *12* in the *Size* list box (you will need to scroll down the list to make this size visible).

f. Click the down-pointing arrow at the right of the *Color* option box (contains the word *Automatic*).

g. At the palette of color choices that displays, click the Blue color.

h. Click OK to close the dialog box.

4. Change the font color for the cells in row 1 by completing the following steps:

a. Select row 1.

b. Click Format and then Cells.

c. At the Format Cells dialog box, make sure the Font tab is selected.

d. Click the down-pointing arrow at the right side of the *Color* option box.

e. At the palette of color choices, click a red color (you choose the red).

f. Click OK to close the dialog box.

5. Select cells B2 through D8 and then change the number formatting to *Currency* with zero decimal places.

6. Select cells A2 through A8 and then click twice on the Increase Indent button on the Formatting toolbar. (This indents the text from the left side of the cells.)

7. Automatically adjust the width of columns A, B, C, and D.

8. Save, print, and then close **sec2x11**.

Inserting/Deleting Cells, Rows, and Columns

New data may need to be included in an existing worksheet. For example, a row or several rows of new data may need to be inserted into a worksheet; or, data may need to be removed from a worksheet.

Inserting Rows

After a worksheet has been created, rows can be added (inserted) to the worksheet. Insert a row with options from the Insert drop-down menu or with options at the Insert dialog box. By default, a row is inserted above the row containing the active cell. To insert a row in a worksheet, make a cell active in the row below where the row is to be inserted, click Insert and then click Rows. If you want to insert more than one row, select the number of rows in the worksheet that you want inserted, click Insert and then click Rows.

HINT
At the Insert dialog box, specify the direction in which cells should move.

Insert Row
Click Insert, Rows.
OR
1. Click Insert, Cells.
2. Click Entire row.
3. Click OK.

You can also insert a row by making a cell active in the row below where the row is to be inserted, clicking Insert, and then clicking Cells. This causes the Insert dialog box to display as shown in Figure 2.11. At the Insert dialog box, click *Entire row*. This inserts an entire row above the active cell.

FIGURE

2.11 *Insert Dialog Box*

exercise 12

INSERTING ROWS IN A WORKSHEET

1. Open **ExcelWorksheet01**.
2. Save the worksheet with Save As and name it **sec2x12**.
3. Add two rows and enter data in the new cells by completing the following steps:
   a. Select rows 7 and 8 in the worksheet.
   b. Click Insert and then Rows.
   c. Type the following data in the specified cells (you do not need to type the dollar sign or the comma in cells containing money amounts):

A7	=	Summit Clinic
B7	=	570
C7	=	33056
D7	=	32500
A8	=	Franklin Center
B8	=	690
C8	=	19745
D8	=	19250

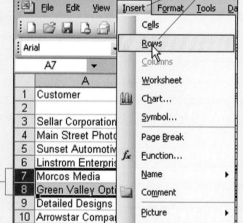

4. Select cells A1 through D12 and then apply an autoformat of your choosing. (Make sure the numbers display properly.)
5. Save, print, and then close **sec2x12**.

QUICK STEPS

Inserting Columns

Insert Column
Click Insert, Column.
OR
1. Click Insert, Cells.
2. Click Entire column.
3. Click OK.

Insert columns in a worksheet in much the same way as rows. Insert a column with options from the Insert drop-down menu or with options at the Insert dialog box. By default, a column is inserted immediately to the left of the column containing the active cell. To insert a column in a worksheet, make a cell active in the column immediately to the right of where the new column is to be inserted, click Insert

EXCEL

and then click Columns. If you want to insert more than one column, select the number of columns in the worksheet that you want inserted, click Insert and then click Columns.

You can also insert a column by making a cell active in the column immediately to the right of where the new column is to be inserted, clicking Insert, and then clicking Cells. This causes the Insert dialog box to display. At the Insert dialog box, click *Entire column*. This inserts an entire column immediately to the left of the active cell.

exercise 13

1. Open **ExcelWorksheet03**.
2. Save the worksheet with Save As and name it **sec2x13**.
3. Add a column to the worksheet and enter data in the new cells by completing the following steps:
   a. Click in any cell in column D.
   b. Click Insert and then Columns.
   c. Type the following data in the specified cells:

	C	D	E
	Planned	Next Year	Prior Year
	0.6	0.55	0.57
	0.39	0.4	0.41
	1.15	1.12	1.2
	1.9	1.85	1.87
	0.2	0.22	0.28
	0.06	0.055	0.06

   Step 3c

D2	=	Next Year
D3	=	0.55
D4	=	0.4
D5	=	1.12
D6	=	1.85
D7	=	0.22
D8	=	0.055

4. Select cells B3 through E8 and then click the Percent Style button on the Formatting toolbar.
5. Select cells A1 through E8 and then apply an autoformat of your choosing.
6. Save, print, and then close **sec2x13**.

Deleting Cells, Rows, or Columns

Specific cells in a worksheet or rows or columns in a worksheet can be deleted. To delete a specific cell, make the cell active, and then press the Delete key. You can also select the cells to be deleted and then press the Delete key. If you use the Delete key to delete cell(s), only the cell text is deleted. The empty cell(s) remains in the worksheet.

If you want to delete the cell(s) as well as the cell text, make the specific cell active or select cells, click Edit, and then click Delete. At the Delete dialog box shown in Figure 2.12, choose what you want deleted, and then click OK.

2.12 *Delete Dialog Box*

The Delete dialog box can also be displayed by positioning the cell pointer in the worksheet, clicking the *right* mouse button, and then clicking *Delete* on the shortcut menu. To delete several rows of cells, select the rows, click Edit, and then click Delete. To delete several columns of cells, select the columns, click Edit, and then click Delete.

Clearing Data in Cells

With the Clear option from the Edit drop-down menu, the contents of selected cells can be cleared. This is useful in a situation where the cells are to remain but the contents need to be changed. To clear cell contents, select the cells, click Edit, point to Clear, and then click All. This deletes the cell contents and the cell formatting. Click Formats to remove formatting from selected cells while leaving the data. Click Contents to remove the contents of the cell, leaving any formatting. You can also click the Delete key to clear the contents of the selected cells.

HINT
One method for clearing the contents of a cell is to right-click the cell and then click Clear Contents at the shortcut menu.

Clear Data in Cells
1. Select cells.
2. Click Edit, Clear, All.

exercise 14

DELETING COLUMNS AND DELETING AND CLEARING ROWS IN A WORKSHEET

1. Open **ExcelWorksheet02**.
2. Save the worksheet with Save As and name it **sec2x14**.
3. Delete column D in the worksheet by completing the following steps:
   a. Click in any cell in column D.
   b. Click Edit and then Delete.
   c. At the Delete dialog box, click *Entire column*.
   d. Click OK or press Enter.
4. Delete row 5 by completing the following steps:
   a. Select row 5.
   b. Click Edit and then Delete.
5. Clear row contents by completing the following steps:
   a. Select rows 5 and 6.
   b. Click Edit, point to Clear, and then click Contents.

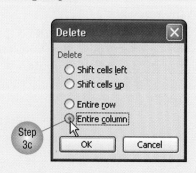

Step 3c

EXCEL

6. Type the following data in the specified cells:

A5	=	Lodging
B5	=	4535
C5	=	5100
A6	=	Entertainment
B6	=	3210
C6	=	3000

Step 6

	A	B	C
1	Expense	Actual	Budget
2	Salaries	126000	126000
3	Commissions	58000	54500
4	Media space	8250	10100
5	Lodging	4535	5100
6	Entertainment	3210	3000
7	Telephone	1450	1500

7. Select cells A1 through C7 and then apply the Accounting 1 autoformat.
8. Clear cell formatting and then apply different formatting by completing the following steps:
   a. Select cells A1 through C1.
   b. Click Edit, point to Clear, and then click Formats.
   c. With cells A1 through C1 still selected, click the Bold button on the Formatting toolbar and then click the Center button.
9. Save, print, and then close **sec2x14**.

Adding Borders and Shading to Cells

The gridlines that display in a worksheet do not print. Borders that will print can be added to cells, however. Add borders with options from the Borders button on the Formatting toolbar or with options from the Format Cells dialog box with the Border tab selected.

To add a border to a cell or selected cells, make the desired cell active or select the desired cells, and then click the Borders button on the Formatting toolbar. By default, a single-line border is added to the bottom of the active cell or the selected cells. To change the style of border, click the down-pointing arrow at the right of the Borders button. This causes a palette of border style choices to display. Click the choice that represents the type of border desired for the cell or selected cells. Clicking the desired border style removes the palette and also applies that border style to the active cell or the selected cells.

Click the down arrow at the right side of the Borders button, click the Draw Borders option, and the Borders toolbar displays. Use buttons on this toolbar to draw, customize, and erase border lines. If you click the Erase button on the Borders toolbar and the mouse pointer turns into an eraser. Use this pointer to erase borders from cells.

QUICK STEPS

Add Border to Cells
1. Select cells.
2. Click Borders button.
   OR
1. Select cells.
2. Click Format, Cells.
3. Click Border tab.
4. Use options in dialog box to apply desired border.
5. Click OK.

Borders

exercise 15

ADDING BORDERS TO CELLS USING THE BORDERS BUTTON

1. Open **ExcelWorksheet01**.
2. Save the worksheet with Save As and name it **sec2x15**.
3. Select row 1 and then turn on bold and change the alignment to center.
4. Select cells B3 through B10 and then change the alignment to center.

5. Add a border to all cells in the worksheet (that contain data) by completing the following steps:

   a. Click the down-pointing arrow at the right side of the Borders button on the Formatting toolbar and then click the Draw Borders option. (The mouse pointer turns into a pencil and the Borders toolbar displays in the worksheet area.)

   b. Click the down-pointing arrow at the right side of the Line Style button on the Borders toolbar and then click the double-line option.

   c. Using the mouse pointer (pencil), draw a double-line border around the outside of the cells containing data.

	A	B	C	D
1	Customer	Job #	Actual	Planned
2				
3	Sellar Corporation	2130	$30,349	$34,109
4	Main Street Photos	1201	$48,290	$48,100
5	Sunset Automotive	318	$34,192	$32,885
6	Linstrom Enterprises	1009	$63,293	$61,220
7	Morcos Media	676	$29,400	$30,500
8	Green Valley Optics	2117	$55,309	$58,394
9	Detailed Designs	983	$12,398	$13,100
10	Arrowstar Company	786	$87,534	$86,905

Step 5c

   d. Change back to a single line by clicking the down-pointing arrow at the right side of the Line Style button on the Borders toolbar, and then clicking the top single-line option.

   e. Turn off the display of the Borders toolbar by clicking the Close button (contains an X) located in the upper right corner of the toolbar.

6. Add a single-line border to specific cells by completing the following steps:

   a. Select cells A1 through D1.

   b. Click the down-pointing arrow at the right of the Borders button on the Formatting toolbar.

   c. At the palette of border style choices that displays, click the Thick Bottom Border option (second option from the left in the middle row).

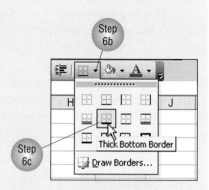

Step 6b

Step 6c

7. Click in cell A1.

8. Save, print, and then close **sec2x15**.

You can also add borders to the active cell or selected cells with options at the Format Cells dialog box with the Border tab selected as shown in Figure 2.13. With options in the *Presets* section, you can remove borders with the *None* option, add only outside borders with the *Outline* option, or click the *Inside* option to add borders to the inside of selected cells. In the *Border* section of the dialog box, specify the side of the cell or selected cells to which you want to apply a border. Choose

EXCEL

the style of line desired for the border with the options that display in the *Style* list box. Add color to border lines with choices from the color palette that displays when you click the down arrow located at the right side of the *Color* option box (contains the word *Automatic*).

2.13 *Format Cells Dialog Box with Border Tab Selected*

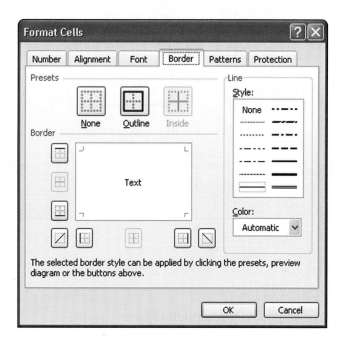

exercise 16

ADDING BORDERS TO CELLS AT THE FORMAT CELLS DIALOG BOX

1. Open **ExcelWorksheet02**.
2. Save the worksheet with Save As and name it **sec2x16**.
3. Select the entire worksheet, display the Format Cells dialog box with the Font tab selected, change the font to 12-point Century (or a similar serif typeface), the color to green (you determine the green), and then close the dialog box.
4. Select row 1 and then turn on bold and change the alignment to center.
5. Select cells B2 through D8, display the Format Cells dialog box with the Number tab selected, change the *Category* option to *Currency* with zero decimal places, and then close the dialog box.
6. Automatically adjust the width of columns A, B, C, and D.
7. Add a green outline border to the worksheet by completing the following steps:
   a. Select cells A1 through D8 (all cells containing data).
   b. Click Format and then Cells.

c. At the Format Cells dialog box, click the Border tab.

d. Click the sixth option from the top in the second column in the *Style* list box.

e. Click the down-pointing arrow located at the right side of the *Color* option box (contains the word *Automatic*).

f. At the palette of color choices, click the same green color that you chose for the font.

g. Click the *Outline* option in the *Presets* section of the dialog box.

h. Click OK to close the dialog box.

8. Click in cell A1.

9. Save, print, and then close **sec2x16**.

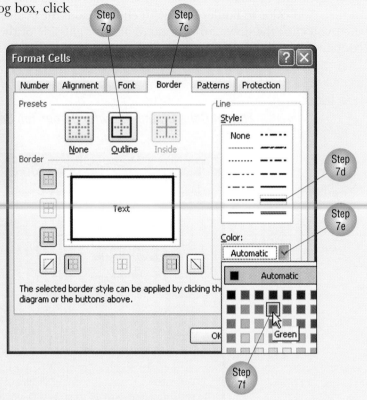

Adding Shading and a Pattern to Cells

Fill Color

To enhance the visual display of cells and data within cells, consider adding shading and/or a pattern to cells. Add color shading to cells in a worksheet by clicking the Fill Color button on the Formatting toolbar. You can also add color shading and/or a pattern to cells in a worksheet with options at the Format Cells dialog box with the Patterns tab selected.

To add color shading using the Fill Color button on the Formatting toolbar, make the desired cell active or select the desired cells, and then click the Fill Color button. By default, the color yellow is added to the cell or selected cells. To add a shading of a different color, click the down-pointing arrow at the right of the Fill Color button, and then click the desired color at the palette that displays.

Add color shading as well as a pattern to the active cell or selected cells with options at the Format Cells dialog box with the Patterns tab selected as shown in Figure 2.14. Choose a color shading for a cell or selected cells by clicking a color choice in the *Color* section. To add a pattern to a cell or selected cells, click the down-pointing arrow at the right of the *Pattern* option box, and then click the desired pattern. When you click a pattern, that pattern displays in the Sample box in the dialog box. The Sample box also displays any chosen color shading.

FIGURE

2.14 *Format Cells Dialog Box with Patterns Tab Selected*

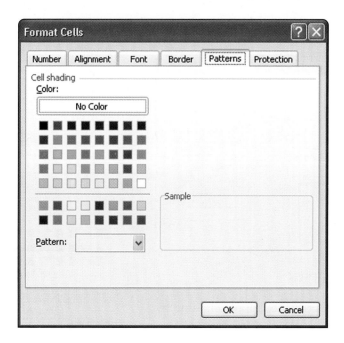

Repeating the Last Action

If you want to apply other types of formatting, such as number, border, or shading formatting to other cells in a worksheet, use the Repeat command by pressing F4 or Ctrl + Y. The Repeat command repeats the last action performed. You can also repeat formatting by clicking Edit and then Repeat. The Repeat option will change depending on the most recent function performed. For example, if you apply shading formatting to a selected cell, click Edit and Repeat Format Cells displays in the drop-down menu.

Repeat Last Action
1. Apply formatting.
2. Press F4; Ctrl + Y; or
   Edit, Repeat.

exercise 17

ADDING SHADING AND A PATTERN TO CELLS

1. Open **ExcelWorksheet08**.
2. Save the worksheet with Save As and name it **sec2x17**.
3. Select cells B3 through D12 and then click the Currency Style button on the Formatting toolbar.
4. Select cells E3 through E12, click the Percent Style button, and then click twice on the Increase Decimal button on the Formatting toolbar.
5. Apply a double-line border around cells by completing the following steps:
    a. Select cells A1 through E12.
    b. Click Format and then Cells.
    c. At the Format Cells dialog box, click the Border tab.

d. Click the double-line option in the *Style* list box.

e. Click the Outline button in the *Presets* section.

f. Click OK to close the dialog box.

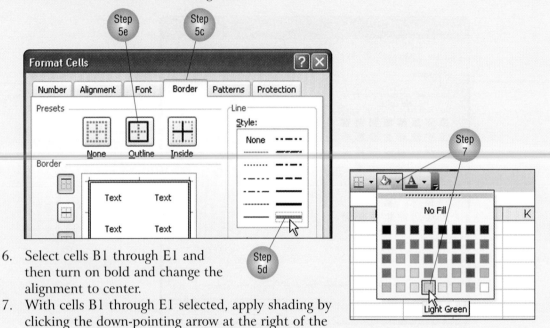

6. Select cells B1 through E1 and then turn on bold and change the alignment to center.

7. With cells B1 through E1 selected, apply shading by clicking the down-pointing arrow at the right of the Fill Color button and then clicking the Light Green color.

8. Repeat the shading by selecting cells A2 through A12 and then pressing F4 or Ctrl + Y.

9. Apply shading to specific cells by completing the following steps:

a. Select cells B3 through E4.

b. Click Format and then Cells.

c. At the Format Cells dialog box, click the Patterns tab.

d. Click the Light Yellow color in the *Color* section.

e. Click OK.

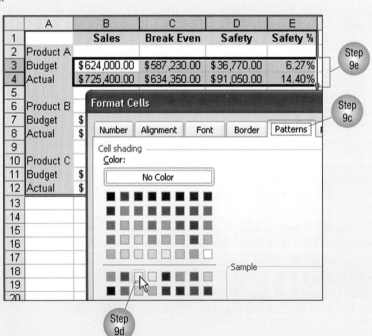

5. Automatically adjust the widths of columns A, B, C, and D.
6. Select cells A1 through D8 and then add a border around the cells (you choose the border-line style).
7. With the cells still selected, add light yellow shading to the selected cells.
8. Select cells A1 through D1 and then add a pattern of your choosing to the cells.
9. Save, print, and then close **sec2sc05**.

Assessment 6

1. Create an Excel worksheet with the information shown in Figure 2.16. You determine the following:
   a. Font
   b. Width of columns
   c. Number formatting
2. Add the following enhancements to the worksheet:
   a. Add a border to all cells in the worksheet containing data.
   b. Add a color shading to all cells in the worksheet containing data.
   c. Add a pattern to column headings (the cells containing *Project, Projected*, and *Actual*).
3. Save the completed worksheet and name it **sec2sc06**.
4. Print and then save **sec2sc06**.

F I G U R E

2.16 **Assessment 6**

CAPITAL PROJECT SUMMARY

Project	Projected	Actual
Rail siding installation	$43,300	$41,200
Cement slabs	$12,000	$13,980
Silos	$28,420	$29,600
Conveying system \	$56,700	$58,200
Modulators	$8,210	$8,100
Winder	$6,400	$7,100

Assessment 7

1. Use the Help feature to learn how to shrink the font size to show all data in a cell. *(Hint: To do this, display the Excel Help task pane, type* Change formatting of text *in the Search for text box and then press Enter. When the results display, click the* Change formatting of text *hyperlink. In the Microsoft Office Excel Help window, click the* Shrink the font size to show all data in a cell *hyperlink.)*
2. Open **ExcelWorksheet03**.
3. Save the worksheet with Save As and name it **sec2sc07**.
4. Select cells A1 through D8 and then change the font size to 12.
5. Select cells A1 through D2 and then shrink the font size to show all data in the selected cells.
6. Save, print, and then close **sec2sc07**.

CHAPTER challenge

You work with a fitness trainer at Exercise for Life Athletic Club. The fitness trainer has asked you to monitor members' activities as they use the club. You decide to create a weekly workout log for the members. Information will be compiled from a daily log sheet that members complete each time they work out. The weekly log will consist of the member's name, number of workouts per week, facilities used (i.e., pool, tennis courts, etc.), and additional fees (if any). Add at least five members (use information about yourself as one of the members) to this weekly log. Save the worksheet and print it.

HELP?

To enhance the appearance of the log, you would like to format the worksheet with an appropriate background. Use the Help feature to learn how to format worksheets with a background. Choose an appropriate background for the workout log and add it to the worksheet. Save the worksheet.

After several weeks of maintaining this workout log in Excel, you decide that the information could be more easily maintained if it were stored in Access. Create a database in Access called **ExerciseforLife** and import the Excel worksheet as an Access table. Save the database and print the newly imported table.

INSERTING FORMULAS IN A WORKSHEET

PERFORMANCE OBJECTIVES

Upon successful completion of Chapter 3, you will be able to:

➤ Insert a formula in a cell using the AutoSum button
➤ Write formulas with mathematical operators
➤ Type a formula in the Formula bar
➤ Copy a formula
➤ Use the Insert Function feature to insert a formula in a cell
➤ Write formulas with the AVERAGE, MAX, MIN, COUNT, PMT, FV, DATE, NOW, and IF functions
➤ Create an absolute and mixed cell reference

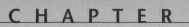

Chapter03S
EXCEL

Excel is a powerful decision-making tool containing data that can be manipulated to answer "what if" situations. Insert a formula in a worksheet and then manipulate the data to make projections, answer specific questions, and use as a planning tool. For example, the manager of a department might use an Excel worksheet to prepare a department budget and then determine the impact on the budget of hiring a new employee or increasing the volume of production.

Insert a formula in a worksheet to perform calculations on values. A formula contains a mathematical operator, value, cell reference, cell range, and a function. Formulas can be written that add, subtract, multiply, and/or divide values. Formulas can also be written that calculate averages, percentages, minimum and maximum values, and much more. Excel includes an AutoSum button on the Standard toolbar that inserts a formula to calculate the total of a range of cells. Insert Function is an Excel feature that offers a variety of functions to create a formula.

Using the AutoSum Button

To perform a calculation in a worksheet, make active the cell in which you want to insert the formula (this cell should be empty). Type the formula in the cell and the formula displays in the cell as well as in the Formula bar. When the formula is completed and you exit the cell, the result of the formula displays in the active cell while the actual formula displays in the Formula bar.

Enter

HINT

Use the AutoSum button to automatically add numbers in a range of cells.

QUICK STEPS

Write Formula Using AutoSum Button

Click AutoSum button on Standard toolbar.

OR

1. Click down-pointing arrow at right of AutoSum button.
2. Click desired function.

You can also enter a formula in the Formula bar located below the Formatting toolbar. To do this, click in the Formula bar text box, type the desired formula, and then press Enter or click the Enter button (contains a green check mark) on the Formula bar.

One of the advantages of using formulas in a worksheet is that cell entries can be changed and the formula will automatically recalculate the values and insert the result in the cell containing the formula. This is what makes an Excel worksheet a decision-making tool.

In addition to typing a formula in a cell, you can also use the AutoSum button on the Standard toolbar. The AutoSum button adds numbers automatically with the SUM function. When you click the AutoSum button, Excel looks for a range of cells containing numbers above the active cell. If no cell above contains numbers, then Excel looks to the left of the active cell. Excel suggests the range of cells to be added. If the suggested range is not correct, drag through the desired range with the mouse, and then press Enter. You can also just double-click the AutoSum button and this will insert the SUM function with the range Excel chooses.

(Note: Before completing computer exercises, delete the ExcelChapter02S folder on your disk. Next, copy the ExcelChapter03S subfolder from the Excel2003Specialist folder on the CD that accompanies this textbook to your disk and then make ExcelChapter03S the active folder.)

exercise 1

ADDING VALUES WITH THE AUTOSUM BUTTON

1. Open **ExcelWorksheet02**.
2. Save the worksheet with Save As and name it **sec3x01**.
3. Calculate the sum of cells by completing the following steps:
   a. Make B9 the active cell.
   b. Click the AutoSum button on the Standard toolbar.
   c. Excel inserts the formula *=SUM(B2:B8)* in cell B9. This is the correct range of cells, so press Enter.
   d. Make C9 the active cell.
   e. Click the AutoSum button on the Standard toolbar.

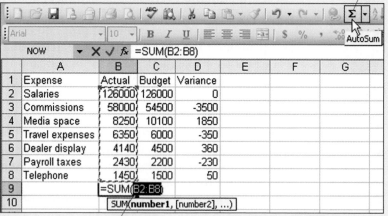

   f. Excel inserts the formula *=SUM(C2:C8)* in cell C9. This is the correct range of cells, so press Enter.
   g. Make D9 the active cell.
   h. Double-click the AutoSum button on the Standard toolbar. (This inserts the formula *=SUM(D2:D8)* in cell D9 and inserts the sum *-1820*.)
4. Select cells A1 through D9 and then apply the Accounting 1 autoformat.

EXCEL

5. Save and then print **sec3x01**.
6. With the worksheet still open, make the following changes to cell entries:

   B4: Change *8,250.00* to *9550*
   D4: Change *1,850.00* to *550*
   B7: Change *2,430.00* to *2050*
   D7: Change *(230.00)* to *150*

7. Save, print, and then close **sec3x01**.

Writing Formulas with Mathematical Operators

The AutoSum button on the Standard toolbar essentially creates the formula for you. You can also write your own formulas using mathematical operators. Commonly used mathematical formulas and their functions are described in Table 3.1.

When writing your own formula, begin the formula with the equals (=) sign. For example, to divide the contents of cell B2 by the contents of cell C2 and insert the result in cell D2, you would make D2 the active cell, and then type =B2/C2.

HINT
After typing a formula in a cell, press the Enter key, the Tab key, Shift + Tab, or click the Enter button on the Formula bar.

TABLE

| 3.1 | **Mathematical Operators** |

Function	Operator
Addition	+
Subtraction	-
Multiplication	*
Division	/
Percent	%
Exponentiation	^

If a formula contains two or more operators, Excel uses the same order of operations used in algebra. From left to right in a formula, this order, called the *order of operations*, is: negations (negative number—a number preceded by -) first, then percents (%), then exponentiations (^), followed by multiplications (*), divisions (/), additions (+), and finally subtractions (-). If you want to change the order of operations, use parentheses around the part of the formula you want calculated first.

Copying a Formula with Relative Cell References

In many worksheets, the same basic formula is used repetitively. In a situation where a formula is copied to other locations in a worksheet, use a *relative cell reference*. Copy a formula containing relative cell references and the cell references change. For example, if you enter the formula *=SUM(A2:C2)* in cell D2 and then

HINT
Display formulas in a worksheet rather than the calculated values by pressing Ctrl + ` (accent grave).

copy it relatively to cell D3, the formula in cell D3 displays as =*SUM(A3:C3)*. (Additional information on cell references is discussed later in this chapter in the "Using an Absolute Cell Reference in a Formula" section.)

To copy a formula relatively in a worksheet, use the Fill option from the Edit drop-down menu. To do this, select the cell containing the formula as well as the cells to which you want the formula copied, and then click Edit. At the Edit drop-down menu, point to Fill. This causes a side menu to display. The choices active in this side menu vary depending on the selected cells. For example, if you select cells down a column, options such as Down and Up will be active. If cells in a row are selected, options such as Right and Left will be active. Click the desired direction and the formula is copied relatively to the selected cells.

exercise 2

FINDING VARIANCES BY INSERTING AND COPYING A FORMULA

1. Open **ExcelWorksheet01**.
2. Save the worksheet with Save As and name it **sec3x02**.
3. Change the width of column A to 19.00.
4. Make cell E1 active and then type Variance.
5. Insert a formula by completing the following steps:
   a. Make E3 the active cell.
   b. Type the formula =D3-C3.
   c. Press Enter.
6. Copy the formula to cells E4 through E10 by completing the following steps:
   a. Select cells E3 through E10.
   b. Click Edit, point to Fill, and then click Down.

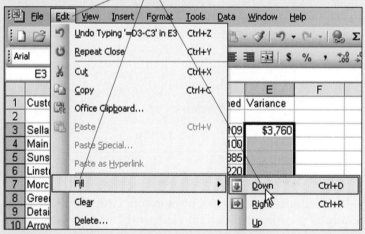

7. Select cells A1 through E10 and then apply the Colorful 1 autoformat.
8. Select cells B3 through B10 and then change the alignment to right.
9. Save and then print **sec3x02**.
10. With the worksheet still open, make the following changes to cell contents:

   C4: Change $48,290 to *46425*
   D6: Change $61,220 to *60000*
   C8: Change $55,309 to *57415*
   C9: Change $12,398 to *14115*

11. Save, print, and then close **sec3x02**.

Copying Formulas with the Fill Handle

Use the fill handle to copy a formula up, down, left, or right within a worksheet. To use the fill handle, insert the desired data in the cell (text, value, formula, and so on). With the cell active, position the mouse pointer (white plus sign) on the fill handle until the mouse pointer turns into a thin black cross. Hold down the left mouse button, drag and select the desired cells, and then release the mouse button. If you are dragging a cell containing a formula, a relative version of the formula is copied to the selected cells.

HINT

Use the fill handle to copy a relative version of a formula.

exercise 3

CALCULATING SALARY BY INSERTING AND COPYING A FORMULA USING THE FILL HANDLE

1. Open **ExcelWorksheet05**.
2. Save the worksheet with Save As and name it **sec3x03**.
3. Make cell D2 active, turn on bold, change the alignment to center, and then type *Salary*.
4. Insert a formula by completing the following steps:
   a. Make D3 the active cell.
   b. Click in the Formula bar and then type =C3*B3.
   c. Click the Enter button on the Formula bar.
5. Copy the formula to cells D4 through D8 by completing the following steps:
   a. Make sure cell D3 is the active cell.
   b. Position the mouse pointer (white plus sign) on the fill handle that displays at the lower right corner of cell D3 until the pointer turns into a thin black cross.
   c. Hold down the left mouse button, drag down to cell D8, and then release the mouse button.
6. Save and then print **sec3x03**.
7. With the worksheet still open, make the following changes to cell contents:

   B4: Change *20* to *28*
   C5: Change *$18.75* to *19.10*
   B7: Change *15* to *24*

8. Save, print, and then close **sec3x03**.

Step 4c · Step 4b

	A		C	D
	NOW	X ✓ fx =C3*B3		
1	January			
2	**Name**	**Hours**	**Rate**	**Salary**
3	Carolyn Bentley	35	$23.15	=C3*B3
4	Lindon Cassini	20	$19.00	

C	D
Rate	**Salary**
$23.15	$810.25
$19.00	$380.00
$18.75	$750.00
$16.45	$394.80
$11.50	$172.50
$11.50	$172.50

Step 5c

Writing a Formula by Pointing

In Exercises 2 and 3, you wrote formulas using cell references such as *=D3-C3*. Another method for writing a formula is to "point" to the specific cells that are to be part of the formula. Creating a formula by pointing is more accurate than typing the cell reference since a mistake can happen when entering the cell reference.

To write a formula by pointing, click the cell that will contain the formula, type the equals sign to begin the formula, and then click the cell you want to reference in the formula. This inserts a moving border around the cell and also changes the mode from Enter to Point. (The word *Point* displays at the left side of the Status bar.) Type the desired mathematical operator and then click the next cell reference.

QUICK STEPS

Write Formula by Pointing
1. Click cell that will contain formula.
2. Type equals sign.
3. Click cell you want to reference in formula.
4. Type desired mathematical operator.
5. Click next cell reference.

Continue in this manner until all cell references are specified and then press the Enter key. This ends the formula and inserts the result of the calculation of the formula in the active cell. When writing a formula by pointing, you can also select a range of cells you want included in a formula.

exercise 4

WRITING A FORMULA BY POINTING THAT CALCULATES PERCENTAGE OF ACTUAL BUDGET

1. Open **ExcelWorksheet02**.
2. Save the worksheet with Save As and name it **sec3x04**.
3. Delete column D.
4. Make cell D1 active and then type % of Actual.
5. Enter a formula by pointing that calculates the percentage of actual budget by completing the following steps:
   a. Make cell D2 active.
   b. Type the equals sign.
   c. Click cell C2. (This inserts a moving border around the cell and the mode changes from Enter to Point.)
   d. Type the forward slash symbol (/).
   e. Click cell B2.
   f. Make sure the formula looks like this =C2/B2 and then press Enter.
6. Make cell D2 active and then click the Percent Style button on the Formatting toolbar.
7. With cell D2 still active, position the mouse pointer on the fill handle, drag down to cell D8, and then release the mouse button.
8. Select cells B2 through C8 and then click the Currency Style button on the Formatting toolbar.
9. Automatically increase the width of column D to accommodate the column heading.
10. Select cells A1 through D8 and then apply the Classic 2 AutoFormat.
11. Save, print, and then close **sec3x04**.

Steps 5a–5e

	A	B	C	D
1	Expense	Actual	Budget	% of Actual
2	Salaries	126000	126000	=C2/B2
3	Commissions	58000	54500	
4	Media space	8250	10100	
5	Travel expenses	6350	6000	
6	Dealer display	4140	4500	
7	Payroll taxes	2430	2200	
8	Telephone	1450	1500	

C	D	
Budget	% of Actual	
126000	100%	
54500	94%	
10100	122%	
6000	94%	
4500	109%	
2200	91%	
1500	103%	

Step 7

Using the Trace Error Button

As you are working in a worksheet, you may occasionally notice a button pop up near the active cell. The general term for this button is **smart tag**. The display of the smart tag button varies depending on the action performed. In Exercise 5, you will insert a formula that will cause a smart tag button, named the Trace Error button, to appear. When the Trace Error button appears, a small dark green triangle also displays in the upper left corner of the cell. Click the Trace Error button and a drop-down list displays with options for updating the formula to include specific cells, getting help on the error, ignoring the error, editing the error in the Formula bar, and completing an error check. In Exercise 5, two of the formulas you insert return the desired results. You will click the Trace Error button, read information on what Excel perceives as the error, and then tell Excel to ignore the error.

Trace Error

EXCEL

exercise 5

1. Open **ExcelWorksheet09**.
2. Save the worksheet with Save As and name it **sec3x05**.
3. Make cell A11 active, type Percentage of, press Alt + Enter, and then type Down Time.
4. Enter a formula by pointing that computes the percentage of equipment down time by completing the following steps:
   a. Make cell B11 active.
   b. Type the equals sign followed by the left parenthesis (=().
   c. Click cell B3. (This inserts a moving border around the cell and the mode changes from Enter to Point.)
   d. Type the minus symbol (-).
   e. Click cell B9.
   f. Type the right parenthesis followed by the forward slash ()/).
   g. Click cell B3.
   h. Make sure the formula looks like this =(B3-B9)/B3 and then press Enter.
5. Make cell B11 active and then click the Percent Style button on the Formatting toolbar.
6. With cell B11 still active, position the mouse pointer on the fill handle, drag across to cell M11, and then release the mouse button.
7. Enter a formula by dragging through a range of cells by completing the following steps:
   a. Click in cell A13, type Hours Available, press Alt + Enter, and then type Jan - June.
   b. Click in cell B13 and then click the AutoSum button on the Standard toolbar.
   c. Select cells B3 through G3.
   d. Click the Enter button on the Formula bar. (This inserts *14,340* in cell B13.)
8. Click in cell A14, type Hours Available, press Alt + Enter, and then type July - Dec.
9. Click in cell B14 and then complete steps similar to those in Steps 7b through 7d to create a formula that totals hours available from July through December (cells H3 through M3). (This inserts *14,490* in cell B14.)
10. Click in cell B13 and notice the Trace Error button that displays. Complete the following steps to read about the error and then tell Excel to ignore the error:

Step 7d

Step 4h

a. Click the Trace Error button.
b. At the drop-down menu that displays, click the *Help on this error* option.
c. Read the information on *Formula Omits Cells in Region* that displays in the Microsoft Excel Help window and then close the window.
d. Click the Trace Error button again and then click *Ignore Error* at the drop-down menu.

11. Remove the dark green triangle from cell B14 by completing the following steps:
    a. Click in cell B14.
    b. Click the Trace Error button and then click *Ignore Error* at the drop-down menu.
12. Save, print, and then close **sec3x05**. (The worksheet will print on two pages. In the next chapter, you will learn about features that control how worksheets are printed.)

Inserting a Formula with the Insert Function Button

In Exercise 1, the AutoSum button inserted a formula that began with =*SUM*. This part of the formula is called a ***function***, which is a built-in formula. Using a function takes less keystrokes when creating a formula. For example, the =*SUM* function saved you from having to type each cell to be included in the formula with the plus (+) symbol between cell entries.

Excel provides other functions for writing formulas. A function operates on what is referred to as an ***argument***. An argument may consist of a constant, a cell reference, or another function (referred to as a nested function). In Exercise 1, when you made cell B10 active and then clicked the AutoSum button, the formula =*SUM(B3:B9)* was inserted in the cell. The cell range *(B3:B9)* is an example of a cell reference argument. An argument may also contain a ***constant***. A constant is a value entered directly into the formula. For example, if you enter the formula =*SUM(B3:B9,100)*, the cell range *B3:B9* is a cell reference argument and *100* is a constant. In this formula, 100 is always added to the sum of the cells. If a function is included in an argument within a function, it is called a ***nested function***. (You will learn about nested functions later in this chapter.)

When a value calculated by the formula is inserted in a cell, this process is referred to as *returning the result*. The term *returning* refers to the process of calculating the formula and the term *result* refers to inserting the value in the cell.

You can type a function in a cell in a worksheet or you can use the Insert Function button on the Formula bar to help you write the formula. When you click the Insert Function button, or click Insert and then Function, the Insert Function dialog box displays as shown in Figure 3.1.

Insert Function

FIGURE

3.1 *Insert Function Dialog Box*

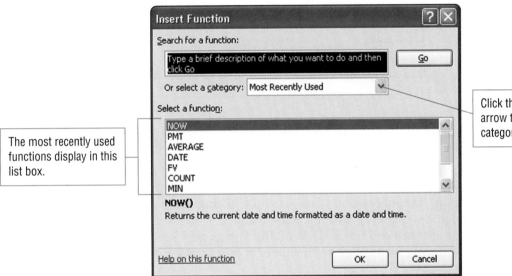

At the Insert Function dialog box, the most recently used functions display in the *Select a function* list box. You can choose a function category by clicking the down arrow at the right side of the *Or select a category* list box, and then clicking the desired category at the drop-down list. Use the *Search for a function* option to locate a specific function.

With the desired function category selected, choose a function in the *Select a function* list box and then click OK. This displays a Function Arguments palette like the one shown in Figure 3.2. At this palette, enter in the *Number1* text box the range of cells you want included in the formula, enter any constants that are to be included as part of the formula, or enter another function. After entering a range of cells, a constant, or another function, click the OK button. More than one argument can be included in a function. If the function you are creating contains more than one argument, press the Tab key to move the insertion point to the *Number2* text box, and then enter the second argument.

HINT
You can also display the Insert Function dialog box by clicking the down-pointing arrow at the right side of the AutoSum button and then clicking More Functions.

HINT
If you need to display a specific cell or cells behind the formula palette, move the palette by clicking and dragging it.

FIGURE

3.2 *Example Function Arguments Palette*

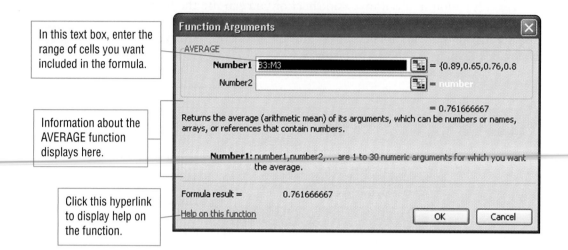

In this text box, enter the range of cells you want included in the formula.

Information about the AVERAGE function displays here.

Click this hyperlink to display help on the function.

Writing Formulas with Functions

Excel includes over 200 functions that are divided into nine different categories including *Financial*, *Date & Time*, *Math & Trig*, *Statistical*, *Lookup & Reference*, *Database*, *Text*, *Logical*, and *Information*. Clicking the AutoSum button on the Standard toolbar automatically adds numbers with the SUM function. The SUM function is included in the *Math & Trig* category. In some sections in this chapter, you will write formulas with functions in other categories including *Statistical*, *Financial*, *Date & Time*, and *Logical*.

Writing Formulas with Statistical Functions

In this section, you will learn to write formulas with the statistical functions AVERAGE, MAX, MIN, and COUNT. The AVERAGE function returns the average (arithmetic mean) of the arguments. The MAX function returns the largest value in a set of values and the MIN function returns the smallest number in a set of values. Use the COUNT function to count the number of cells that contain numbers within the list of arguments.

Finding Averages

A common function in a formula is the AVERAGE function. With this function, a range of cells is added together and then divided by the number of cell entries. In Exercise 6 you will use the AVERAGE function, which will add all test scores for a student and then divide that number by the total number of tests. You will use the Insert Function feature to simplify the creation of the formula containing an AVERAGE function.

One of the advantages to using formulas in a worksheet is the ability to easily manipulate data to answer certain questions. In Exercise 6 you will learn the impact of retaking certain tests on the final average score.

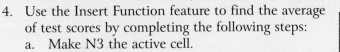

1. Open **ExcelWorksheet06**.
2. Save the worksheet with Save As and name it **sec3x06**.
3. Make cell N1 the active cell, turn on bold, and then type Average.
4. Use the Insert Function feature to find the average of test scores by completing the following steps:
    a. Make N3 the active cell.
    b. Click the Insert Function button on the Formula bar.
    c. At the Insert Function dialog box, click the down-pointing arrow at the right side of the *Or select a category* options box, and then click *Statistical* at the drop-down list.
    d. Click *AVERAGE* in the *Select a function* list box.

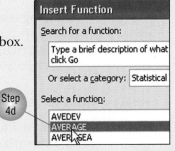

Step 4b

Step 4d

	A	B	C
1	**Name**	Test 1	Test 2
2			
3	Arnson, Patrick	89%	65%
4	Barclay, Jeanine	78%	66%

Insert Function

Search for a function:

Type a brief description of what click Go

Or select a category: Statistical

Select a function:

AVEDEV
AVERAGE
AVERAGEA

Insert Function

Search for a function:

Type a brief description of what you want to do and then click Go

Or select a category: Most Recently Used

Most Recently Used
All
Financial
Date & Time
Math & Trig
Statistical
Lookup & Reference
Database

Step 4c

Select a function:

AVERAGE
NOW
PMT
DATE
FV
COUNT

Function Arguments

AVERAGE

Number1 B3:M3

Number2

Step 4f

M	N
Test 12	Average
69%	76%
91%	84%
49%	66%
98%	90%
73%	76%
79%	80%
97%	92%
49%	57%
88%	76%
89%	91%
94%	95%
56%	41%
76%	80%
94%	94%
88%	79%
95%	92%
77%	76%
86%	79%

Step 5c

    e. Click OK.
    f. At the Function Arguments palette, make sure *B3:M3* displays in the *Number1* text box. (If not, type **B3:M3** in the *Number1* text box.)
    g. Click OK.
5. Copy the formula by completing the following steps:
    a. Make cell N3 active.
    b. Position the mouse pointer on the fill handle until the pointer turns into a thin black cross.
    c. Hold down the left mouse button, drag down to cell N20, and then release the mouse button.
6. Save and then print **sec3x06**. (The worksheet will print on two pages.)
7. After viewing the averages of test scores, you notice that a couple of people have a low average. You decide to see what happens to the average score if students make up tests where they scored the lowest. You decide that a student can make up to a 70% on a retake of the test. Make the following changes to test scores to see how the changes will affect the test average.

    L5: Change *45%* to *70%*
    M5: Change *49%* to *70%*

C10: Change *45%* to *70%*
M10: Change *49%* to *70%*
C14: Change *0%* to *70%*
I14: Change *0%* to *70%*
J14: Change *0%* to *70%*

8. Save, print, and then close **sec3x06**. (Compare the test averages for Jack Calahan, Stephanie Flanery, and Kathleen Kwieciak to see what the effect of retaking the tests has on their final test averages.)

When a formula such as the AVERAGE formula you inserted in a cell in Exercise 6 calculates cell entries, it ignores certain cell entries. The AVERAGE function will ignore text in cells and blank cells (not zeros). For example, in the worksheet containing test scores, a couple of cells contained a *0%* entry. This entry was included in the averaging of the test scores. If you did not want that particular test to be included in the average, enter text in the cell such as *N/A* (for *not applicable*) or leave the cell blank.

Finding Maximum and Minimum Values

The MAX function in a formula returns the maximum value in a cell range and the MIN function returns the minimum value in a cell range. As an example, you could use the MAX and MIN functions in a worksheet containing employee hours to determine which employee worked the most number of hours and which worked the least. In a worksheet containing sales commissions, you could use the MAX and MIN functions to determine the salesperson who earned the most commission dollars and the one who earned the least.

Insert a MAX and MIN function into a formula in the same manner as an AVERAGE function. In Exercise 7, you will use the Insert Function feature to insert MAX and MIN functions in cells to determine the highest test score average and the lowest test score average.

exercise 7

FINDING MAXIMUM AND MINIMUM VALUES IN A WORKSHEET

1. Open **sec3x06**.
2. Save the worksheet with Save As and name it **sec3x07**.
3. Type the following in the specified cells:

   A22: Turn on bold and then type Highest Test Average.
   A23: Turn on bold and then type Lowest Test Average.
   A24: Turn on bold and then type Average of All Tests.

4. Automatically adjust the width of column A.
5. Insert a formula to identify the highest test score average by completing the following steps:
   a. Make cell B22 active.
   b. Click the Insert Function button on the Formula bar.

c. At the Insert Function dialog box, make sure *Statistical* is selected in the *Or select a category* option box. (If not, click the down-pointing arrow at the right side of the *Or select a category* option box and then click *Statistical* at the drop-down list.)

d. Click *MAX* in the *Select a function* list box. (You will need to scroll down the list to display *MAX*.)

e. Click OK.

f. At the Function Arguments palette, type N3:N20 in the *Number1* text box.

g. Click OK.

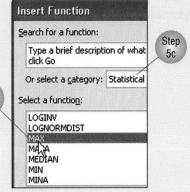

Step 5c

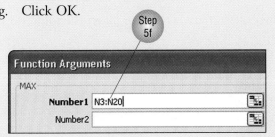

Step 5f

Step 5d

6. Insert a formula to identify the lowest test score average by completing the following steps:

a. Make cell B23 active.

b. Click the Insert Function button on the Formula bar.

c. At the Insert Function dialog box, make sure *Statistical* is selected in the *Or select a category* option box, and then click *MIN* in the *Select a function* list box. (You will need to scroll down the list to display *MIN*.)

d. Click OK.

e. At the Function Arguments palette, type N3:N20 in the *Number1* text box, and then click OK.

7. Insert a formula to determine the average of all test scores by completing the following steps:

a. Make cell B24 active.

b. Click the Insert Function button on the Formula bar.

c. At the Insert Function dialog box, make sure *Statistical* is selected in the *Or select a category* option box and then click *AVERAGE* in the *Select a function* list box.

d. Click OK.

e. At the Function Arguments palette, type N3:N20 in the *Number1* text box, and then click OK.

8. Save and then print **sec3x07**. (The worksheet will print on two pages.)

9. Change the *70%* values (which were previously *0%*) in cells C14, I14, and J14 to *N/A*. (This will cause the average of test scores for Kathy Kwieciak to increase and will change the minimum number and average of all test scores.)

10. Save, print, and then close **sec3x07**.

Counting Numbers in a Range

Use the COUNT function to count the numeric values in a range. For example, in a range of cells containing cells with text and cells with numbers, you can count how many cells in the range contain numbers. In Exercise 8, you will use the COUNT function to specify the number of students taking the midterm test and the number taking the final test. In this worksheet, a cell is left blank if a student did not take a test. If a value such as *0%* was entered into the cell, the COUNT function would count this as a cell with a number.

exercise 8

1. Open **ExcelWorksheet19**.
2. Save the worksheet and name it **sec3x08**.
3. Make cell A22 active.
4. Type Number of students, press Alt + Enter, and then type completing the midterm.
5. Make cell B22 active.
6. Insert a formula counting the number of students who have taken the midterm test by completing the following steps:
   a. Click the Insert Function button on the Formula bar.
   b. At the Insert Function dialog box, make sure *Statistical* is selected in the *Or select a category* option box. (If not, click the down-pointing arrow at the right side of the *Or select a category* option box and then click *Statistical* at the drop-down list.)
   c. Scroll down the list of functions in the *Select a function* list box until COUNT is visible and then double-click *COUNT*.
   d. At the Function Arguments palette, type **B3:B20** in the *Value1* text box.
   e. Click OK.

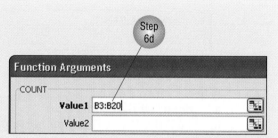

Step 6d

7. Count the number of students who have taken the final test by completing the following steps:
   a. Make cell A23 active.
   b. Type Number of students, press Alt + Enter, and then type completing the final.
   c. Make cell B23 active.

20	Pherson, Douglas	69%	82%
21			
22	Number of students completing the midterm	16	
23	Number of students completing the final	15	
24			

Step 4

Step 7b

8. Insert a formula counting the number of students who have taken the final test by completing the following steps:
   a. Click the Insert Function button on the Formula bar.
   b. At the Insert Function dialog box, make sure *Statistical* is selected in the *Or select a category* option box.
   c. Scroll down the list of functions in the *Select a function* list box until COUNT is visible and then double-click *COUNT*.
   d. At the Function Arguments palette, type **C3:C20** in the *Value1* text box, and then click OK.
9. Save and then print **sec3x08**.
10. Add test scores by completing the following steps:
    a. Make cell B14 active and then type 68.
    b. Make cell C14 active and then type 70.
    c. Make cell C19 active and then type 55.
    d. Press Enter.
11. Save, print, and then close **sec3x08**.

Writing Formulas with Financial Functions

In this section, you will learn to write formulas with the financial functions PMT and FV. The PMT function calculates the payment for a loan based on constant payments and a constant interest rate. Use the FV function to return the future value of an investment based on periodic, constant payments and a constant interest rate.

Finding the Periodic Payments for a Loan

The PMT function finds the periodic payment for a loan based on constant payments and a constant interest rate. The PMT function contains the arguments Nper, Pv, Fv, and Type. The Nper argument is the number of payments that will be made to an investment or loan, Pv is the current value of amounts to be received or paid in the future, Fv is the value of a loan or investment at the end of all periods, and Type determines whether calculations will be based on payments made in arrears (at the end of each period) or in advance (at the beginning of each period).

CALCULATING PAYMENTS

1. Open **ExcelWorksheet20**.
2. Save the worksheet with Save As and name it **sec3x09**.
3. The owner of Real Photography is interested in purchasing a new developer and needs to determine monthly payments on three different models. Insert a formula that calculates monthly payments and then copy that formula by completing the following steps:
   a. Make cell E7 active.
   b. Click the Insert Function button on the Formula bar.
   c. At the Insert Function dialog box, click the down-pointing arrow at the right side of the *Or select a category* option box and then click *Financial* at the drop-down list.
   d. Scroll down the *Select a function* option box until *PMT* is visible and then double-click *PMT*.
   e. At the Function Arguments palette, type **C7/12** in the *Rate* text box. (This tells Excel to divide the interest rate by 12 months.)
   f. Press the Tab key. (This moves the insertion point to the *Nper* text box.)
   g. Type **D7**. (This is the total number of months in the payment period.)
   h. Press the Tab key. (This moves the insertion point to the *Pv* text box.)
   i. Type **-B7**. (Excel displays the result of the PMT function as a negative number since the loan represents a negative cash flow to the borrower. Insert a minus sign before *B7* to show the monthly payment as a positive number rather than a negative number.)
   j. Click OK. (This closes the palette and inserts the monthly payment of *$316.98* in cell E7.)

Step 3e   Step 3g   Step 3i

Function Arguments

PMT

Rate   C7/12   = 0.007083333
Nper   D7   = 60
Pv   -B7   = -15450
Fv   = number
Type   = number

k. Copy the formula in cell E7 down to cells E8 and E9.
4. Insert a formula in cell F7 that calculates the total amount of the payments by completing the following steps:
   a. Make cell F7 active.
   b. Type =E7*D7 and then press Enter.
   c. Make cell F7 active and then copy the formula down to cells F8 and F9.
5. Insert a formula in cell G7 that calculates the total amount of interest paid by completing the following steps:
   a. Make cell G7 active.
   b. Type =F7-B7 and then press Enter.
   c. Make cell G7 active and then copy the formula down to cells G8 and G9.
6. Save, print, and then close **sec3x09**.

Monthly Payments	Total Payments	Total Interest
$316.98	$ 19,018.82	$ 3,568.82
$615.39	$ 36,923.60	$ 6,928.60
$711.92	$ 42,715.42	$ 8,015.42

Step 5c

Finding the Future Value of a Series of Payments

The FV function calculates the future value of a series of equal payments or an annuity. Use this function to determine information such as how much money can be earned in an investment account with a specific interest rate and over a specific period of time.

exercise 10

FINDING THE FUTURE VALUE OF AN INVESTMENT

1. Open **ExcelWorksheet21**.
2. Save the worksheet with Save As and name it **sec3x10**.
3. The owner of Real Photography has decided to save money to purchase a new developer and wants to compute how much money can be earned by investing the money in an investment account that returns 9% annual interest. The owner determines that $1,200 per month can be invested in the account for three years. Determine the future value of the investment account by completing the following steps:
   a. Make cell B6 active.
   b. Click the Insert Function button on the Formula bar.
   c. At the Insert Function dialog box, make sure *Financial* displays in the *Or select a category* option box.
   d. Click *FV* in the *Select a function* list box.
   e. Click OK.
   f. At the Function Arguments palette, type **B3/12** in the *Rate* text box.
   g. Press the Tab key.
   h. Type **B4** in the *Nper* text box.
   i. Press the Tab key.
   j. Type **B5** in the *Pmt* text box.
   k. Click OK. (This closes the palette and also inserts the future value of *$49,383.26* in cell B6.)

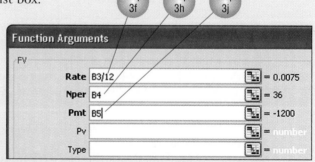

Step 3f   Step 3h   Step 3j

Function Arguments

FV

Rate	B3/12		= 0.0075
Nper	B4		= 36
Pmt	B5		= -1200
Pv			= number
Type			= number

EXCEL

4. Save and then print **sec3x10**.
5. The owner decides to determine the future return after two years. To do this, change the amount in cell B4 from *36* to *24* and then press Enter. (This recalculates the future investment amount in cell B6.)
6. Save, print, and then close **sec3x10**.

	A	B	
1	**REAL PHOTOGRAPHY**		
2	**Future Value of Investment**		
3	Rate	9%	Step 5
4	Number of Months	24	
5	Monthly Payment	$ (1,200.00)	
6	Future Value	$31,426.16	

Writing Formulas with Date and Time Functions

In this section, you will learn to write formulas with the date and time functions NOW and DATE. The NOW function returns the serial number of the current date and time. The DATE function returns the serial number that represents a particular date. Excel can make calculations using dates because the dates are represented as serial numbers. To calculate a date's serial number, Excel counts the days since the beginning of the twentieth century. The date serial number for January 1, 1900, is 1. The date serial number for January 1, 2000, is 36,526.

HINT
Ctrl + ; is the shortcut key to insert the current date in the active cell.

exercise 11

USING THE DATE AND NOW FUNCTIONS

1. Open **ExcelWorksheet23**.
2. Save the worksheet with Save As and name it **sec3x11**.
3. This worksheet establishes overdue dates for accounts. Enter a formula in cell D5 that returns the serial number for the date March 21, 2005, by completing the following steps:
   a. Make cell D5 active.
   b. Click the Insert Function button on the Formula bar.
   c. At the Insert Function dialog box, click the down-pointing arrow at the right side of the *Or select a category* option box and then click *Date & Time* at the drop-down list.
   d. Double-click *DATE* in the *Select a function* list box.
   e. At the Function Arguments palette, type **2005** in the *Year* text box.
   f. Press the Tab key and then type **03** in the *Month* text box.
   g. Press the Tab key and then type **21** in the *Day* text box.
   h. Click OK.

Function Arguments — Step 3e
DATE
Year 2005 — Step 3f
Month 03
Day 21 — Step 3g

4. Complete steps similar to those in Step 3 to enter the following dates as serial numbers in the specified cells:

D6	=	March 27, 2005
D7	=	April 2, 2005
D8	=	April 10, 2005

5. Enter a formula in cell F5 that inserts the due date (the purchase date plus the number of days in the Terms column) by completing the following steps:
   a. Make cell F5 active.

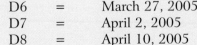

b.   Type =D5+E5 and then press Enter.
c.   Make cell F5 active and then copy the
     formula down to cells F6, F7, and F8.
6.   Make cell A10 active and then type your name.
7.   Insert the current date and time as a serial
     number by completing the following steps:
   a.   Make cell A11 active.
   b.   Click the Insert Function button on the
        Formula bar.
   c.   At the Insert Function dialog box, make sure *Date & Time* displays
        in the *Or select a category* option box.
   d.   Scroll down the *Select a function* list box until *NOW* is visible and then double-
        click *NOW*.
   e.   At the Function Arguments palette telling you that the function takes no argument,
        click OK.
   f.   With cell A11 still active, click the Align Left button on the Formatting toolbar.
8.   Save, print, and then close **sec3x11**.

Purchase Date	Terms	Due Date
3/21/2005	30	4/20/2005
3/27/2005	15	4/11/2005
4/2/2005	15	4/17/2005
4/10/2005	30	5/10/2005

Step
5c

Writing a Formula with the IF Logical Function

The IF function is considered a **conditional function**. With the IF function you
can perform conditional tests on values and formulas. A question that can be
answered with true or false is considered a **logical test**. The IF function makes a
logical test and then performs a particular action if the answer is true and another
action if the answer is false.

For example, an IF function can be used to write a formula that calculates a
salesperson's bonus as 10% if the quota of $100,000 is met or exceeded, and
zero if the quota is less than $100,000. That formula would look like this:
=IF(quota=>100000,quota*0.1,0). The formula contains three parts—the condition
or logical test *IF(quota=>100000)*, action taken if the condition or logical test is
true *(quota*0.1)*, and the action taken if the condition or logical test is false *(0)*.
Commas separate the condition and the actions. In the bonus formula, if the
quota is equal to or greater than $100,000, then the quota is multiplied by 10%.
If the quota is less than $100,000, then the bonus is zero.

In Exercise 12, you will write a formula with cell references rather than cell
data. The formula in Exercise 12 is *=IF(C2>B2,C2*0.15,0)*. In this formula the
condition or logical test is whether or not the number in cell C2 is greater than
the number in cell B2. If the condition is true and the number is greater, then the
number in cell C2 is multiplied by 0.15 (providing a 15% bonus). If the condition
is false and the number in cell C2 is less than the number in cell B2, then nothing
happens (no bonus). Notice how commas are used to separate the logical test
from the actions.

Editing a Formula

Enter

Edit a formula by making active the cell containing the formula and then editing
the formula in the cell or in the Formula bar text box. After editing the formula,
press Enter or click the Enter button on the Formula bar and Excel will recalculate
the result of the formula.

EXCEL

1. Open **ExcelWorksheet10**.
2. Save the worksheet with Save As and name it **sec3x12**.
3. Write a formula with the IF function by completing the following steps. (The formula will determine if the quota has been met and, if it has, will insert the bonus [15% of the actual sales]. If the quota has not been met, the formula will insert a zero.)
   a. Make cell D2 active.
   b. Type =IF(C2>B2,C2*0.15,0) and then press Enter.
   c. Make cell D2 active and then use the fill handle to copy the formula to cells D3 through D7.
   d. With cells D2 through D7 selected, click the Currency Style button on the Formatting toolbar.
4. Print the worksheet.
5. Revise the formula so it will insert a 25% bonus if the quota has been met by completing the following steps:
   a. Make cell D2 active.
   b. Click in the Formula bar, edit the formula so it displays as =IF(C2>B2,C2*0.25,0), and then click the Enter button on the Formula bar.

C	D
Actual Sales	**Bonus**
$ 103,295.00	15494.25
$ 129,890.00	0
$ 133,255.00	19988.25
$ 94,350.00	14152.5
$ 167,410.00	25111.5
$ 109,980.00	

Step 3c

D
Bonus
$ 25,823.75
$ -
$ 33,313.75
$ 23,587.50
$ 41,852.50
$ -

Step 5b

DATE		fx	=IF(C2>B2,C2*0.25,0)
	A	B	IF(logical_test, **[value_if_true]**, [value_if_false])
1	**Salesperson**	Enter uota	**Actual Sales**	**Bonus**
2	Allejandro	$ 95,500.00	$ 103,295.00	2,C2*0.25,0)

   c. Copy the formula down to cells D3 through D7.
6. Save, print, and then close **sec3x12**.

Step 5c

Writing a Nested IF Condition

In Exercise 12, the IF function had only two possible actions—the actual sales times 15% or a zero. In a formula where more than two actions are required, use nested IF functions. For example, in Exercise 13, you will write a formula with IF conditions that has four possible actions—a letter grade of A, B, C, or D. When writing nested IF conditions, insert symbols such as commas, quotation marks, and parentheses in the proper locations. If you want an IF condition to insert text, insert quotation marks before and after the text. The formula you will be writing in Exercise 13 is shown below.

=IF(E2>89,"A",IF(E2>79,"B",IF(E2>69,"C",IF(E2>59,"D"))))

This formula begins with the condition =IF(E2>89,"A",. If the number in cell E2 is greater than 89, then the condition is met and the grade of A is returned. The formula continues with a nested condition, IF(E2>79,"B",. If the number in cell E2 does not meet the first condition (greater than 89), then Excel looks to the next condition—is the number in cell E2 greater than 79? If it is, then the grade of B is inserted in cell E2. The formula continues with another nested condition,

HINT

If you enter a complicated formula in a worksheet, consider protecting the worksheet. To do this, click Tools, point to Protection, and then click Protect Sheet. At the Protect Sheet dialog box, enter a password, and then click OK.

IF(E2>69,"C",. If the number in cell E2 does not match the first condition, Excel looks to the second condition, and if that condition is not met, then Excel looks to the third condition. If the number in cell E2 is greater than 69, then the grade of C is inserted in cell E2. The final nested condition is IF(E2>59,"D". If the first three conditions are not met but this one is, then the grade of D is inserted in cell E2. The four parentheses at the end of the formula end each condition in the formula.

exercise 13

1. Open **ExcelWorksheet11**.
2. Save the worksheet with Save As and name it **sec3x13**.
3. Insert a formula to average the scores by completing the following steps:
   a. Make cell E2 active.
   b. Type =AVERAGE(B2:D2) and then press Enter.
   c. Make cell E2 active and then copy the formula down to cells E3 through E6.
   d. With cells E2 through E6 still selected, click the Decrease Decimal button on the Formatting toolbar five times.
4. Insert a formula with nested IF conditions by completing the following steps:
   a. Make cell F2 active.
   b. Type =IF(E2>89,"A",IF(E2>79,"B",IF(E2>69,"C",IF(E2>59,"D")))) and then press Enter.

E	F	G	H	I	J
Average	**Grade**				
78	=IF(E2>89,"A",IF(E2>79,"B",IF(E2>69,"C",IF(E2>59,"D"))))				
90					
88					
98					
67					

Step 4b

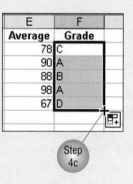

Step 4c

E	F
Average	**Grade**
78	C
90	A
88	B
98	A
67	D

   c. Make cell F2 active and then use the fill handle to copy the formula down to cells F3 through F6.
   d. With cells F2 through F6 still selected, click the Center button on the Formatting toolbar.
5. Save, print, and then close **sec3x13**.

As you typed the formula with nested IF conditions in Step 4b of Exercise 13, did you notice that the parentheses were different colors? Each color represents a condition. The four right parentheses at the end of the formula ended each of the conditions and each matched in color a left parenthesis. If an average in column E in sec3x13 is less than 59, the nested formula inserts *FALSE* in the cell. If you want the formula to insert a letter grade, such as *F,* instead of *FALSE,* include another nested IF condition in the formula. A maximum of seven IF functions can be nested in a formula.

EXCEL

Using Absolute and Mixed Cell References in Formulas

A reference identifies a cell or a range of cells in a worksheet and can be relative, absolute, or mixed. Relative cell references refer to cells relative to a position in a formula. Absolute references refer to cells in a specific location. When a formula is copied, a relative cell reference adjusts while an absolute cell reference remains constant. A mixed cell reference does both—either the column remains absolute and the row is relative or the column is relative and the row is absolute. Distinguish between relative, absolute, and mixed cell references using the dollar sign ($). Type a dollar sign before the column and/or row cell reference in a formula to specify that the column or row is an absolute cell reference.

Using an Absolute Cell Reference in a Formula

In this chapter you have learned to copy a relative formula. For example, if the formula =SUM(A2:C2) in cell D2 is copied relatively to cell D3, the formula changes to =SUM(A3:C3). In some situations, you may want a formula to contain an absolute cell reference, which always refers to a cell in a specific location. In Exercise 14, you will add a column for projected job earnings and then perform "what if" situations using a formula with an absolute cell reference.

To identify an absolute cell reference, insert a $ symbol before the row and also the column. For example, the absolute cell reference C12 would be typed as $C$12 in a formula.

exercise 14

INSERTING AND COPYING A FORMULA WITH AN ABSOLUTE CELL REFERENCE

1. Open **ExcelWorksheet01**.
2. Save the worksheet with Save As and name it **sec3x14**.
3. Delete columns B and D by completing the following steps:
   a. Click the column B header (the letter *B* at the top of the column).
   b. Hold down the Ctrl key and then click the column D header. (This selects column B and column D.)
   c. Click Edit and then Delete.
4. Type **Projected** in cell C1.
5. Center and bold the text in cells A1 through C1.
6. Determine the effect on actual job earnings with a 20% increase by completing the following steps:
   a. Type **% Increase/Decrease** in cell A12.
   b. Type **1.2** in cell B12 and then press Enter. (This number will be used in a formula to determine a 20% increase.)
   c. Make cell B12 active and then change the number formatting to General. (To do this, click Format and then Cells. At the Format Cells dialog box, click the Number tab, click *General* in the *Category* list box, and then click OK.)
   d. Make cell C3 active, type the formula =B3*$B$12, and then press Enter.
   e. Make cell C3 active and then use the fill handle to copy the formula to cells C4 through C10.

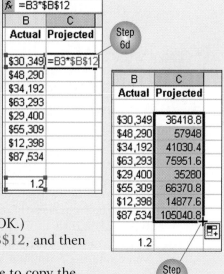

EXCEL

f. Select cells B3 through C10 and then click the Currency Style button on the Formatting toolbar.

g. With cells B3 through C10 still selected, click twice on the Decrease Decimal button on the Formatting toolbar.

7. Save and then print the worksheet.

8. With the worksheet still open, determine the effect on actual job earnings with a 10% decrease by completing the following steps:

a. Make cell B12 active.

b. Type 0.9 and then press Enter.

9. Save and then print **sec3x14**.

10. Determine the effects on actual job earnings with a 10% increase. (To do this, type 1.1 in cell B12.)

11. Save, print, and then close **sec3x14**.

B	C
Actual	**Projected**
$ 30,349	$ 27,314
$ 48,290	$ 43,461
$ 34,192	$ 30,773
$ 63,293	$ 56,964
$ 29,400	$ 26,460
$ 55,309	$ 49,778
$ 12,398	$ 11,158
$ 87,534	$ 78,781
0.9	

Step 8b

Using a Mixed Cell Reference in a Formula

The formula you created in Step 6d in Exercise 14 contained a relative cell reference (B3) and an absolute cell reference ($B$12). A formula can also contain a mixed cell reference. In a mixed cell reference either the column remains absolute and the row is relative or the column is relative and the row is absolute. In Exercise 15, you will create the formula =$A3*B$2. In the first cell reference in the formula, $A3, the column is absolute and the row is relative. In the second cell reference, B$2, the column is relative and the row is absolute. The formula containing the mixed cell references allows you to fill in the column and row data using only one formula.

Identify an absolute or mixed cell reference by typing a dollar sign before the column and/or row reference or press the F4 function key to cycle through the various cell references. For example, type =A3 in a cell, press F4, and the cell reference changes to =$A$3. Press F4 again and the cell reference changes to =A$3. The next time you press F4, the cell reference changes to =$A3. Press it again to change the cell reference back to =A3.

exercise 15

DETERMINING SIMPLE INTEREST USING A FORMULA WITH MIXED CELL REFERENCES

1. Open **ExcelWorksheet12**.

2. Save the worksheet with Save As and name it **sec3x15**.

3. Make cell B3 the active cell and then insert a formula containing mixed cell references by completing the following steps:

a. Type =A3 and then press the F4 function key three times. (This changes the cell reference to $A3.)

b. Type *B2 and then press the F4 function key twice. (This changes the cell reference to B$2.)

c. Make sure the formula displays as =$A3*B$2 and then press Enter.

	A	B	C
1		SIMPLE INTER
2		$ 1,000	$ 2,000
3	5%	=$A3*B$2	
4	6%		
5	7%		

Step 3c

EXCEL

4. Copy the formula down and to the right by completing the following steps:
   a. Make cell B3 active and then use the fill handle to copy the formula down to cell B13.
   b. Make cell B3 active and then use the fill handle to copy the formula across to cell F3.

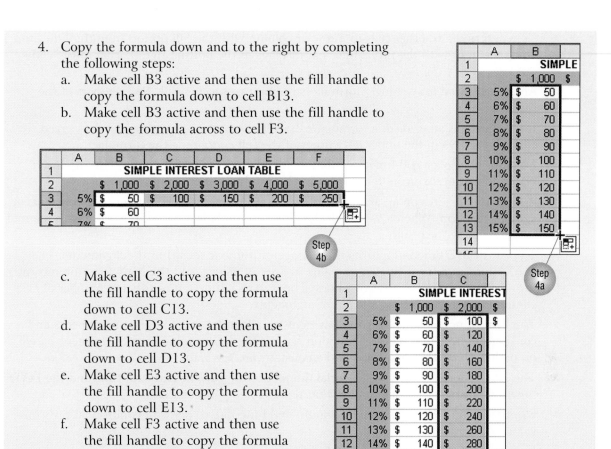

   c. Make cell C3 active and then use the fill handle to copy the formula down to cell C13.
   d. Make cell D3 active and then use the fill handle to copy the formula down to cell D13.
   e. Make cell E3 active and then use the fill handle to copy the formula down to cell E13.
   f. Make cell F3 active and then use the fill handle to copy the formula down to cell F13.

5. Save, print, and then close **sec3x15**.

Step 4b

Step 4a

Step 4c

You only had to type one formula in Exercise 15 to create the data in the simple interest table. The mixed cell references allowed you to copy the formula down columns and across rows.

CHAPTER summary

➤ Type a formula in a cell and the formula displays in the cell as well as in the Formula bar. If cell entries are changed, a formula will automatically recalculate the values and insert the result in the cell.

➤ Use the AutoSum button on the Standard toolbar to automatically add numbers in rows or columns.

➤ Create your own formula with commonly used operators such as addition (+), subtraction (-), multiplication (*), division (/), percent (%), and exponentiation (^). When writing a formula, begin with the equals (=) sign.

➤ Copy a formula to other cells in a row or column with the Fill option from the Edit drop-down menu or with the fill handle that displays in the bottom right corner of the active cell.

➤ Another method for writing a formula is to point to specific cells that are part of the formula.

➤ If Excel detects an error in a formula, a Trace Error button appears and a dark green triangle displays in the upper left corner of the cell containing the formula.

➤ Excel includes over 200 functions that are divided into nine categories. Use the Insert Function feature to create formulas using built-in functions.

➤ A function operates on an argument, which may consist of a cell reference, a constant, or another function. When a value calculated by a formula is inserted in a cell, this is referred to as returning the result.

➤ The AVERAGE function returns the average (arithmetic mean) of the arguments. The MAX function returns the largest value in a set of values, and the MIN function returns the smallest number in a set of values. The COUNT function counts the number of cells containing numbers within the list of arguments.

➤ The PMT function calculates the payment for a loan based on constant payments and a constant interest rate. The FV function returns the future value of an investment based on periodic, constant payments and a constant interest rate.

➤ The NOW function returns the serial number of the current date and time and the DATE function returns the serial number that represents a particular date.

➤ Use the IF function, considered a conditional function, to perform conditional tests on values and formulas.

➤ Use nested IF functions in a formula where more than two actions are required.

➤ A reference identifies a cell or a range of cells in a worksheet and can be relative, absolute, or mixed. Identify an absolute cell reference by inserting a $ symbol before the column and row. Cycle through the various cell reference options by typing the cell reference and then pressing F4.

FEATURES summary

FEATURE	BUTTON	MENU	KEYBOARD
AutoSum function	Σ ▾	Insert, Function, SUM	
Insert Function dialog box	*fx*	Insert, Function	
Cycle through cell reference options			F4

EXCEL

CONCEPTS check

Completion: On a blank sheet of paper, indicate the correct term, symbol, or command for each description.

1. When typing a formula, begin the formula with this sign.
2. Click this button on the Standard toolbar to automatically add numbers in cells.
3. This is the operator for division that is used when writing a formula.
4. This is the operator for multiplication that is used when writing a formula.
5. This is the name of the small black box located at the bottom right corner of a cell that can be used to copy a formula to adjacent cells.
6. A function operates on this, which may consist of a constant, a cell reference, or another function.
7. This function returns the largest value in a set of values.
8. This function finds the periodic payment for a loan based on constant payments and a constant interest rate.
9. This function returns the serial number of the current date and time.
10. This function is considered a conditional function.
11. To identify an absolute cell reference, type this symbol before the column and row.
12. Suppose that cell B2 contains the budgeted amount and cell C2 contains the actual amount. Write the formula (including the IF conditions) that would insert the word *under* if the actual amount was less than the budgeted amount and insert the word *over* if the actual amount was greater than the budgeted amount.

SKILLS check

Assessment 1

1. Create a worksheet with the information shown in Figure 3.3 with the following specifications:
   a. Type the data shown in Figure 3.3 with the appropriate formatting.
   b. Insert the formula to calculate the difference (actual amount minus the budget amount) and then copy the formula down to the other cells.
   c. Use AutoSum to insert the total amounts.
   d. Format the numbers in cells as currency with zero decimal places.
2. Save the worksheet and name it **sec3sc01**.
3. Print and then close **sec3sc01**.

3.3 *Assessment 1*

SUMMARY OF PERFORMANCE

	Actual	Budget	Difference
Northeast division	2,505,250	2,250,000	
Southeast division	1,895,200	1,550,000	
Northwest division	2,330,540	2,200,000	
Southwest division	1,850,340	1,950,500	
Total			

Assessment 2

1. Open **ExcelWorksheet13**.
2. Save the worksheet with Save As and name it **sec3sc02**.
3. Make the following changes to the worksheet:
   a. Determine the average monthly sales using the AVERAGE function.
   b. Format the numbers in cell B3 through H8 as currency with zero decimal places.
   c. Automatically adjust columns B through H.
4. Save, print, and then close **sec3sc02**.

Assessment 3

1. Open **sec3sc02**.
2. Save the worksheet with Save As and name it **sec3sc03**.
3. Make the following changes to the worksheet:
   a. Total each monthly column. (Create an appropriate title for the row and resize column widths, if necessary.)
   b. Use the MAX function to determine the highest monthly total (for cells B3 through G8). (You determine where you want this maximum monthly total to appear in the worksheet. Be sure to include a cell title.)
   c. Use the MIN function to determine the lowest monthly total (for cells B3 through G8). (You determine where you want this minimum monthly total to appear in the worksheet. Be sure to include a cell title.)
4. Save, print, and then close **sec3sc03**.

Assessment 4

1. Open **ExcelWorksheet24**.
2. Save the worksheet with Save As and name it **sec3sc04**.
3. The manager of Clearline Manufacturing is interested in refinancing a loan for either $125,000 or $300,000 and wants to determine the monthly payments, total payments, and total interest paid. Insert a formula with the following specifications:
   a. Make cell E5 active.
   b. Use the Insert Function button on the Formula bar to insert a formula using the PMT function. At the formula palette, enter the following:

$$\begin{aligned} \text{Rate} &= \text{C5/12} \\ \text{Nper} &= \text{D5} \\ \text{Pv} &= \text{-B5} \end{aligned}$$

  c. Copy the formula in cell E5 down to cells E6 through E8.

4. Insert a formula in cell F5 that multiplies the amount in E5 by the amount in D5.

5. Copy the formula in cell F5 down to cells F6 through F8.

6. Insert a formula in cell G5 that subtracts the amount in B5 from the amount in F5. (The formula is **=F5-B5**.)

7. Copy the formula in cell G5 down to cells G6 through G8.

8. Save, print, and then close **sec3sc04**.

Assessment 5

1. Open **ExcelWorksheet21**.
2. Save the worksheet with Save As and name it **sec3sc05**.
3. Make the following changes to the worksheet:
   a. Change the percentage in cell B3 from *9%* to *10%*.
   b. Change the number in cell B4 from *36* to *60*.
   c. Change the amount in cell B5 from *($1,200)* to *-500*.
   d. Use the FV function to insert a formula that calculates the future value of the investment. *(**Hint: For help with the formula, refer to Exercise 10.**)*
4. Save, print, and then close **sec3sc05**.

Assessment 6

1. Open **ExcelWorksheet14**.
2. Save the worksheet with Save As and name it **sec3sc06**.
3. Make the following changes to the worksheet:
   a. Insert a formula using an absolute reference to determine the projected quotas at 10% of the current quotas.
   b. Save and then print **sec3sc06**.
   c. Determine the projected quotas at 15% of the current quota by changing cell A14 to *15% Increase* and cell B14 to *1.15*.
   d. Save and then print **sec3sc06**.
   e. Determine the projected quotas at 20% of the current quota.
4. Save, print, and then close **sec3sc06**.

Assessment 7

1. Learn about specific options in the Options dialog box by completing the following steps:
   a. Open a blank workbook and then display the Options dialog box by clicking Tools and then Options.
   b. At the Options dialog box, click the View tab.
   c. Read information about the options in the *Window options* section of the dialog box. (To do this, click the Help button [displays with a question mark] that displays in the upper right corner of the dialog box. At the Microsoft Office Excel Help window, click the <u>View</u> hyperlink. Scroll down the window and read information about the options in the Window options section.)
   d. Close the blank workbook.
2. After reading information about the options in the Window options section, complete the following steps:

a. Open **sec3sc04**.
b. Save the worksheet with Save As and name it **sec3sc07**.
c. Display the formulas in the worksheet (rather than the results) using information you learned from the Options dialog box.

3. Save, print, and then close **sec3sc07**.

CHAPTER challenge

You are a loan officer for Loans R Us. You work in the department that specializes in home loans. To quickly determine monthly payments for potential customers, create a worksheet that displays the following labels: Price of Home, Down Payment, Loan Amount, Interest Rate, Term of Loan, and Monthly Payment. Use a formula to calculate the loan amount. Use the PMT function to determine the Monthly Payment. Insert amounts of your choosing for the other parts. In addition to calculating the monthly payment, customers whose down payment is less than 10% of the price of the home will be required to purchase private mortgage insurance. In another area of the worksheet, use the IF function to determine if the customer would have to purchase insurance. If the customer's down payment is less than 10%, display "purchase insurance" in the cell. If customer's down payment is 10% or greater, "no insurance necessary" should appear in the cell. Use cell references whenever possible. Format the worksheet so that it is easy to read and understand. Save the file and print it.

When a customer is required to purchase private mortgage insurance, you would like to provide information to the customer quickly concerning this insurance. Use the Help feature to learn about creating hyperlinks in Excel. Locate a helpful Web site that specializes in private mortgage insurance. Create a hyperlink in the worksheet that will jump to the Web site. Save the file again.

Once a loan has been approved and finalized, a letter will be sent to the customer explaining the details of the loan. Use a letter template in Word to create a letter that will be sent to a customer. Copy and link the information in the worksheet created in the first part of the Chapter Challenge to the customer letter. Save the letter and print it.

EXCEL

ENHANCING A WORKSHEET

PERFORMANCE OBJECTIVES

Upon successful completion of Chapter 4, you will be able to:
- ➤ Create headers and footers
- ➤ Change worksheet margins
- ➤ Center a worksheet horizontally and vertically on the page
- ➤ Insert a page break in a worksheet
- ➤ Print gridlines and row and column headings
- ➤ Hide and unhide a worksheet, column, or row
- ➤ Set and clear a print area
- ➤ Specify more than one print area in Page Break Preview
- ➤ Change the print quality
- ➤ Complete a spelling check on a worksheet
- ➤ Find and replace data and cell formatting in a worksheet
- ➤ Sort data in cells in ascending and descending order
- ➤ Filter a list using AutoFilter
- ➤ Plan and create a worksheet

Excel contains features you can use to enhance and control the formatting of a worksheet. In this chapter, you will learn how to create headers and footers, change worksheet margins, print column and row titles, print gridlines, and center a worksheet horizontally and vertically on the page. You will also learn how to complete a spell check on text in a worksheet, find and replace specific data and formatting in a worksheet, sort and filter data, and plan and create a worksheet.

Formatting a Worksheet Page

Worksheets, by default, are printed in portrait orientation with default top and bottom margins of 1 inch and left and right margins of .75 inch. These settings can be changed with options at the Page Setup dialog box. The Page Setup dialog box contains several tabs for controlling the appearance of the worksheet page.

Controlling the Page Layout

The Page Setup dialog box with the Page tab selected as shown in Figure 4.1 provides options for controlling the layout of the worksheet on the page. To display this dialog box, click File and then Page Setup. You can also display the Page Setup dialog box while in Print Preview by clicking the Setup button. At the Page Setup dialog box, make sure the Page tab is selected.

FIGURE

4.1 *Page Setup Dialog Box with Page Tab Selected*

Control how information is printed on the page with options in this section.

Adjust the size of the data on the page by percentage with options in this section.

Choose printing options in this section.

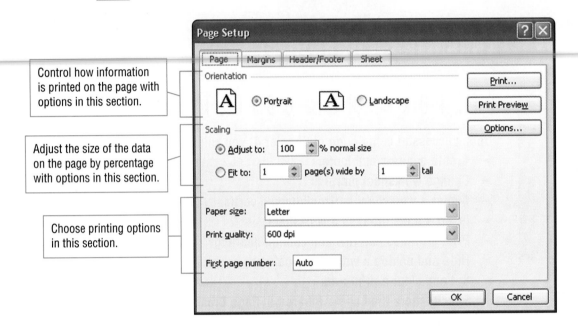

Control how information is printed on the page with choices in the *Orientation* section of the Page Setup dialog box. The two choices in the *Orientation* section are represented by sample pages. A sample page that is taller than it is wide shows how the default orientation (*Portrait*) prints data on the page. The other choice, *Landscape*, will rotate the data and print it on a page that is wider than it is tall. The landscape orientation might be useful in a worksheet that contains more columns than rows.

With options in the *Scaling* section of the Page Setup dialog box, you can adjust the size of the data in the worksheet by percentage. You can also specify on how many pages you want the data to fit. For example, if a worksheet contains too many columns to print on one page, choosing *Fit to* and leaving *1* as the number of pages will cause the display percentage to be decreased until the columns all fit on one page.

By default, an Excel worksheet is printed on standard paper, which is 8.5 inches wide and 11 inches long. Change this paper size with options from the Paper size drop-down list. Paper size choices will vary depending on the selected printer. To view the list of paper sizes, click the down-pointing arrow at the right of the *Paper size* option box.

Depending on the printer you are using, you may or may not have choices for setting the print quality. The data that displays in the *Print quality* option box will

EXCEL

vary depending on the selected printer. To view a list of print quality choices, click the down-pointing arrow at the right side of the *Print quality* option box. Choose a higher dpi (dots per inch) number to improve the quality of the print.

The worksheets you have printed so far have not been numbered. If you turn on page numbering (discussed in the "Inserting Headers/Footers" section), the first worksheet page is numbered 1 and any additional pages are incrementally numbered. With the *First page number* option, you can specify a different beginning page number. To do this, select *Auto* in the *First page number* text box, and then type the new starting number.

Inserting Headers/Footers

Use options at the Page Setup dialog box with the Header/Footer tab selected as shown in Figure 4.2 to insert text that will print at the top and/or bottom of each page of the worksheet. Click the down-pointing arrow after the *Header* option box and a drop-down list displays with options for inserting the user's name, workbook name, current date, and page number. The same list will display if you click the down-pointing arrow at the right of the *Footer* option box.

HINT

Delete all headers and footers by selecting the *(none)* option at the Header drop-down list or the Footer drop-down list.

FIGURE

4.2 *Page Setup Dialog Box with Header/Footer Tab Selected*

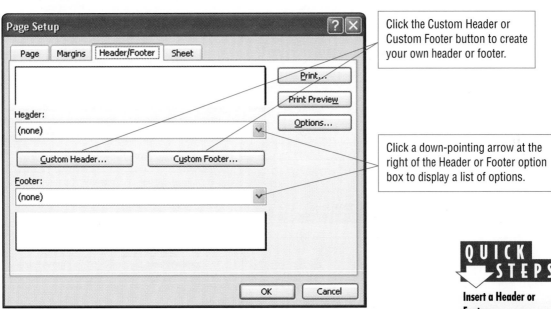

Click the Custom Header or Custom Footer button to create your own header or footer.

Click a down-pointing arrow at the right of the Header or Footer option box to display a list of options.

QUICK STEPS

Insert a Header or Footer
1. Click File, Page Setup.
2. Click Header/Footer tab.
3. Use options to insert desired header or footer.
4. Click OK.

(Note: Before completing computer exercises, delete the ExcelChapter03S folder on your disk. Next, copy the ExcelChapter04S subfolder from the Excel2003Specialist folder on the CD that accompanies this textbook to your disk and then make ExcelChapter04S the active folder.)

exercise 1

1. Open **ExcelWorksheet06**.
2. Save the worksheet with Save As and name it **sec4x01**.
3. Change the orientation of the worksheet and insert a header and footer by completing the following steps:
   a. Click File and then Page Setup.
   b. At the Page Setup dialog box, click the Page tab.
   c. Click the *Landscape* option.
   d. Click twice on the up-pointing arrow at the right side of the *Adjust to* text box. (This inserts *110* in the text box.)
   e. Click the Header/Footer tab.
   f. At the Page Setup dialog box with the Header/Footer tab selected, click the down-pointing arrow at the right of the *Header* option box, and then click **sec4x01** in the drop-down list box. (If **sec4x01** is not visible in the list box, scroll down the list box.)

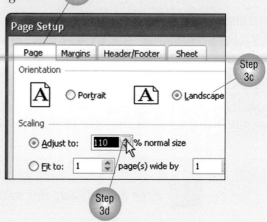

Step 3b

Step 3c

Step 3d

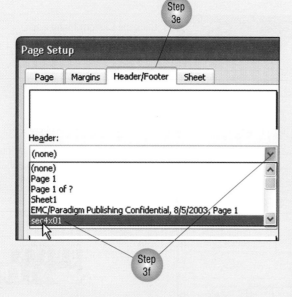

Step 3e

Step 3f

Step 3g

   g. Click the down-pointing arrow at the right of the *Footer* option box and then click *Page 1* at the drop-down list box. (If *Page 1* is not visible in the list box, scroll down the list box.)
   h. Click OK to close the Page Setup dialog box.
4. Save and then preview **sec4x01**.
5. Print **sec4x01**. (Before printing this worksheet, check with your instructor to determine if your printer can print in landscape orientation.)

EXCEL

6. With **sec4x01** still open, change the page orientation, scale the size of the worksheet so it fits on one page, and change the beginning page number to 3 by completing the following steps:
    a. Click File and then Page Setup.
    b. At the Page Setup dialog box, click the Page tab.
    c. Click the *Portrait* option.
    d. Click the *Fit to* option.
    e. Select *Auto* that displays in the *First page number* text box and then type 3.
    f. Click OK to close the dialog box.
7. Save, preview, print, and then close **sec4x01**.

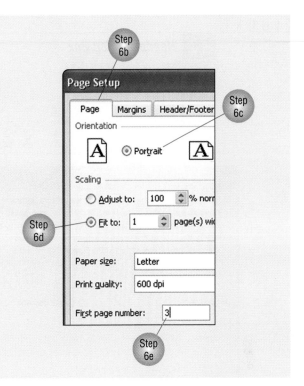

Creating Custom Headers/Footers

If you want to create a custom header, click the Custom Header button at the Page Setup dialog box with the Header/Footer tab selected. This displays the Header dialog box shown in Figure 4.3. Create a custom footer by clicking the Custom Footer button. This displays the Footer dialog box containing the same options as the Header dialog box. The Header dialog box and Footer dialog box contain a toolbar with buttons for customizing header/footer text; inserting text such as a page number, date, time, and path and file name; and inserting a picture. Buttons on this toolbar are identified in Figure 4.3.

To insert text in a custom header or footer, click in the desired section text box (such as *Left section*, *Center section*, or *Right section*) and then click the button on the toolbar that inserts the desired text or type the desired text. For example, to insert the workbook file name and path at the top center of the page, click in the *Center section* text box, and then click the Path & File button on the toolbar.

QUICK STEPS

Insert a Custom Header
1. Click File, Page Setup.
2. Click Header/Footer tab.
3. Click Custom Header button.
4. Type or insert desired data.
5. Click OK.
6. Click OK.

QUICK STEPS

Insert a Custom Footer
1. Click File, Page Setup.
2. Click Header/Footer tab.
3. Click Custom Footer button.
4. Type or insert desired data.
5. Click OK.
6. Click OK.

4.3 *Header Dialog Box*

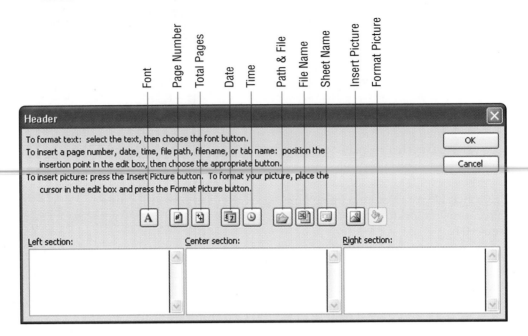

exercise 2

1. Open **ExcelWorksheet06**.
2. Save the worksheet with Save As and name it **sec4x02**.
3. Delete row 2.
4. Insert the text *Average* in cell N1.
5. Insert a formula in cell N2 that averages the percentages in cells B2 through M2.
6. Copy the formula in cell N2 relatively to cells N3 through N19.
7. Insert a header and footer in the worksheet by completing the following steps:
   a. Click File and then Page Setup.
   b. At the Page Setup dialog box, click the Header/Footer tab.
   c. At the Page Setup dialog box with the Header/Footer tab selected, click the Custom Header button.
   d. At the Header dialog box, click in the text box below *Right section*, and then type your name.
   e. Click OK to close the Header dialog box.
   f. At the Page Setup dialog box, click the Custom Footer button.
   g. At the Footer dialog box, click in the text box below *Center section*, and then click the File Name button on the toolbar.

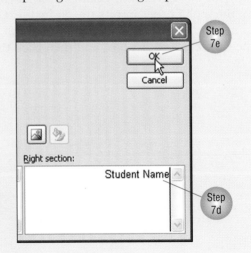

Step 7e

Step 7d

EXCEL

h. Click OK to close the Footer dialog box.
i. Click OK to close the Page Setup dialog box.
8. Save, preview, print, and then close **sec4x02**.

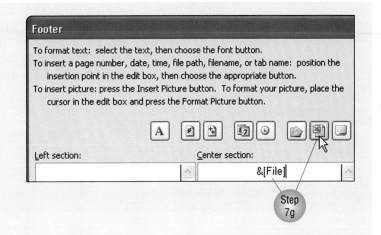

Step 7g

Changing Worksheet Margins

Excel uses 1-inch top and bottom margins for a worksheet and 0.75-inch left and right margins. You can change these default margins at the Page Setup dialog box with the Margins tab selected as shown in Figure 4.4.

QUICK STEPS

Change Worksheet Margins
1. Click File, Page Setup.
2. Click Margins tab.
3. Change the top, left, right, and/or bottom measurements.
4. Click OK.

FIGURE

4.4 *Page Setup Dialog Box with Margins Tab Selected*

Changes made to margin measurements are reflected in the sample worksheet page.

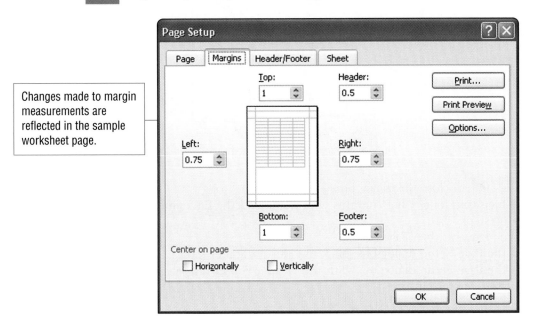

A worksheet page showing the cells and margins displays in the dialog box. As you increase or decrease the Top, Bottom, Left, or Right margin measurements, the sample worksheet page reflects the change. You can also increase or decrease the measurement from the top of the page to the header with the *Header* option or the measurement from the footer to the bottom of the page with the *Footer* option.

exercise 3

CHANGING WORKSHEET MARGINS

1. Open **ExcelWorksheet02**.
2. Save the worksheet with Save As and name it **sec4x03**.
3. Select cells A1 through D8 and then apply the Accounting 2 autoformat.
4. Change the orientation of the worksheet and change the worksheet margins by completing the following steps:
   a. Click File and then Page Setup.
   b. At the Page Setup dialog box, click the Page tab.
   c. Click the *Landscape* option.
   d. Click the Margins tab.
   e. At the Page Setup dialog box with the Margins tab selected, click the up-pointing arrow at the right of the *Top* text box until *3.5* displays.
   f. Click the up-pointing arrow at the right of the *Left* text box until *3.5* displays.

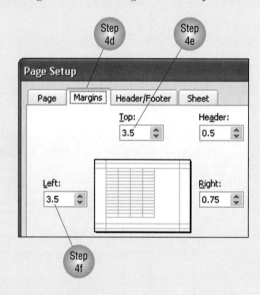

   g. Click OK to close the dialog box.
5. Create a custom footer that contains your name and the file name by completing the following steps:
   a. Click File and then Page Setup.
   b. At the Page Setup dialog box, click the Header/Footer tab.
   c. At the Page Setup dialog box with the Header/Footer tab selected, click the Custom Footer button.

d. At the Footer dialog box, click in the text box below *Left section*, and then type your name.

e. Click in the text box below *Right section* and then click the File Name button on the toolbar.

f. Click OK to close the Footer dialog box.

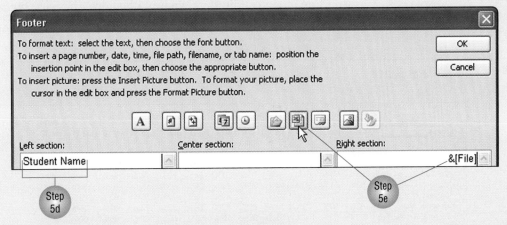

g. Click OK to close the Page Setup dialog box.

6. Save, preview, print, and then close **sec4x03**.

Centering a Worksheet Horizontally and/or Vertically

By default, worksheets print in the upper left corner of the page. You can center a worksheet on the page by changing the margins; however, an easier method for centering a worksheet is to use the *Horizontally* and/or *Vertically* options that display at the bottom of the Page Setup dialog box with the Margins tab selected. If you choose one or both of these options, the worksheet page in the *Preview* section displays how the worksheet will print on the page.

QUICK STEPS

Center Worksheet Horizontally/Vertically
1. Click File, Page Setup.
2. Click Margins tab.
3. Click *Horizontally* option and/or click *Vertically* option.
4. Click OK.

exercise 4

HORIZONTALLY AND VERTICALLY CENTERING A WORKSHEET

1. Open **ExcelWorksheet03**.
2. Save the worksheet with Save As and name it **sec4x04**.
3. Select cells B3 through D8 and then click the Percent Style button on the Formatting toolbar.
4. Select cells A1 through D8 and then apply the Colorful 2 autoformat.
5. Horizontally and vertically center the worksheet by completing the following steps:
   a. Click File and then Page Setup.
   b. At the Page Setup dialog box, click the Margins tab.
   c. Click the *Horizontally* option. (This inserts a check mark.)
   d. Click the *Vertically* option. (This inserts a check mark.)
   e. Click OK to close the dialog box.
6. Save, preview, print, and then close **sec4x04**.

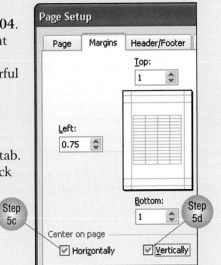

Insert Page Break
1. Select column or row.
2. Click Insert, Page Break.

Inserting and Removing Page Breaks

The default left and right margins of .75 inch allow a total of 7 inches of cells across the page (8.5 inches minus 1.5 inches equals 7 inches). If a worksheet contains more than 7 inches of cells across the page, a page break is inserted in the worksheet and the remaining columns are moved to the next page. A page break displays as a broken line along cell borders. Figure 4.5 shows the page break in ExcelWorksheet06. (The location of your page break may vary.)

F I G U R E

4.5 *Page Break*

	A	B	C	D	E	F	G	H	I	J	K	L	M	N
1	Name	Test 1	Test 2	Test 3	Test 4	Test 5	Test 6	Test 7	Test 8	Test 9	Test 10	Test 11	Test 12	
2														
3	Arnson, Patrick	89%	65%	76%	89%	98%	65%	76%	87%	55%	78%	67%	69%	
4	Barclay, Jeanine	78%	66%	87%	90%	92%	82%	100%	84%	67%	86%	82%	91%	
5	Calahan, Jack	65%	71%	64%	66%	70%	81%	64%	59%	76%	76%	45%	49%	
6	Cumpston, Kurt	89%	91%	90%	93%	86%	80%	84%	93%	95%	81%	96%	98%	
7	Dimmitt, Marian	78%	73%	81%	82%	67%	69%	82%	72%	85%	83%	71%	73%	
8	Donovan, Nancy	82%	89%	79%	74%	80%	82%	86%	72%	74%	82%	76%	79%	
9	Fisher-Edwards, Teri	89%	93%	100%	91%	86%	90%	88%	86%	100%	98%	90%	97%	
10	Flanery, Stephanie	58%	45%	63%	51%	60%	59%	63%	52%	66%	67%	53%	49%	
11	Heyman, Grover	78%	75%	87%	88%	64%	76%	70%	67%	55%	87%	82%	88%	
12	Herbertson, Wynn	92%	80%	93%	90%	86%	84%	95%	100%	98%	88%	95%	89%	
13	Jewett, Troy	98%	94%	99%	89%	100%	93%	100%	95%	96%	91%	87%	94%	
14	Kwieciak, Kathleen	55%	0%	42%	65%	72%	40%	65%	0%	0%	48%	52%	56%	
15	Leibrand, Maxine	78%	69%	83%	87%	84%	69%	80%	82%	88%	79%	83%	76%	
16	Markovits, Claude	89%	93%	84%	100%	95%	92%	95%	100%	89%	94%	98%	94%	
17	Moonstar, Siana	73%	87%	67%	83%	90%	84%	73%	81%	75%	65%	84%	88%	
18	Nyegaard, Curtis	90%	89%	84%	85%	93%	85%	100%	94%	98%	93%	100%	95%	
19	Oglesbee, Randy	65%	55%	73%	90%	87%	67%	85%	77%	85%	73%	78%	77%	
20	Pherson, Douglas	69%	82%	87%	74%	70%	82%	84%	85%	66%	77%	91%	86%	
21														
22														
23														

A1 ▼ *fx* Name

Page Break

\Sheet1 / Sheet2 / Sheet3 /

A page break also displays horizontally in a worksheet. By default, a worksheet can contain approximately 9 inches of cells vertically down the page. This is because the paper size is set by default at 11 inches. With the default top and bottom margins of 1 inch, this allows 9 inches of cells to print on one page.

Excel automatically inserts a page break in a worksheet. You can insert your own if you would like more control over what cells print on a page. To insert your own page break, select the column or row, click Insert, and then click Page Break. A page break is inserted immediately left of the selected column or immediately above the selected row. If you want to insert both a horizontal and vertical page break at the same time, make a cell active, click Insert, and then click Page Break. This causes a horizontal page break to be inserted immediately above the active cell, and a vertical page break to be inserted at the left side of the active column. To remove a page break, select the column or row or make the desired cell active, click Insert and then click Remove Page Break.

The page break automatically inserted by Excel may not be visible initially in a worksheet. One way to display the page break is to preview the worksheet. When you close the Print Preview screen, the page break will display in the worksheet. In Print Preview, click the Next button on the Preview bar to display the next page in the worksheet. Click the Previous button to display the previous page in the worksheet.

Excel provides a Page Break view that will display worksheet pages and page breaks. To display this view, click View and then Page Break Preview. This causes the worksheet to display similarly to the worksheet shown in Figure 4.6. The word *Page* along with the page number is displayed in gray behind the cells in the worksheet. A blue line displays indicating the page break. You can move the page break by positioning the arrow pointer on the blue line, holding down the left mouse button, dragging the line to the desired location, and then releasing the mouse button. To return to the Normal view, click View and then Normal.

FIGURE

4.6 **Worksheet in Page Break Preview**

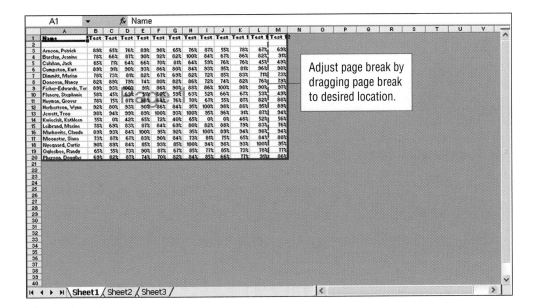

Adjust page break by dragging page break to desired location.

exercise 5

INSERTING A PAGE BREAK IN A WORKSHEET

1. Open **ExcelWorksheet06**.
2. Save the worksheet with Save As and name it **sec4x05**.
3. View the default page break inserted automatically by Excel by completing the following steps:
   a. Click the Print Preview button on the Standard toolbar.
   b. After previewing the worksheet, click the Close button.
   c. At the worksheet, click the right scroll arrow at the right side of the horizontal scroll bar until columns L and M are visible. The default page break should display between columns L and M. (The default page break displays as a dashed line. The location of the page break may vary slightly.)
4. Select the entire worksheet and then change the font to 12-point Century (or a similar serif typeface such as Garamond).
5. If necessary, automatically adjust the width of column A.
6. Select columns B through M and then drag one of the selected column boundaries to the right until the column width displays as *9.00* in the yellow box.

7. Insert a page break between columns F and G by completing the following steps:
   a. Select column G.
   b. Click Insert and then Page Break.
   c. Click once in any cell in column F.

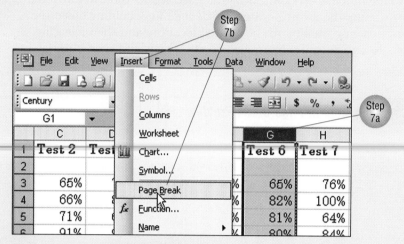

8. View the worksheet in Page Break Preview by completing the following steps:
   a. Click View and then Page Break Preview.
   b. View the pages and page breaks in the worksheet.
   c. Click View and then Normal to return to the Normal view.
9. Horizontally and vertically center the worksheet by completing the following steps:
   a. Click File and then Page Setup.
   b. At the Page Setup dialog box, click the Margins tab.
   c. Click the *Horizontally* option. (This inserts a check mark.)
   d. Click the *Vertically* option. (This inserts a check mark.)
   e. Click OK to close the dialog box.
10. Save, preview, print, and then close **sec4x05**.

Print Column and Row Titles
1. Click File, Page Setup.
2. Click Sheet tab.
3. Type row range in *Rows to repeat at top* option.
4. Type column range in *Columns to repeat at left* option.
5. Click OK.

Printing Column and Row Titles on Multiple Pages

Columns and rows in a worksheet are usually titled. For example, in ExcelWorksheet06, column titles include *Name*, *Test 1*, *Test 2*, *Test 3*, and so on. Row titles include the names of the people who have taken the tests. If a worksheet prints on more than one page, having column and/or row titles printing on each page can be useful. For example, when you printed sec4x05, the names of the people did not print on the second page. This makes matching test scores with names difficult.

You can print column and/or row titles on each page of a worksheet. To do this, click File and then Page Setup. At the Page Setup dialog box, click the Sheet tab. This displays the dialog box as shown in Figure 4.7.

4.7 *Page Setup Dialog Box with Sheet Tab Selected*

Type the row range in this text box.

Type the column range in this text box.

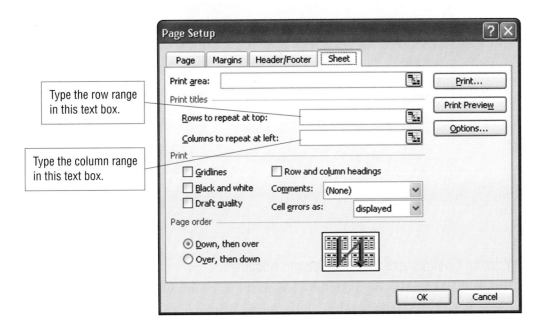

At the Page Setup dialog box with the Sheet tab selected, specify the range of row cells you want to print on every page in the *Rows to repeat at top* text box. Type a cell range using a colon. For example, if you want cells A1 through J1 to print on every page, you would type **A1:J1** in the *Rows to repeat at top* text box. Type the range of column cells you want to print on every page in the *Columns to repeat at left* text box.

exercise 6

PRINTING COLUMN TITLES ON EACH PAGE OF A WORKSHEET

1. Open **ExcelWorksheet06**.
2. Save the worksheet with Save As and name it **sec4x06**.
3. Select the entire worksheet and then change the font to 12-point Garamond (or a similar serif typeface).
4. If necessary, automatically adjust the width of column A.
5. Select columns B through M and then drag one of the selected column boundaries to the right until the column width displays as *8.00* in the yellow box above the mouse pointer. (This will change the width of columns B through M to *8.00*.)
6. Select row 1 and then change the alignment to center.
7. Specify that you want column titles to print on each page by completing the following steps:
   a. Click File and then Page Setup.
   b. At the Page Setup dialog box, click the Sheet tab.
   c. At the Page Setup dialog box with the Sheet tab selected, click in the *Columns to repeat at left* text box.

d.   Type A1:A20.
e.   Click OK to close the dialog box.

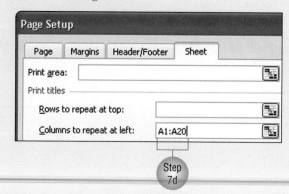

Step
7d

8.   Save, preview, print, and then close **sec4x06**.

Printing Gridlines and Row and Column Headings

Print Gridlines
1. Click File, Page Setup.
2. Click Sheet tab.
3. Click *Gridlines* option.
4. Click OK.

The gridlines that create the cells in a worksheet, by default, do not print. If you would like these gridlines to print, display the Page Setup dialog box with the Sheet tab selected, and then click *Gridlines* in the *Print* section. This inserts a check mark in the check box. At the Page Setup dialog box with the Sheet tab selected, you can also click *Row and column headings* and the row numbers and column letters will print with the worksheet.

If you are printing with a color printer, you can print the worksheet in black and white. To do this, display the Page Setup dialog box with the Sheet tab selected, and then click *Black and white*. This option is located in the *Print* section of the dialog box.

exercise 7

PRINTING GRIDLINES AND ROW AND COLUMN HEADINGS

1. Open **ExcelWorksheet05**.
2. Save the worksheet with Save As and name it **sec4x07**.
3. Insert the text *Total* in cell D2.
4. Merge and center cells A1 through D1. (You must click the Merge and Center button twice.)
5. Make cell D3 active and then insert a formula that multiplies the contents of cell C3 with B3.
6. Copy the formula in cell D3 relatively to cells D4 through D8.
7. Specify that the gridlines and row and column headings are to print by completing the following steps:
    a.   Click File and then Page Setup.
    b.   At the Page Setup dialog box, click the Sheet tab.

C	D	
ary		
Rate	Total	
$23.15	$810.25	
$19.00	$380.00	
$18.75	$750.00	
$16.45	$394.80	
$11.50	$172.50	
$11.50	$172.50	

Step
6

c. At the Page Setup dialog box with the Sheet tab selected, click the *Gridlines* check box in the *Print* section to insert a check mark.

d. Click the *Row and column headings* check box in the *Print* section to insert a check mark.

8. With the Page Setup dialog box still displayed, click the Margins tab.

9. At the Page Setup dialog box with the Margins tab selected, click the *Horizontally* option, click the *Vertically* option, and then click OK to close the dialog box.

10. Save, preview, print, and then close **sec4x07**.

Page Setup

Page | Margins | Header/Footer | Sheet

Print area:

Print titles

Rows to repeat at top:

Columns to repeat at left:

Print

Step 7c → ☑ Gridlines ☑ Row and column headings
☐ Black and white   Comments: (None)
☐ Draft quality   Cell errors as: displayed

Step 7d

Hiding and Unhiding Columns/Rows

If a worksheet contains columns and/or rows of sensitive data or data that you are not using or do not want to view, consider hiding the columns and/or rows. To hide columns in a worksheet, select the columns to be hidden, click Format, point to Column, and then click Hide. To hide selected rows, click Format, point to Row, and then click Hide. To make a hidden column visible, select the column to the left and the column to the right of the hidden column, click Format, point to Column, and then click Unhide. To make a hidden row visible, select the row above and the row below the hidden row, click Format, point to Row, and then click Unhide.

If the first row or column is hidden, use the Go To feature to make the row or column visible. To do this, click Edit and then Go To. At the Go To dialog box, type **A1** in the *Reference* text box, and then click OK. At the worksheet, click Format, point to either Column or Row, and then click Unhide.

You can also unhide columns or rows using the mouse. If a column or row is hidden, the gray boundary line in the column or row header displays as a slightly thicker gray line. To unhide a column, position the mouse pointer on the slightly thicker gray line that displays in the column header until the mouse pointer changes to left- and right-pointing arrows with a double line between. (Make sure the mouse pointer displays with two lines between the arrows. If a single line displays, you will simply change the size of the visible column.) Hold down the left mouse button, drag to the right until the column displays at the desired width, and then release the mouse button. Unhide a row in a similar manner. Position the mouse pointer on the slightly thicker gray line in the row header until the mouse pointer changes to up- and down-pointing arrows with a double line between. Drag down to display the row and then release the mouse button. If two or more adjacent columns or rows are hidden, you will need to unhide each column or row separately.

QUICK STEPS

Hide Columns
1. Select columns.
2. Click Format, Column, Hide.

QUICK STEPS

Hide Rows
1. Select rows.
2. Click Format, Row, Hide.

1. Open **ExcelWorksheet26**.
2. Save the worksheet with Save As and name it **sec4x08**.
3. Hide the rows containing rental information on the forklift by completing the following steps:
   a. Click cell A9 to make it the active cell.
   b. Click Format, point to Row, and then click Hide.
   c. Click cell A16 to make it the active cell.
   d. Click Format, point to Row, and then click Hide.

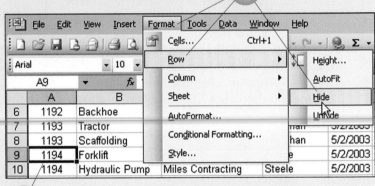

4. Hide the column containing the names of the service representatives by completing the following steps:
   a. Click cell D3 to make it the active cell.
   b. Click Format, point to Column, and then click Hide.
5. Create a custom footer that prints your name at the left margin and the file name at the right margin. *(Hint: For assistance, refer to Exercise 3, Step 5.)*
6. Save and then print **sec4x08**.

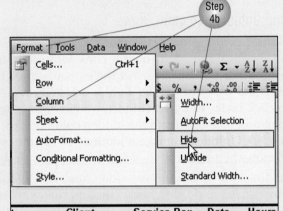

7. Unhide row 9 by completing the following steps:
   a. Select rows 8 and 10.
   b. Click Format, point to Row, and then click Unhide.
8. Unhide row 16 by completing the following steps:

a. Position the mouse pointer on the thicker gray line that displays between rows 15 and 17 in the header row until the pointer turns into arrows pointing up and down with a double line between.

b. Hold down the left mouse button, drag down until *Height: 12.75 (17 pixels)* displays in the yellow box above the mouse pointer, and then release the mouse button.

8	1193	Scaffolding	A
9	1194	Forklift	M
10	1194	Hydraulic Pump	M
11	1195	Pressure Sprayer	E
12	1196	Sandblaster	B
13	1196	Pressure Sprayer	B
1	Height: 12.75 (17 pixels)	ader	C
15	1197	Flatbed Truck	C
16			
17			
18			

Step 8b

9. Save, print, and then close **sec4x08**.

Printing a Specific Area of a Worksheet

Use the Print Area feature to select and print specific areas in a worksheet. To use this feature, select the cells you want to print, click File, point to Print Area, and then click Set Print Area. This inserts a border around the selected cells. Click the Print button on the Standard toolbar and the cells within the border are printed.

You can specify more than one print area in a worksheet in Page Break Preview. To do this, display the worksheet in Page Break Preview. Select the first group of cells, click File, point to Print Area, and then click Set Print Area. Select the next group of cells, right-click in the selected cells, and then click Add to Print Area at the shortcut menu. Clear a print area by clicking File, pointing to Print Area, and then clicking Clear Print Area.

Each area specified as a print area will print on a separate page. If you want nonadjacent print areas to print on the same page, consider hiding columns and/or rows in the worksheet to bring the areas together.

Changing Print Quality

Most printers have more than one level of print quality. The print quality choices vary with printers and may include options such as *High, Medium, Low,* and *Draft.* Print quality choices are available at the Page Setup dialog box with the Page tab selected. At this dialog box, click the down-pointing arrow at the right side of the *Print quality* option, and then click the desired print quality at the drop-down list.

1. Open **ExcelWorksheet06**.
2. Specify a print area by completing the following steps:
   a. Select cells A1 through B20.
   b. Click File, point to Print Area, and then click Set Print Area.
   c. With the border surrounding the cells A1 through B20, click the Print button on the Standard toolbar.
   d. Clear the print area by clicking File, pointing to Print Area, and then clicking Clear Print Area.
3. Suppose you want to print all of the student names and just the percentages for Test 6 and you want the information to print on one page. To do this, hide columns B through F and select the print area by completing the following steps:
   a. Select columns B through F.
   b. Click Format, point to Column, and then click Hide.
   c. Select cells A1 through G20. (Columns A and G are now adjacent.)
   d. Click File, point to Print Area, and then click Set Print Area.
4. Change the print quality and print the specified print area by completing the following steps:
   a. Click File and then Page Setup.
   b. At the Page Setup dialog box, click the Page tab.
   c. At the Page Setup dialog box with the Page tab selected, click the down-pointing arrow at the right side of the *Print quality* option, and then click *Draft* (or a similar quality or lower *dpi*) at the drop-down list.
   d. Click the Print button.
   e. At the Print dialog box, click OK.
5. Clear the print area by making sure cells A1 through G20 are selected, clicking File, pointing to Print Area, and then clicking Clear Print Area.
6. With cells A1 through G20 selected, make the hidden columns visible by clicking Format, pointing to Column, and then clicking Unhide.
7. Close **ExcelWorksheet06** without saving the changes.

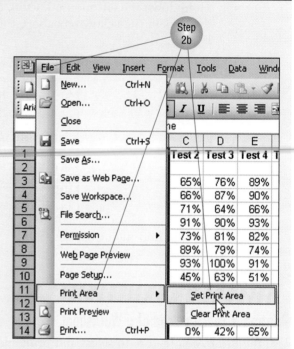

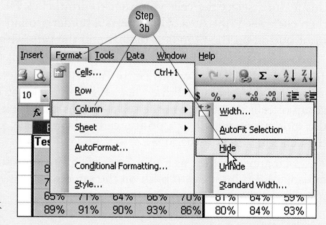

Customizing Print Jobs

The Print dialog box provides options for customizing a print job. Display the Print dialog box shown in Figure 4.8 by clicking File and then Print. Use options at the Print dialog box to print a specific range of cells, selected cells, or multiple copies of a workbook.

FIGURE

4.8   *Print Dialog Box*

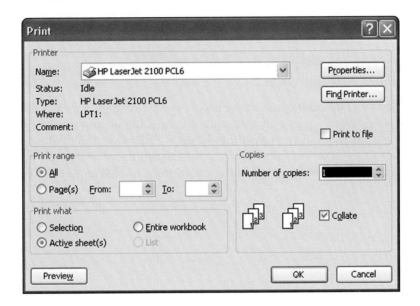

At the Print dialog box, the currently selected printer name displays in the *Name* option box. If other printers are installed, click the down-pointing arrow at the right side of the *Name* option box to display a list of printers.

The *Active sheet(s)* option in the *Print what* section is selected by default. At this setting, the currently active worksheet will print. If you want to print an entire workbook that contains several worksheets, click *Entire workbook* in the *Print what* section. Click the *Selection* option in the *Print what* section to print the currently selected cells.

If you want more than one copy of a worksheet or workbook printed, change to the desired number of copies with the *Number of copies* option in the *Copies* section. If you want the copies collated, make sure the *Collate* check box in the *Copies* section contains a check mark.

A worksheet within a workbook can contain more than one page. If you want to print specific pages of a worksheet within a workbook, click *Page(s)* in the *Print range* section, and then specify the desired page numbers in the *From* and *To* text boxes.

If you want to preview the worksheet before printing, click the Preview button that displays at the bottom left corner of the dialog box. This displays the worksheet as it will appear on the printed page. After viewing the worksheet, click the Close button that displays toward the top of the Preview screen.

exercise 10

1. Open **ExcelWorksheet24**.
2. Print selected cells by completing the following steps:
   a. Select cells A4 through D8.
   b. Click File and then Print.
   c. At the Print dialog box, click *Selection* in the *Print what* section.
   d. Click OK.
3. Close **ExcelWorksheet24**.

Spelling

Complete a Spelling Check
1. Click Spelling button on Standard toolbar.
2. Replace or ignore selected word.

Completing a Spelling Check

To spell check text in a worksheet using Excel's spell checking feature, make the first cell in the worksheet active, and then click the Spelling button on the Standard toolbar or click Tools and then Spelling. Figure 4.9 displays the Spelling dialog box. At this dialog box, you can click a button to tell Excel to ignore a word or you can replace a misspelled word with a word from the *Suggestions* list box.

FIGURE

4.9 *Excel Spelling Dialog Box*

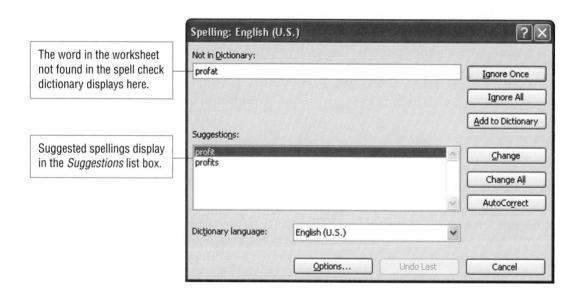

The word in the worksheet not found in the spell check dictionary displays here.

Suggested spellings display in the *Suggestions* list box.

EXCEL

Using Undo and Redo

Excel includes an Undo button on the Standard toolbar that will reverse certain commands or delete the last data typed in a cell. For example, if you apply an autoformat to selected cells in a worksheet and then decide you want the autoformatting removed, click the Undo button on the Standard toolbar. If you decide you want the autoformatting back again, click the Redo button on the Standard toolbar.

Undo   Redo

In addition to the Undo and Redo buttons on the Standard toolbar, you can use options from the Edit drop-down menu to undo or repeat actions. The first two options at the Edit drop-down menu will vary depending on the last action completed. For example, if you just clicked the Currency Style button on the Formatting toolbar and then displayed the Edit drop-down menu, the first option displays as Undo Style and the second option displays as Repeat Style. If you decide you do not want the currency style applied, click Edit and then Undo Style. You can also just click the Undo button on the Standard toolbar.

HINT
Ctrl + Z is the keyboard command to Undo a command.

exercise 11

SPELL CHECKING AND FORMATTING A WORKSHEET

1. Open **ExcelWorksheet04**.
2. Save the worksheet with Save As and name it **sec4x11**.
3. Complete a spelling check on the worksheet by completing the following steps:
   a. Make sure cell A1 is the active cell.
   b. Click the Spelling button on the Standard toolbar.
   c. Click the Change button as needed to correct misspelled words in the worksheet.
   d. At the message telling you the spelling check is completed, click OK.

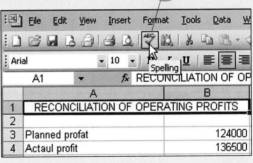

4. Select the entire worksheet and then change the font to 11-point Univers (or a similar sans serif typeface such as Tahoma).
5. Select cells A1 through B12 and then apply the Accounting 4 autoformat.
6. Select cells B3 through B12 and then click the Currency Style button on the Formatting toolbar.
7. With cells B3 through B12 still selected, click twice the Decrease Decimal button on the Formatting toolbar.
8. Make cell B4 active and then add a single-line border at the bottom of the cell. (To do this, click the down-pointing arrow at the right side of the Borders button on the Formatting toolbar and then click the Bottom Border option.)
9. Make cell B5 active and then add a double-line border at the bottom of the cell. (To do this, click the down-pointing arrow at the right side of the Borders button on the Formatting toolbar and then click the Bottom Double Border option.)
10. Make cell B10 active and then add a single-line border at the bottom of the cell.
11. Make cell B12 active and then add a double-line border at the bottom of the cell.
12. Select row 1 and then turn on bold.

13. Select cells A1 through B12 and then add a pale blue color shading.
14. After looking at the worksheet with the pale blue color shading, you decide you want to remove it. To do this, click the Undo button on the Standard toolbar.
15. Save, print, and then close **sec4x11**.

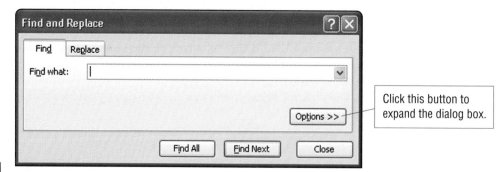

Finding and Replacing Data in a Worksheet

Excel provides a Find feature you can use to look for specific data and either replace it with nothing or replace it with other data. This feature is particularly helpful in a large worksheet with data you want to find quickly. Excel also includes a find and replace feature. Use this to look for specific data in a worksheet and replace with other data.

To find specific data in a worksheet, click Edit and then Find. This displays the Find and Replace dialog box with the Find tab selected as shown in Figure 4.10. Type the data you want to find in the *Find what* text box and then click the Find Next button. Continue clicking the Find Next button to move to the next occurrence of the data. Ctrl + F is the keyboard command to display the Find and Replace dialog box with the Find tab selected.

Find Data
1. Click Edit, Find.
2. Type data in *Find what* text box.
3. Click Find Next button.

FIGURE

4.10 *Find and Replace Dialog Box with Find Tab Selected*

Find and Replace

| Find | Replace |

Find what: |

Click this button to expand the dialog box.

Options >>

Find All   Find Next   Close

Find and Replace Data
1. Click Edit, Replace.
2. Type data in *Find what* text box.
3. Type data in *Replace with* text box.
4. Click Replace button or Replace All button.

To find specific data in a worksheet and replace it with other data, click Edit and then Replace. This displays the Find and Replace dialog box with the Replace tab selected as shown in Figure 4.11. Enter the data for which you are looking in the *Find what* text box. Press the Tab key or click in the *Replace with* text box and then enter the data that is to replace the data in the *Find what* text box. Ctrl + H is the keyboard command to display the Find and Replace dialog box with the Replace tab selected.

EXCEL

FIGURE

4.11   *Find and Replace Dialog Box with Replace Tab Selected*

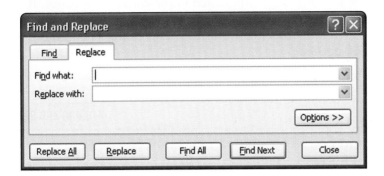

Click the Find Next button to tell Excel to find the next occurrence of the data. Click the Replace button to replace the data and find the next occurrence. If you know that you want all occurrences of the data in the *Find what* text box replaced with the data in the *Replace with* text box, click the Replace All button. Click the Close button to close the Replace dialog box.

Display additional find and replace options by clicking the Options button. This expands the dialog box as shown in Figure 4.12. By default, Excel will look for any data that contains the same characters as the data in the *Find what* text box, without concern for the characters before or after the entered data. For example, in Exercise 12, you will be looking for test scores of 0%. If you do not specify to Excel that you want to find cells that contain only *0%*, Excel will stop at any cell containing *0%*. In this example, Excel would stop at a cell containing *90%* or a cell containing *100%*. To specify that the only data that should be contained in the cell is what is entered in the *Find what* text box, click the Options button to expand the dialog box, and then insert a check mark in the *Match entire cell contents* check box.

HINT

If the Find and Replace dialog box obstructs your view of the worksheet, move the box by clicking and dragging the Title bar.

FIGURE

4.12   *Expanded Find and Replace Dialog Box*

Search the active worksheet or the entire workbook with the *Within* option.

With this option you can search by rows or by columns.

Use these two Format buttons to search for specific cell formatting and replace with other cell formatting.

If the *Match case* option is active (contains a check mark), Excel will look for only that data that exactly matches the case of the data entered in the *Find what* text box. Remove the check mark from this check box if you do not want Excel to find exact case matches. Excel will search in the current worksheet. If you want Excel to search an entire workbook, change the *Within* option to *Workbook*. Excel, by default, searches by rows in a worksheet. This can be changed to *By Columns* with the *Search* option.

exercise 12

1. Open **ExcelWorksheet06**.
2. Save the worksheet with Save As and name it **sec4x12**.
3. Find all occurrences of *0%* in the worksheet and replace with *70%* by completing the following steps:
    a. Click Edit and then Replace.
    b. At the Find and Replace dialog box with the Replace tab selected, type *0%* in the *Find what* text box.
    c. Press the Tab key (this moves the insertion point to the *Replace with* text box).
    d. Type *70%*.
    e. Click the Options button to display additional options. (If additional options already display, skip this step.)
    f. Click the *Match entire cell contents* option to insert a check mark in the check box.
    g. Click the Replace All button.
    h. At the message telling you that Excel has completed the search and has made three replacements, click OK.
    i. Click the Options button to decrease the size of the Find and Replace dialog box and then close the dialog box.

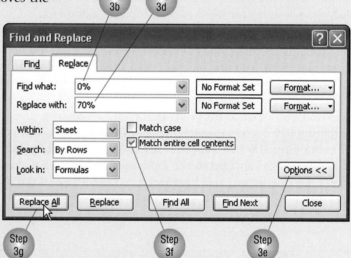

4. Select the entire worksheet and then change the font to 10-point Century (or a similar serif typeface).
5. Automatically adjust the width of columns A through M.
6. Display the Page Setup dialog box with the Page tab selected, click the *Landscape* option, and then close the dialog box.
7. Print, save, and then close **sec4x12**.

Finding and Replacing Cell Formatting

Use the *Format* options at the expanded Find and Replace dialog box (see Figure 4.12) to search for specific cell formatting and replace with other formatting. Click the down-pointing arrow at the right side of the Format button and a drop-down menu displays. Click the *Format* option and the Find Format dialog box displays with

EXCEL

the Number, Alignment, Font, Border, Patterns, and Protection tabs. Specify formatting at this dialog box. Click the *Choose Format From Cell* option and the mouse pointer displays with a pointer tool attached. Click in the cell containing the desired formatting and the formatting displays in the Preview box to the left of the Format button. Click the *Clear Find Format* option and any formatting in the Preview box is removed.

exercise 13

FINDING AND REPLACING CELL FORMATTING

1. Open **ExcelWorksheet28**.
2. Save the worksheet with Save As and name it **sec4x13**.
3. Search for orange shading and replace it with light purple shading by completing the following steps:
   a. Click Edit and then Replace.
   b. At the Find and Replace dialog box with the Replace tab selected, make sure the dialog box is expanded. (If not, click the Options button.)
   c. Select and then delete any text that displays in the *Find what* text box.
   d. Select and then delete any text that displays in the *Replace with* text box.
   e. Make sure the boxes immediately preceding the two Format buttons display with the text *No Format Set*. (If not, click the down-pointing arrow at the right of the Format button, and then click the *Clear Find Format* option at the drop-down list. Do this for each Format button.)
   f. Click the down-pointing arrow at the right side of the top Format button (the one at the far right side of the *Find what* text box) and then click Format at the drop-down menu.
   g. At the Find Format dialog box, click the Patterns tab.
   h. Click the Light Orange color (as shown below on the left).
   i. Click OK to close the dialog box.
   j. Click the down-pointing arrow at the right side of the second Format button (the one at the far right side of the *Replace with* text box and then click Format at the drop-down menu.
   k. At the Replace Format dialog box with the Patterns tab selected, click the Light Purple color (as shown at the far right).
   l. Click OK to close the dialog box.
   m. At the Find and Replace dialog box, click the Replace All button.
   n. At the message telling you that Excel has completed the search and made replacements, click OK.

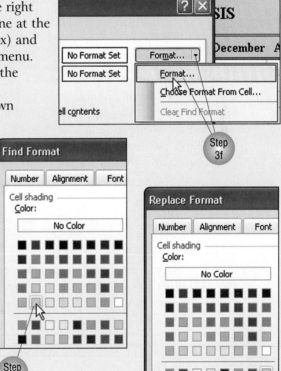

4. Complete steps similar to those in Steps 3f through 3n to search for light yellow shading and replace it with light green shading.

5. Search for 11-point Times New Roman formatting and replace with 10-point Arial formatting by completing the following steps:

   a. Clear formatting from the top Format button by clicking the down-pointing arrow and then clicking the *Clear Find Format* option at the drop-down menu.

   b. Clear formatting from the bottom Format button by clicking the down-pointing arrow and then clicking *Clear Replace Format*.

   c. Click the down-pointing arrow at the right side of the top Format button and then click Format at the drop-down menu.

   d. At the Find Format dialog box, click the Font tab.

   e. Click *Times New Roman* in the *Font* list box (you will need to scroll down the list to display this typeface).

   f. Click *11* in the *Size* text box.

   g. Click OK to close the dialog box.

   h. Click the down-pointing arrow at the right side of the second Format button and then click Format at the drop-down menu.

   i. At the Find Format dialog box with the Font tab selected, click *Arial* in the *Font* list box.

   j. Click *10* in the *Size* list box.

   k. Click OK to close the dialog box.

   l. At the Find and Replace dialog box, click the Replace All button.

   m. At the message telling you that Excel has completed the search and made replacements, click OK.

6. At the Find and Replace dialog box, remove formatting from both Format buttons.

7. Click the Close button to close the Find and Replace dialog box.

8. Click in cell H3 and then insert a formula that finds the average of cells B3 through G3.

9. Copy the formula in cell H3 down to cells H4 through H8.

10. Copying the formula removed the double-line border at the bottom of cell H8. Replace the border by clicking the down-pointing arrow at the right side of the Borders button on the Formatting toolbar and then clicking the Bottom Double Border option at the drop-down palette.

11. Save, print, and then close **sec4x13**.

Sorting Data

Sort Ascending

Sort Descending

Excel is primarily a spreadsheet program, but it also includes some basic database functions. With a database program, you can alphabetize information or arrange numbers numerically. Data can be sorted by columns in a worksheet. By default, Excel will sort special symbols such as *, /, @, and # first, numbers second, and letters third. Sort data in a worksheet using the Sort Ascending or Sort Descending buttons on the Standard toolbar or at the Sort dialog box.

Sorting Data Using Buttons on the Standard Toolbar

To sort data in a worksheet using the buttons on the Standard toolbar, open the worksheet, select the cells containing data you want to sort, and then click the Sort Ascending button (sorts text A through Z; sorts numbers lowest to highest) or the Sort Descending button (sorts text Z through A; sorts numbers highest to lowest). If you select more than one column in a worksheet, Excel will sort the data in the first selected column.

exercise 14

SORTING DATA USING THE SORT ASCENDING AND SORT DESCENDING BUTTONS

1. Open **ExcelWorksheet03**.
2. Save the worksheet with Save As and name it **sec4x14**.
3. Merge and center the data in cell A1 across cells A1 through D1.
4. Bold the data in cell A1.
5. Bold the data in cells B2 through D2.
6. Automatically adjust the width of columns A through D.
7. Select cells B3 through D8 and then click the Percent Style button on the Formatting toolbar.
8. Sort the data in the first column alphabetically in ascending order by completing the following steps:
   a. Select cells A3 through D8.
   b. Click the Sort Ascending button on the Standard toolbar.

Step 8b

Sort Ascending

A3   *fx* Stockholder's equity ratio

	A	B	C	D	E	F	G
1	ANALYSIS OF FINANCIAL CONDITION						
2		Actual	Planned	Prior Year			
3	Stockholder's equity ratio	62%	60%	57%			
4	Bond holder's equity ratio	45%	39%	41%			
5	Liability liquidity ratio	122%	115%	120%			
6	Fixed obligation security ratio	196%	190%	187%			
7	Fixed interest ratio	23%	20%	28%			
8	Earnings ratio	7%	6%	6%			

Step 8a

9. Save and print **sec4x14**.
10. Sort the data in the first column alphabetically in descending order by completing steps similar to those in Step 8, except click the Sort Descending button on the Standard toolbar.
11. Save, print, and then close **sec4x14**.

Sorting Data at the Sort Dialog Box

If you want to sort data in a column other than the first selected column, use the Sort dialog box. If you select just one column in a worksheet and then click the Sort Ascending or Sort Descending button on the Standard toolbar, only the data in that column is sorted. If this data is related to data to the left or right of the data in the column, that relationship is broken. For example, if you sort cells B3 through B8 in sec4x13, the percentages for *Bondholder's equity ratio* are now *23%, 39%,* and *41%,* when they should be *45%, 39%,* and *41%.*

QUICK STEPS

Sort Data
1. Select cells.
2. Click Sort Ascending button or Sort Descending button.
   OR
1. Select cells.
2. Click Data, Sort.
3. Specify options at Sort dialog box.
4. Click OK.

Use the Sort dialog box to sort data and maintain the relationship of all cells. To sort using the Sort dialog box, select the cells you want sorted, click Data, and then click Sort. This displays the Sort dialog box shown in Figure 4.13.

F I G U R E

4.13 *Sort Dialog Box*

The data displayed in the *Sort by* option box will vary depending on what you have selected. Generally, the data that displays is the title of the first column of selected cells. If the selected cells do not have a title, the data may display as *Column A*. Use this option to specify what column you want sorted. Using the Sort dialog box to sort data in a column maintains the relationship of the data.

exercise 15

SORTING DATA USING THE SORT DIALOG BOX

1. Open **sec4x14**.
2. Save the worksheet with Save As and name it **sec4x15**.
3. Sort the percentages in cells B3 through B8 in ascending order and maintain the relationship to the other data by completing the following steps:
   a. Select cells A3 through D8.
   b. Click Data and then Sort.
   c. At the Sort dialog box, click the down-pointing arrow at the right of the *Sort by* option box, and then click *Actual* from the drop-down list.
   d. Make sure *Ascending* is selected in the *Sort by* section of the dialog box. If not, click *Ascending*.
   e. Click OK to close the dialog box.
4. Save and then print **sec4x15**.
5. Sort the percentages in cells B3 through B8 in *descending* order and maintain the relationship of the data by completing steps similar to those in Step 3.
6. Save, print, and then close **sec4x15**.

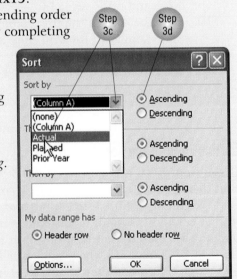

Step 3c   Step 3d

Sorting More than One Column

When sorting data in cells, you can sort in more than one column. For example, in Exercise 16, you will be sorting the average test scores in ascending order and then sorting the names of the students alphabetically. In this sort, the test averages are sorted first and then students with the same average are sorted alphabetically within that average. For example, the worksheet contains several average scores of 76%. Students within that average are sorted alphabetically—not all students.

To sort in more than one column, select all columns in the worksheet that need to remain relative, and then display the Sort dialog box. At the Sort dialog box, specify the first column you want sorted in the *Sort by* option box, and then specify the second column in the first *Then by* text box. In Excel, you can sort in up to three columns. If you want to sort the data in a third column, you would specify that in the second *Then by* option box.

exercise 16

1. Open **ExcelWorksheet06**.
2. Save the worksheet with Save As and name it **sec4x16**.
3. Select and then delete row 2.
4. Sort the Test 1 percentages in cells B2 through B19 in ascending order and then sort alphabetically by the names in the first column by completing the following steps:
   a. Select cells A2 through M19.
   b. Click Data and then Sort.
   c. At the Sort dialog box, click the down-pointing arrow at the right side of the *Sort by* option box, and then click *Test 1* from the drop-down list.
   d. Make sure *Ascending* is selected in the *Sort by* section of the dialog box. If not, click *Ascending*.
   e. Click the down-pointing arrow at the right of the first *Then by* option box and then click *Name* in the drop-down list.
   f. Make sure *Ascending* is selected in the first *Then by* section.
   g. Click OK to close the dialog box.

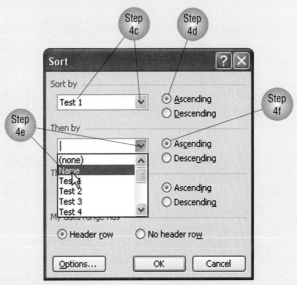

5. Display the Page Setup dialog box with the Page tab selected, click the *Landscape* option, and then close the dialog box.
6. Print the worksheet. (Notice how the names of the students with the same Test 1 percentages are alphabetized.)
7. Save and then close **sec4x16**.

Creating a List

QUICK STEPS

Create a List
1. Click Data, List, Create List.
2. Click OK at Create List dialog box.

A list in an Excel worksheet is a series of rows that contain related data such as a specific customer name, invoice number, product, and so forth. Each column in a list must be labeled and contain specific information. For example, in Exercise 17 you will identify cells in a worksheet as a list that contains specific columns of information including a column for invoice numbers, a column for equipment, another for client, and so on.

To identify a list in a worksheet, click Data on the Menu bar, point to List, and then click Create List. This displays the Create List dialog box and also inserts a moving border around all cells in the worksheet. If you want all selected cells included in the list, click the OK button. If your worksheet contains cells that you do not want included in the list (such as cells containing headings or titles), first select the cells you want included in the list and then click Data, point to List, and then click Create List. At the Create List dialog box, click OK. When you select specific cells, you must make sure that the first row is the row containing column labels.

When you click OK at the Create List dialog box, the dialog box is removed from the screen and a button containing a down arrow is inserted at the right side of each column label cell. Click this down arrow and a drop-down list displays with options for sorting and filtering records in the list.

exercise 17

CREATING AND SORTING A LIST

1. Open **ExcelWorksheet27**.
2. Save the worksheet with Save As and name it **sec4x17**.
3. Create a list by completing the following steps:
   a. Select cells A2 through F14.
   b. Click Data on the Menu bar, point to List, and then click Create List.
   c. At the Create List dialog box, click OK. (This removes the dialog box and inserts a button containing a down-pointing arrow at the right side of each cell containing a column label.)
4. Sort the client numbers in ascending order by clicking the button containing the down arrow located at the right side of the *Client #* cell (the # symbol is not visible) and then clicking *Sort Ascending* at the drop-down list.
5. Save and then print **sec4x17**.
6. Sort the rates in descending order by clicking the button containing the down-pointing arrow located at the right side of the *Rate* cell and then click *Sort Descending* at the drop-down list.
7. Save, print, and then close **sec4x17**.

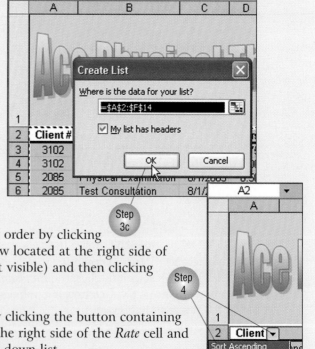

Filtering a List

You can place a restriction, called a *filter*, on data in a worksheet to isolate temporarily a specific list. You can apply only one filter to a worksheet at a time. You can filter data in a worksheet by first creating a list or by using the AutoFilter feature. To use the AutoFilter feature, click in a cell containing data you want to filter, click Data, point to Filter, and then click AutoFilter. This causes a down arrow to appear in each column label in the worksheet as shown in Figure 4.14. Unlike creating a list, the AutoFilter feature automatically searches for column labels—you do not need to first select the cells.

To filter a list, click the down-pointing arrow in the heading you want to filter. This causes a drop-down list to display with options to filter all records in the list, display the top 10 records, create a custom filter, or select an entry that appears in one or more of the cells in the list.

QUICK STEPS

Filter a List
1. Click Data, Filter, AutoFilter.
2. Click down-pointing arrow of heading to filter.
3. Click desired option at drop-down list.

FIGURE
4.14 Using AutoFilter

Activate the AutoFilter feature and down-pointing triangles display in column heading.

	Invoice	Equipment	Client	Service R	Date	Hour	Ra	Tota
3	1190	Backhoe	Lakeside Trucking	Monahan	5/1/2003	8	$75	$ 600
4	1190	Front Loader	Lakeside Trucking	Monahan	5/1/2003	8	$65	$ 520
5	1191	Trencher	Martin Plumbing	Steele	5/1/2003	4	$45	$ 180
6	1192	Backhoe	Country Electrical	Leuke	5/1/2003	16	$75	$1,200
7	1193	Tractor	Able Construction	Monahan	5/2/2003	5	$55	$ 275
8	1193	Scaffolding	Able Construction	Monahan	5/2/2003	5	$25	$ 125
9	1194	Forklift	Miles Contracting	Steele	5/2/2003	10	$70	$ 700
10	1194	Hydraulic Pump	Miles					
11	1195	Pressure Sprayer	Ever					
12	1196	Sandblaster	Barri					
13	1196	Pressure Sprayer	Barri					
14	1197	Front Loader	Cas					
15	1197	Flatbed Truck	Cas					
16	1198	Forklift	Allie					

Click the down-pointing triangle in the Service Rep column, click *Monahan* at the drop-down list, and only those rows containing *Monahan* display.

	Invoice	Equipment	Client	Service R	Date	Hour	Ra	Tota
3	1190	Backhoe	Lakeside Trucking	Monahan	5/1/2003	8	$75	$ 600
4	1190	Front Loader	Lakeside Trucking	Monahan	5/1/2003	8	$65	$ 520
7	1193	Tractor	Able Construction	Monahan	5/2/2003	5	$55	$ 275
8	1193	Scaffolding	Able Construction	Monahan	5/2/2003	5	$25	$ 125
16	1198	Forklift	Allied Builders	Monahan	5/3/2003	6	$70	$ 420
17								

The Top 10 option displays in a list that contains values rather than text. Click *(Top 10...)* and the Top 10 AutoFilter dialog box displays as shown in Figure 4.15. With options at this dialog box, you can choose to show the top values, the bottom values, and the number you want filtered.

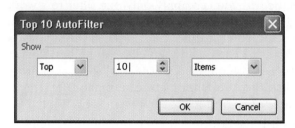

4.15 *Top 10 AutoFilter Dialog Box*

When you filter a list, the down-pointing arrow in the column heading turns blue as well as the row number for the selected rows. This color indicates that rows in the worksheet have been filtered. To deactivate AutoFilter, click Data, point to Filter, and then click AutoFilter.

exercise 18

FILTERING LISTS USING AUTOFILTER

1. Open **ExcelWorksheet26**.
2. Save the worksheet with Save As and name it **sec4x18**.
3. Apply the AutoFilter by clicking Data, pointing to Filter, and then clicking AutoFilter. (This causes down-pointing arrows to appear in heading cells.)
4. Filter and then print a list of rows containing companies renting a forklift by completing the following steps:
   a. Click the down-pointing arrow at the right side of the *Equipment* heading.
   b. Click *Forklift* at the drop-down list.
   c. Print the list by clicking the Print button on the Standard toolbar.
   d. Redisplay all cells containing data by clicking the down-pointing arrow at the right side of the *Equipment* heading and then clicking *(All)* at the drop-down list.
5. Filter and then print a list of rows containing equipment rented by the service representative Monahan by completing the following steps:
   a. Click the down-pointing arrow at the right side of the *Service Rep* heading.
   b. Click *Monahan* at the drop-down list.
   c. Click the Print button.
   d. Redisplay all cells containing data by clicking the down-pointing arrow at the right side of the *Service Rep* heading and then clicking *(All)* at the drop-down list.

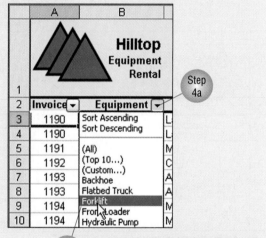

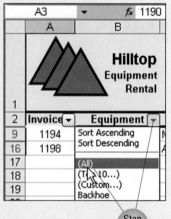

6. Filter and then print a list of rows containing only the client *Cascade Enterprises* by completing steps similar to those in Steps 4 or 5. (Make sure you return the list to *(All)*.)
7. Display the top 3 highest totals by completing the following steps:
   a. Click the down-pointing arrow at the right side of the *Total* heading and then click *(Top 10...)* at the drop-down list.
   b. At the Top 10 AutoFilter dialog box, select *10* in the middle text box and then type *3*.
   c. Click OK.
   d. Click the Print button to print the list.

   e. Click the down-pointing arrow at the right side of the *Total* heading and then click *(All)* at the drop-down list.
8. Deactivate AutoFilter by clicking Data, pointing to Filter, and then clicking AutoFilter.
9. Save, print, and then close **sec4x18**.

Planning a Worksheet

The worksheets you have worked with so far basically have already been planned. If you need to plan a worksheet yourself, some steps you can follow are listed below. These are basic steps—you may think of additional steps or additional information to help you plan a worksheet.

- **Step 1: Identify the purpose of the worksheet.** The more definite you are about your purpose, the easier organizing your data into an effective worksheet will be. Consider things such as the purpose of the worksheet, the intended audience, the desired output or results, and the data required.

- **Step 2: Design the worksheet.** To do this, you need to determine how the data is to be organized, the titles of columns and rows, and how to emphasize important information. Designing the worksheet also includes determining any calculations that need to be performed.

- **Step 3: Create a sketch of the worksheet.** A diagram or sketch can help create a logical and well-ordered worksheet. With a sketch, you can experiment with alternative column and row configurations and titles and headings. When creating a sketch, start with the heading or title of the worksheet, which should provide a quick overview of what the data represents in the worksheet. Determine appropriate column and row titles that clearly identify the data.

- **Step 4: Enter the data in the worksheet.** Type the data in the worksheet, including the worksheet title, column titles, row titles, and data within cells. Enter any required formulas into the worksheet and then format the worksheet to make it appealing and easy to read.

- **Step 5: Test the worksheet data.** After preparing the worksheet and inserting any necessary formulas, check the data to be sure that the calculations are performed correctly. Consider verifying the formula results by completing the formula on a calculator.

1. Look at the data shown in Figure 4.16. (The first paragraph is simply a description of the data—do not include this in the worksheet.) After reviewing the data, complete the following steps:
   a. Create a sketch of how you think the worksheet should be organized.
   b. Create a worksheet from the sketch. (Be sure to include the necessary formula to calculate the total costs.)
   c. Apply formatting to enhance the appearance of the worksheet.
2. Save the worksheet and name it **sec4x19**.
3. Print and then close **sec4x19**.

FIGURE

4.16 *Exercise 19*

The following data itemizes budgeted direct labor hours and dollars by department for planning purposes. This data is prepared quarterly and sent to the plant manager and production manager.

DIRECT LABOR BUDGET

	Labor Rate	Total Hours	Total Costs
April			
Assembly	12.75	723	
Electronics	16.32	580	
Machining	27.34	442	
May			
Assembly	12.75	702	
Electronics	16.32	615	
Machining	27.34	428	
June			
Assembly	12.75	694	
Electronics	16.32	643	
Machining	27.34	389	

CHAPTER summary

➤ By default, a worksheet prints on the page in portrait orientation. This can be changed to landscape orientation at the Page Setup dialog box with the Page tab selected.

➤ Adjust the percentage size of data in a worksheet with options in the *Scaling* section of the Page Setup dialog box with the Page tab selected.

➤ Change the paper size with the *Paper size* option at the Page Setup dialog box with the Page tab selected.

➤ Create a header and/or footer for worksheet pages with options at the Page Setup dialog box with the Header/Footer tab selected.

➤ Create a custom header at the Header dialog box and create a custom footer at the Footer dialog box.

➤ Excel uses 1-inch top and bottom margins and .75-inch left and right margins for a worksheet. Change these default margins at the Page Setup dialog box with the Margins tab selected.

➤ Center a worksheet horizontally and/or vertically on a page with options at the Page Setup dialog box with the Margins tab selected.

➤ Insert a page break in a worksheet with Insert and then Page Break.

➤ Print column and row titles on every page of a multiple-page worksheet with options at the Page Setup dialog box with the Sheet tab selected.

➤ Print gridlines, column letters, and row numbers with options at the Page Setup dialog box with the Sheet tab selected.

➤ You can hide and unhide columns or rows in a worksheet.

➤ Use the Print Area feature to select and print specific areas in a worksheet. Specify more than one print area in Page Break Preview.

➤ Change the print quality for most printers with options at the Properties dialog box. Print quality choices are available at the Page Setup dialog box with the Page tab selected.

➤ Use options at the Print dialog box to print a specific range of cells, selected cells, or multiple copies of a workbook.

➤ Complete a spelling check on a worksheet by clicking the Spelling button on the Standard toolbar or clicking Tools and then Spelling.

➤ Click the Undo button to reverse certain commands or delete the last data typed in a cell. Click the Redo button to repeat the last command or action, if possible.

➤ Find data with options at the Find and Replace dialog box with the Find tab selected, and find and replace data in a worksheet with options at the Find and Replace dialog box with the Replace tab selected.

➤ Use options at the expanded Find and Replace dialog box to search for specific cell formatting and replace with other formatting.

➤ Sort the first column of selected cells with the Sort Ascending or Sort Descending buttons on the Standard toolbar.

➤ Use the Sort dialog box to sort in a column other than the first column, to maintain the relationship of the data, or to sort in more than one column.

➤ A list in an Excel worksheet is a series of rows that contain related data. Once you identify a list in a worksheet, you can sort and filter the information in the list.

➤ Use the AutoFilter feature to isolate temporarily a specific list. With the AutoFilter, you can filter all records in the list, display the top 10 records, create a custom filter, or select an entry that appears in one or more of the cells in the list.

➤ Plan a worksheet by completing these basic steps: identify the purpose of the worksheet, design the worksheet, create a sketch of the worksheet, enter the data in the worksheet, and test the worksheet data.

FEATURES summary

FEATURE	BUTTON	MENU	KEYBOARD
Page Setup dialog box		File, Page Setup	
Header dialog box		File, Page Setup, Header/Footer tab, Custom Header	
Footer dialog box		File, Page Setup, Header/Footer tab, Custom Footer	
Insert page break		Insert, Page Break	
Hide columns		Format, Column, Hide	
Hide rows		Format, Row, Hide	
Unhide columns		Format, Column, Unhide	
Unhide rows		Format, Row, Unhide	
Set a print area		File, Print Area, Set Print Area	
Clear a print area		File, Print Area, Clear Print Area	
Print dialog box		File, Print	Ctrl + P
Spelling dialog box		Tools, Spelling	F7
Undo command		Edit, Undo	Ctrl + Z

FEATURE	BUTTON	MENU	KEYBOARD
Redo command	↻ ▾	Edit, Redo	Ctrl + Y
Find and Replace dialog box		Edit, Find or Edit, Replace	Ctrl + F or Ctrl + H
Sort column in ascending order	A↓Z↓		
Sort column in descending order	Z↓A↓		
Sort dialog box		Data, Sort	
Create a list		Data, List, Create List	Ctrl + L
Activate/Deactivate AutoFilter		Data, Filter, AutoFilter	

CONCEPTS check

Completion: On a blank sheet of paper, indicate the correct term, symbol, or command for each description.

1. By default, a worksheet prints in this orientation on a page.
2. Change the page orientation at the Page Setup dialog box with this tab selected.
3. This is the default paper size.
4. Display the Header dialog box by clicking this button at the Page Setup dialog box with the Header/Footer tab selected.
5. This is the worksheet default top and bottom margin measurement.
6. This is the worksheet default left and right margin measurement.
7. A worksheet can be horizontally and/or vertically centered with options at the Page Setup dialog box with this tab selected.
8. Click this to insert a page break in a worksheet.
9. Print gridlines with an option at the Page Setup dialog box with this tab selected.
10. To make a hidden column visible, select these columns, click Format, point to Column, and then click Unhide.
11. Use this feature to print specific areas in a worksheet.
12. To complete a spelling check on a worksheet, click this button on the Standard toolbar.
13. To display the Sort dialog box, click Sort from this drop-down menu.
14. Use this feature to isolate temporarily a specific list of rows in a worksheet containing related data.
15. List the steps you would complete to print column titles in a multiple-page worksheet.
16. List the steps you would complete to find all occurrences of *January* in a worksheet and replace with *July*.

SKILLS check

Assessment 1

1. Open **ExcelWorksheet28**.
2. Save the worksheet with Save As and name it **sec4sc01**.
3. Make the following changes to the worksheet:
   a. Insert a formula in cell H3 that averages the amounts in cells B3 through G3.
   b. Copy the formula in cell H3 down to cells H4 through H8.
   c. Copying the formula removed the double-line border at the bottom of cell H8. Use the Borders button to insert a double-line border at the bottom of cell H8.
   d. Change the orientation of the worksheet to landscape.
   e. Change the top margin to 3 inches and the left margin to 1.5 inches.
4. Save, print, and then close **sec4sc01**.

Assessment 2

1. Open **ExcelWorksheet06**.
2. Save the worksheet with Save As and name it **sec4sc02**.
3. Make the following changes to the worksheet:
   a. Select the worksheet and then change the font to 11-point Garamond (or a similar serif typeface).
   b. Automatically adjust columns A through M.
   c. Delete row 2.
   d. Create a footer that prints *Page x* (where *x* represents the correct page number) at the bottom center of the page.
   e. Create a custom header that prints your name at the left margin and the text *Excel Test Scores* at the right margin.
4. Save the worksheet again with the same name (**sec4sc02**).
5. Print the worksheet so the column titles (names) print on both pages.
6. Close **sec4sc02**.

Assessment 3

1. Open **ExcelWorksheet13**.
2. Save the worksheet with Save As and name it **sec4sc03**.
3. Make the following changes to the worksheet:
   a. Delete column H.
   b. Type Total in cell A9.
   c. Make cell B9 active and then use the AutoSum button to sum the amounts in B3 through B8.
   d. Copy the formula in cell B9 to cells C9 through G9.
4. Print the worksheet including gridlines and the row and column headings.
5. Save and then close **sec4sc03**.

Assessment 4

1. Open **ExcelWorksheet26**.
2. Save the worksheet with Save As and name it **sec4sc04**.
3. Make the following changes to the worksheet:
   a. Find all occurrences of cells containing *75* and replace with *90*.

b. Find all occurrences of cells containing *20* and replace with *25*.

c. Find all occurrences of *Barrier Concrete* and replace with *Lee Sand and Gravel*.

4. Save the worksheet again with the same name (**sec4sc04**).

5. Print the worksheet horizontally and vertically centered on the page.

6. Close **sec4sc04**.

Assessment 5

1. Open **ExcelWorksheet06**.

2. Print student names and scores for Test 12 on one page by completing the following steps:

a. Hide columns B through L.

b. Specify A1 through M20 as a print area.

c. Print the print area. (Make sure the cells print on one page.)

d. Clear the print area.

e. Make columns B through L visible.

3. Close **ExcelWorksheet06** without saving the changes.

Assessment 6

1. Open **ExcelWorksheet23**.

2. Save the worksheet with Save As and name it **sec4sc06**.

3. Search for 11-point Arial formatting and replace with 12-point Garamond formatting (or another serif typeface such as Century or Times New Roman).

4. Search for 10-point Arial formatting and replace with 11-point Garamond formatting (or the typeface you chose in Step 3) with a light yellow background color.

5. Save, print, and then close **sec4sc06**. (This worksheet will contain blank cells in columns D and F.

Assessment 7

1. Open **ExcelWorksheet27**.

2. Save the worksheet with Save As and name it **sec4sc07**.

3. Select cells A3 through F14 and then click the Sort Ascending button on the Standard toolbar.

4. Print the worksheet horizontally and vertically centered on the page.

5. With the worksheet still open, select cells A3 through F14, and then sort the text in column B (Treatment) in ascending order (do this at the Sort dialog box).

6. Print the worksheet horizontally and vertically centered on the page.

7. With the worksheet still open, select cells A3 through F14, and then sort by the *Client #* in ascending order and then by *Treatment* in ascending order. (This is one sort.)

8. Save the worksheet again with the same name (**sec4sc07**).

9. Print the worksheet horizontally and vertically centered on the page.

10. Close **sec4sc07**.

Assessment 8

1. Open **ExcelWorksheet27**.

2. Save the worksheet with Save As and name it **sec4sc08**.

3. Filter and then print a list of rows containing only the treatment *Physical Therapy*. (After printing, return the list to *(All)*.)

4. Filter and then print a list of rows containing only the client number *2085*. (After printing, return the list to *(All)*.)

5. Filter and then print a list of rows containing the top 2 highest rates.
6. After printing, return the list to *(All)*. ***(Hint: Excel will display the three highest rates because there is a tie.)***
7. Save, print, and then close **sec4sa08**.

Assessment 9

1. Using the Ask a Question text box on the Menu bar, ask the question *What is Excel's default sorting order?*
2. Display information on default sort orders. After reading and printing the information presented, create a worksheet containing a summary of the information. Create the worksheet with the following features:
   a. Create a title for the worksheet.
   b. Set the data in cells in a serif typeface and change the data color.
   c. Add borders to the cells (you determine the border style).
   d. Add a color shading to cells (you determine the color—make it complementary to the data color).
   e. Create a custom footer that prints your name at the left margin and the file name at the right margin.
3. Save the completed worksheet and name it **sec4sc09**.
4. Print and then close **sec4sc09**.

CHAPTER challenge

You have been hired by See It Again video store. The store manager would like you to create and maintain a list of the store's videos and DVDs using Excel. The list should include the name of the movie, type of movie (comedy, horror, drama, etc.), rating, checkout date, return date, and any other fields you feel would be appropriate. Add at least 10 movies and their associated information to the list. Sort the list by movie names. Save and print the file.

A customer has entered the store and wants a list of the comedy and drama movies. Use the Help feature to learn about creating a custom filter that filters more than one criterion. Then use the custom filter to filter the comedy and drama movies. Print the results.

Business continues to grow for See It Again. You have spoken with the manager about maintaining the list of information in Access, since it is a more powerful database application, and Excel is limited in the database features it can use. Many of the individuals who maintain the current list are more familiar with Excel, so the transition from using Excel to Access will be gradual. Therefore, the information will be maintained in both Excel and Access. Create a database in Access called **SeeItAgain** and link the Excel list as a table. By linking the information, changes made in one application will take effect in the other application. Save the database and print the table.

WORK IN Progress

Preparing and Formatting a Worksheet

ASSESSING proficiency

In this unit, you have learned to create, save, print, edit, and format Excel worksheets; create and insert formulas; and enhance worksheets with features such as headers and footers, page numbering, sorting, and filtering.

(Note: Before completing computer exercises, delete the ExcelChapter04S folder on your disk. Next, copy the ExcelUnit01S subfolder from the Excel2003Specialist folder on the CD that accompanies this textbook to your disk and then make ExcelUnit01S the active folder.)

Assessment 1

1. Create the Excel worksheet shown in Figure U1.1. Format the cells as you see them in the figure. (Include a formula in cell D3 that subtracts the Quota sales from the Actual sales and then copy the formula down to cells D4 through D9.) *(Hint: The formula should look like this: =C3-B3.)*
2. Print the worksheet with gridlines and centered horizontally and vertically on the page.
3. Save the completed worksheet and name it **seu1pa01**.
4. Close **seu1pa01**.

	A	B	C	D	E
1	SALES QUOTA REPORT				
2	Salesperson	Quota	Actual	Over/(Under)	
3	Chavis	$55,000	$63,450		
4	Hampton	$85,000	$74,000		
5	Martindale	$48,000	$51,250		
6	Enriquez	$93,000	$86,300		
7	Gorham	$45,000	$45,000		
8	Kline	$75,000	$78,560		
9	McGuinness	$65,000	$71,450		
10					

FIGURE U1.1 • Assessment 1

Assessment 2

1. Open **seu1pa01**.
2. Save the worksheet with Save As and name it **seu1pa02**.
3. Make the following changes to the worksheet:

a. Add a row above row 7.
b. Type the following data in the specified cells:

A7	=	Dillinger
B7	=	95000
C7	=	89650

c. Make cell E2 the active cell and then type % of Quota.
d. Insert a formula in cell E3 that divides the actual amount by the quota. Copy this formula down to the other cells. (The result will be a decimal point. Select the decimal numbers that are a result of the formula and then click the Percent Style button on the Formatting toolbar.)
e. Select cells A1 through E10 and then apply an autoformat of your choosing.

4. Save, print, and then close **seu1pa02**.

Assessment 3

1. Open **seu1pa01**.
2. Save the worksheet with Save As and name it **seu1pa03**.
3. Make the following changes to the worksheet:
    a. Type Quota Met in cell E2.
    b. Select cells A1 through E1 and then merge and center the cells. (To do this, click the Merge and Center button twice.)
    c. Increase the height of row 1 to 30.00.
    d. Increase the height of row 2 to 24.00.
    e. Vertically center the text in cell A1. *(Hint: To do this, make cell A1 active, click Format, and then click Cells. At the Format Cells dialog box, click the Alignment tab. Click the down-pointing triangle at the right of the* Vertical *option and then click* Center *at the drop-down list.)*
    f. Vertically center the text in cells A2 through E2.
    g. Change the width of column A to 16.00 and the width of columns B, C, D, and E to 14.00.
    h. Set the text in cell A1 in 14-point Arial bold.
    i. Set the text in cells A2 through E2 in 12-point Arial bold.
    j. Insert a formula in cell E3 that inserts the word *YES* if the quota is met and inserts *NO* if the quota is not met. *(Hint: Use the IF function to write the formula, which should look like this:* **=IF(D3>=0,"YES",IF(D3<0,"NO")).)**
    k. Copy the formula in cell E3 down to cells E4 through E9.
    l. Center align the text in cells E3 through E9.
    m. Select cells A1 through E9 and then apply an outline border to the selected cells.
    n. Select cells A2 through E2 and then apply to the cells a top and bottom border and light gray shading.
    o. Select cells A4 through E4 and then apply light yellow shading.
    p. Apply the light yellow shading to cells A6 through E6 and cells A8 through E8.
4. Hide column D and then print the worksheet.
5. Redisplay column D.
6. Create the custom footer that prints your name at the left margin and *Annual Report* at the right margin.
7. Save and then close **seu1pa03**.

Copying Selected Cells

Copying selected cells can be useful in worksheets that contain repetitive data. To copy cells, select the cells, and then click the Copy button on the Standard toolbar. Click the cell where you want the first selected cell copied and then click the Paste button on the Standard toolbar.

Selected cells can also be copied using the mouse and the Ctrl key. To do this, select the cells to be copied, and then position the mouse pointer on any border around the selected cells until it turns into an arrow pointer. Hold down the Ctrl key and the left mouse button, drag the outline of the selected cells to the desired location, release the left mouse button, and then release the Ctrl key.

You can also use the Copy and Paste options from the Edit drop-down menu to copy selected cells in a worksheet. To do this, select the cells, click Edit, and then click Copy. Click the cell where you want the first selected cell copied, click Edit, and then click Paste.

Copy

HINT

Ctrl + C is the keyboard command to copy selected data.

Copy and Paste Cells
1. Select cells.
2. Click Copy button.
3. Click desired cell.
4. Click Paste button.

exercise 2

COPYING SELECTED CELLS IN A WORKSHEET

1. Open **ExcelWorksheet05**.
2. Save the worksheet with Save As and name it **sec5x02**.
3. Type Total in cell D2.
4. Make cell D3 active and then insert a formula that multiplies the contents of cell C3 with the contents of cell B3.
5. Copy the formula in cell D3 down to cells D4 through D8.
6. Select cells A1 through D1.
7. Click the Merge and Center button on the Formatting toolbar. (This splits the cells.)
8. Click the Merge and Center button again. (This merges cells A1 through D1.)
9. Copy and paste cells by completing the following steps:
   a. Select cells A1 through D8.
   b. Position the mouse pointer on any boundary of the selected cells until it turns into an arrow pointer with a four-headed arrow attached.
   c. Hold down the Ctrl key and then the left mouse button.
   d. Drag the outline of the selected cells so the top left corner of the outline is positioned at the top of cell A10.
   e. Release the left mouse button and then the Ctrl key.
10. Change the contents of the following cells to the specified data:

    A10: From *January* to *February*
    B12: From *35* to *40*
    B14: From *40* to *32*
    B16: From *15* to *30*

11. Select cells A1 through D8 and then apply the Colorful 2 autoformat.
12. Select cells A10 through D17 and then apply the Colorful 2 autoformat.
13. Save, print, and then close **sec5x02**.

Step 9d

	A	B	C	D
1	January			
2	Name	Hours	Rate	Total
3	Carolyn Bentley	35	$23.15	$810.25
4	Lindon Cassini	20	$19.00	$380.00
5	Michelle DeFord	40	$18.75	$750.00
6	Javier Farias	24	$16.45	$394.80
7	Deborah Gould	15	$11.50	$172.50
8	William Jarman	15	$11.50	$172.50
9				
10				
11				
12				
13				
14				
15				
16				
17				
18			A10:D17	
19				

Using the Office Clipboard

Copy and Paste Multiple Items

1. Click Edit, Office Clipboard.
2. Select desired cells.
3. Click Copy button.
4. Continue selecting desired cells and then clicking the Copy button.
5. Make active the desired cell.
6. Click item in Clipboard task pane that you want inserted in the worksheet.
7. Continue pasting desired items from the Clipboard task pane.

Use the Office Clipboard feature to collect and paste multiple items. You can collect up to 24 different items and then paste them in various locations. To use the Office Clipboard feature, display the Clipboard task pane, by clicking Edit on the Menu bar and then clicking Office Clipboard, or by pressing Ctrl + C twice. You can also display the Clipboard task pane by clicking the Other Task Panes button (displays with a down-pointing arrow at the right side) located at the top of the task pane and then clicking Clipboard at the drop-down menu. The Clipboard task pane displays at the right side of the screen in a manner similar to what you see in Figure 5.1.

The Clipboard task pane holds up to 24 items. After that number, items are discarded beginning with the oldest item.

FIGURE

5.1 *Clipboard Task Pane*

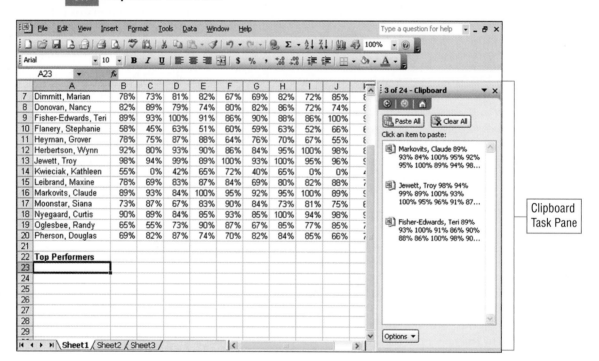

Select data or an object you want to copy and then click the Copy button on the Standard toolbar. Continue selecting text or items and clicking the Copy button. To insert an item, position the insertion point in the desired location and then click that item in the Clipboard task pane. If the copied item is text, the first 50 characters display. When all desired items are inserted, click the Clear All button to remove any remaining items.

exercise 3

1. Open **ExcelWorksheet06**.
2. Save the worksheet with Save As and name it **sec5x03**.
3. Make cell A22 the active cell, turn on bold, and then type Top Performers.
4. Display the Clipboard task pane by clicking Edit and then Office Clipboard.
5. Collect several rows of cells and then paste them by completing the following steps:
   a. Click the row header for row 9 (this selects the entire row).
   b. Click the Copy button on the Standard toolbar.
   c. Click the row header for row 13 and then click the Copy button on the Standard toolbar.
   d. Click the row header for row 16 and then click the Copy button on the Standard toolbar.

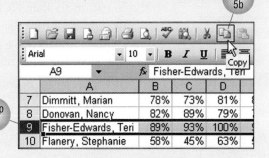

6. Paste the copied cells by completing the following steps:
   a. Make cell A23 active.
   b. Click the item in the Clipboard task pane representing row 13 (the row for Jewett).
   c. Make cell A24 active.
   d. Click the item in the Clipboard task pane representing row 16 (the row for Markovits).
   e. Make cell A25 active.
   f. Click the item in the Clipboard task pane representing row 9 (the row for Fisher-Edwards).
7. Click the Clear All button located toward the top of the Clipboard task pane.
8. Close the Clipboard task pane by clicking the Close button (contains an *X*) located in the upper right corner of the task pane.

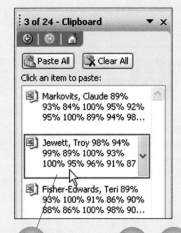

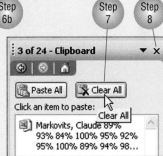

9. Create a custom footer that prints your name at the left margin and the file name at the right margin.
10. Print the worksheet in landscape orientation.
11. Save the worksheet.
12. Close **sec5x03**.

Creating a Workbook with Multiple Worksheets

Up to this point, each workbook you have created has contained one worksheet. A workbook can contain several worksheets. You can create a variety of worksheets within a workbook for related data. For example, a workbook may contain a worksheet for the expenses for each salesperson in a company and another worksheet for the monthly payroll for each department within the company. Another example is recording sales statistics for each quarter in individual worksheets within a workbook.

HINT
By default, a workbook contains three worksheets. You can change this number with the *Sheets in new workbook* option at the Options dialog box with the General tab selected.

The copy and paste features can be useful in creating more than one worksheet within a workbook. These features are helpful if some data within each worksheet is consistent. For example, you can create a worksheet containing information on a product and then copy this information to another worksheet where you would change data in specific cells.

To copy selected cells to a new worksheet, select the cells, click the Copy button on the Standard toolbar, click the worksheet tab (displayed immediately above the Status bar) representing the desired worksheet, and then click the Paste button.

By default, a workbook contains three worksheets named *Sheet1*, *Sheet2*, and *Sheet3*. (Later in this chapter, you will learn how to change these default names.) You can insert additional worksheets in a workbook. To do this, click the worksheet tab that you want to follow the new worksheet, click Insert, and then click Worksheet. For example, if you want to insert a new worksheet between *Sheet1* and *Sheet2*, click the *Sheet2* tab to make it active, click Insert, and then click Worksheet. The new worksheet, by default, is named *Sheet4*.

Printing a Workbook Containing Multiple Worksheets

In Exercise 4, you will create a workbook that contains four worksheets. When printing this workbook, by default, Excel will print the worksheet currently displayed. If you want to print all worksheets in a workbook, display the Print dialog box by clicking File and then Print. At the Print dialog box, click *Entire workbook* in the *Print what* section, and then click OK.

Another method for printing specific worksheets within a workbook is to select the tabs of the worksheets you want to print. To do this, open the desired workbook, hold down the Ctrl key, and then click the desired tabs. If the tabs are adjacent, you can use the Shift key.

QUICK STEPS

Insert Worksheet
1. Click worksheet tab that you want to follow the new worksheet.
2. Click Insert, Worksheet.

HINT

Print specific worksheets in a workbook by selecting the desired worksheet tabs.

QUICK STEPS

Print all Worksheets in a Workbook
1. Click File, Print.
2. Click *Entire workbook*.
3. Click OK.

exercise 4

COPYING CELLS TO DIFFERENT WORKSHEETS

1. Open **ExcelWorksheet34**.
2. Save the worksheet with Save As and name it **sec5x04**.
3. Add a fourth worksheet by clicking Insert and then Worksheet. (This adds a *Sheet4* tab before the *Sheet1* tab.)
4. Click *Sheet1* to make worksheet 1 active and then make the following changes to the worksheet:
   a. Insert the formula **=B3-C3** in cell D3 to subtract the amount in C3 from the amount in B3.
   b. Copy the formula in cell D3 down to cells D4 through D9.
5. Copy cells and paste them into worksheets 2, 3, and 4 by completing the following steps:
   a. Click the Select All button that displays immediately to the left of the column A header and immediately above the row 1 header.
   b. Click the Copy button on the Standard toolbar.
   c. Click the *Sheet2* tab that displays immediately above the Status bar.
   d. At worksheet 2, make sure cell A1 is the active cell, and then click the Paste button.

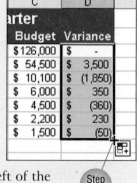

    e. Click the *Sheet3* tab that displays immediately above the Status bar.

    f. At worksheet 3, make sure cell A1 is the active cell, and then click the Paste button.

    g. Click the *Sheet4* tab.

    h. At worksheet 4, make sure cell A1 is the active cell, and then click the Paste button.

6. Click the *Sheet2* tab and then make the following changes to cell entries in worksheet 2:

> A1: From *First Quarter* to *Second Quarter*
> B4: From *58,000* to *60,500*
> C4: From *54,500* to *58,500*
> B8: From *2,430* to *2,510*
> C8: From *2,200* to *2,350*

7. Click the *Sheet3* tab and then make the following changes to cell entries in worksheet 3:

> A1: From *First Quarter* to *Third Quarter*
> B4: From *58,000* to *60,200*
> C4: From *54,500* to *60,500*
> B8: From *2,430* to *2,500*
> C8: From *2,200* to *2,550*

8. Click the *Sheet4* tab and then make the following changes to cell entries in worksheet 4:

> A1: From *First Quarter* to *Fourth Quarter*
> B4: From *58,000* to *61,000*
> C4: From *54,500* to *60,500*
> B8: From *2,430* to *2,550*
> C8: From *2,200* to *2,500*

9. Save the workbook again with the same name (**sec5x04**).

10. Print all of the worksheets in the workbook by completing the following steps:

    a. Make sure no cells are selected (just an active cell).

    b. Click File and then Print.

    c. At the Print dialog box, click *Entire workbook* in the *Print what* section.

    d. Click OK. (Each worksheet will print on a separate piece of paper.)

11. Close **sec5x04**.

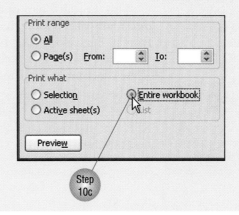

Step 10c

Managing Worksheets

Right-click a sheet tab and a shortcut menu displays as shown in Figure 5.2 with the options Insert, Delete, Rename, Move or Copy, Select All Sheets, Tab Color, and View Code. Use these options to manage worksheets in a workbook. For example, remove a worksheet by clicking the Delete option. Move or copy a worksheet by clicking the Move or Copy option. Clicking this option causes a Move or Copy dialog box to display where you specify what sheet you want to move or copy the selected sheet. By default, Excel names worksheets in a workbook *Sheet1, Sheet2, Sheet3,* and so on. To rename a worksheet, click the Rename option (this selects the default sheet name), and then type the desired name.

HINT
Use the tab scroll buttons, located to the left of the sheet tabs, to bring into view any worksheet tabs not currently visible.

5.2 *Sheet Tab Shortcut Menu*

Move or Copy a Worksheet
1. Right-click sheet tab.
2. Click Move or Copy.
3. At Move or Copy dialog box, click desired worksheet name in *Before sheet* list box.
4. Click OK.
   OR
Drag worksheet tab to the desired position (hold down Ctrl key while dragging to copy).

Recolor Sheet Tab
1. Right-click sheet tab.
2. Click Tab Color.
3. Click desired color.
4. Click OK.

HINT

Copy a worksheet in a workbook by holding down the Ctrl key and then dragging a tab from one location to another.

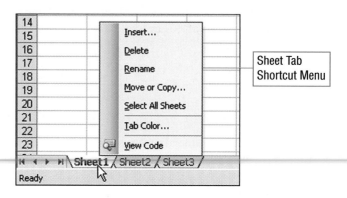

In addition to the shortcut menu options, you can use the mouse to move or copy worksheets. To move a worksheet, position the mouse pointer on the worksheet tab, hold down the left mouse button (a page icon displays next to the mouse pointer), drag the page icon to the desired position, and then release the mouse button. For example, to move *Sheet2* tab after *Sheet3* tab you would position the mouse pointer on the *Sheet2* tab, hold down the left mouse button, drag the page icon so it is positioned after the *Sheet3* tab, and then release the mouse button. To copy a worksheet, hold down the Ctrl key while dragging the sheet tab.

Use the Tab Color option at the shortcut menu to apply a color to a worksheet tab. Right-click a worksheet tab, click Tab Color at the shortcut menu, and the Format Tab Color dialog box displays. At this dialog box, click the desired color and then click OK. Only a strip of color displays at the bottom of the active sheet tab. If the sheet tab is not the active tab, the entire tab displays with the selected color.

You can manage more than one worksheet at a time by first selecting the worksheets. To select adjacent worksheet tabs, click the first tab, hold down the Shift key, and then click the last tab. To select nonadjacent worksheet tabs, click the first tab, hold down the Ctrl key, and then click any other tabs you want selected.

exercise 5

SELECTING, DELETING, RENAMING, AND CHANGING THE COLOR OF WORKSHEET TABS

1. Open **sec5x04**.
2. Save the workbook with Save As and name it **sec5x05**.
3. Delete worksheets 3 and 4 by completing the following steps:
   a. Click the left mouse button on *Sheet3* that displays at the bottom of the workbook window.
   b. Hold down the Ctrl key, click *Sheet4*, and then release the Ctrl key.
   c. Position the arrow pointer on the *Sheet4* tab and then click the *right* mouse button.

d. At the shortcut menu that displays, click Delete.

   e. At the message telling you that the selected sheets will be permanently deleted, click the Delete button.

4. Rename worksheets 1 and 2 by completing the following steps:

   a. Right-click the *Sheet1* tab and then click Rename.

   b. Type **First Quarter** and then press Enter.

   c. Right-click the *Sheet2* tab and then click Rename.

   d. Type **Second Quarter** and then press Enter.

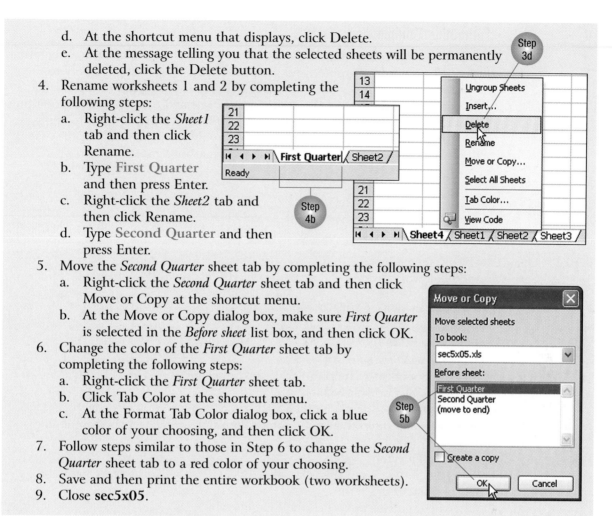

5. Move the *Second Quarter* sheet tab by completing the following steps:

   a. Right-click the *Second Quarter* sheet tab and then click Move or Copy at the shortcut menu.

   b. At the Move or Copy dialog box, make sure *First Quarter* is selected in the *Before sheet* list box, and then click OK.

6. Change the color of the *First Quarter* sheet tab by completing the following steps:

   a. Right-click the *First Quarter* sheet tab.

   b. Click Tab Color at the shortcut menu.

   c. At the Format Tab Color dialog box, click a blue color of your choosing, and then click OK.

7. Follow steps similar to those in Step 6 to change the *Second Quarter* sheet tab to a red color of your choosing.

8. Save and then print the entire workbook (two worksheets).

9. Close **sec5x05**.

Hiding a Worksheet in a Workbook

In a workbook containing multiple worksheets, you can hide a worksheet that may contain sensitive data or data you do not want to display or print with the workbook. To hide a worksheet in a workbook, click Format, point to Sheet, and then click Hide. To make a hidden worksheet visible, click Format, point to Sheet, and then click Unhide. At the Unhide dialog box shown in Figure 5.3, double-click the name of the hidden worksheet you want to display.

HINT
If the Hide command is unavailable, the workbook is protected from change.

FIGURE

5.3 *Unhide Dialog Box*

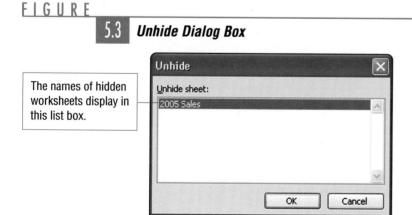

The names of hidden worksheets display in this list box.

Hide a Worksheet
Click Format, Sheet, Hide.

Unhide a Worksheet
Click Format, Sheet, Unhide.

Formatting Multiple Worksheets

When you apply formatting to a worksheet, such as changing margins, orientation, or inserting a header or footer, and so on, the formatting is applied only to the active worksheet. If you want formatting to apply to multiple worksheets in a workbook, select the tabs of the desired worksheets and then apply the formatting. For example, if a workbook contains three worksheets and you want to apply formatting to the first and second worksheets only, select the tabs for the first and second worksheets and then apply the formatting.

exercise 6

HIDING A WORKSHEET AND FORMATTING MULTIPLE WORKSHEETS

1. Open **ExcelWorksheet41**.
2. Save the workbook with Save As and name it **sec5x06**. (This workbook contains three worksheets.)
3. Make the following changes to the worksheet tabs:
   a. Rename *Sheet1* to *2003 Sales*.
   b. Rename *Sheet2* to *2004 Sales*.
   c. Rename *Sheet3* to *2005 Sales*.
4. Hide the *2005 Sales* worksheet by completing the following steps:
   a. Click the *2005 Sales* worksheet tab.
   b. Click Format, point to Sheet, and then click Hide.
5. Change the margins and insert a custom footer to multiple worksheets by completing the following steps:
   a. Click the *2003 Sales* tab.
   b. Hold down the Shift key and then click the *2004 Sales* tab. (This selects both tabs.)
   c. Click File and then Page Setup.
   d. At the Page Setup dialog box, click the Margins tab.
   e. At the Page Setup dialog box with the Margins tab selected, change the *Top* margin measurement to *2* and the *Left* margin measurement to *2.25*.
   f. Click the Header/Footer tab.
   g. At the Page Setup dialog box with the Header/Footer tab selected, click the Custom Footer button.
   h. At the Footer dialog box, type your name in the *Left section* text box, insert the page number in the *Center section* text box, and insert the file name in the *Right section* text box.
   i. Click OK to close the Footer dialog box.

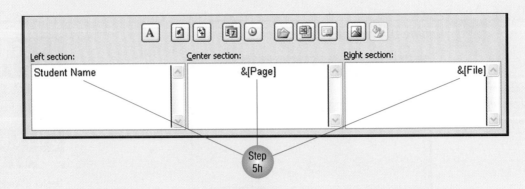

Step
5h

j. Click OK to close the Page Setup dialog box.

6. Print the entire workbook (except the hidden worksheet) by displaying the Print dialog box, clicking *Entire workbook* in the *Print what* section, and then clicking OK.

7. Unhide the *2005 Sales* worksheet by completing the following steps:

   a. Click Format, point to Sheet, and then click Unhide.

   b. At the Unhide dialog box, make sure *2005 Sales* is selected in the *Unhide sheet* list box, and then click OK.

8. Save and then close **sec5x06**.

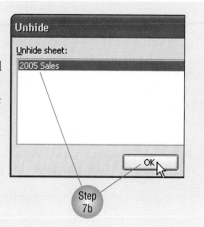

Splitting a Worksheet into Windows and Freezing and Unfreezing Panes

In some worksheets, not all cells display at one time in the worksheet area (such as ExcelWorksheet06). When working in worksheets with more cells than can display at one time, you may find splitting the worksheet window into panes helpful. Split the worksheet window into panes with the Split option from the Window drop-down menu or use the split bars that display at the top of the vertical scroll bar and at the right side of the horizontal scroll bar. Figure 5.4 identifies these split bars.

Split a Worksheet
Click Window, Split.
OR
Drag horizontal and/or vertical split bars.

FIGURE

5.4 Split Bars

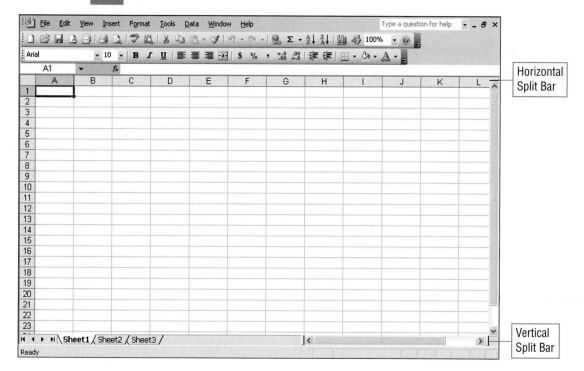

To split a window with the split bar located at the top of the vertical scroll bar, position the mouse pointer on the split bar until it turns into a double-headed arrow with a short double line in the middle. Hold down the left mouse button, drag down the thick gray line that displays until the pane is the desired size, and then release the mouse button. Split the window vertically with the split bar at the right side of the horizontal scroll bar.

To split a worksheet window with the Window drop-down menu, click Window and then Split. This causes the worksheet to split into four window panes as shown in Figure 5.5. The windows are split by thick gray lines (with a three-dimensional look). To remove a split from a worksheet window, click Window, Remove Split; or, drag the split bars to the upper left corner of the worksheet.

HINT

Restore a split window by double-clicking anywhere on the split bar that divides the panes.

FIGURE

5.5 **Split Window**

A window pane will display the active cell. As the insertion point is moved through the pane, another active cell with a blue background may display. This additional active cell displays when the insertion point passes over one of the gray lines that creates the pane. As you move through a worksheet, you may see both active cells—one with a normal background and one with a blue background. If you make a change to the active cell, the change is made in both. If you want only one active cell to display, freeze the window panes by clicking Window and then Freeze Panes. With panes frozen, only the display of the pane with the active cell will change. To unfreeze panes, click Window and then Unfreeze Panes.

Using the mouse, you can move the thick gray lines that divide the window into panes. To do this, position the mouse pointer on the line until it turns into a double-headed arrow with a double line in the middle. Hold down the left mouse button, drag the outline of the gray line to the desired location, and then release the mouse button. If you want to move both the horizontal and vertical lines at the same time, position the mouse pointer on the intersection of the thick gray lines until it turns into a four-headed arrow. Hold down the left mouse button, drag the thick gray lines in the desired direction, and then release the mouse button.

c. Click OK.

5. Hide and unhide workbooks by completing the following steps:

a. Click the ExcelWorksheet01 title bar to make it the active workbook.

b. Click Window and then Hide.

c. Click the ExcelWorksheet04 title bar to make it the active workbook.

d. Click Window and then Hide.

e. Click Window and then Unhide.

f. At the Unhide dialog box, click *ExcelWorksheet01* in the list box, and then click OK.

g. Click Window and then Unhide.

h. At the Unhide dialog box, make sure **ExcelWorksheet04** is selected in the list box, and then click OK.

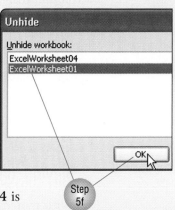

Step 5f

6. Close all of the open workbooks by holding down the Shift key, clicking File, and then clicking Close All. (If a message displays asking you to save the worksheet, click No.)

Sizing and Moving Workbooks

The Maximize and Minimize buttons in the upper right corner of the active workbook window can be used to change the size of the window. The Maximize button is the button in the upper right corner of the active workbook immediately to the left of the Close button. (The Close button is the button containing the *X*.) The Minimize button is located immediately to the left of the Maximize button.

Maximize   Minimize

Close   Restore

If you arrange all open workbooks and then click the Maximize button in the active workbook, the active workbook expands to fill the screen. In addition, the Maximize button changes to the Restore button. To return the active workbook back to its size before it was maximized, click the Restore button.

Clicking the Minimize button causes the active workbook to be reduced and positioned as a button on the Taskbar. In addition, the Minimize button changes to the Restore button. To maximize a workbook that has been reduced, click the button on the Taskbar representing the workbook.

exercise **11**

MINIMIZING, MAXIMIZING, AND RESTORING WORKBOOKS

1. Open **ExcelWorksheet01**.

2. Maximize **ExcelWorksheet01** by clicking the Maximize button at the right side of the workbook Title bar. (The Maximize button is the button at the right side of the Title bar, immediately to the left of the Close button.)

3. Open **ExcelWorksheet03** and **ExcelWorksheet05**.

4. Make the following changes to the open workbooks:

a. Tile the workbooks.

b. Make **ExcelWorksheet01** the active workbook (Title bar displays with a blue background [the background color may vary depending on how Windows is customized]).

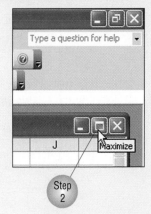

Step 2

c. Minimize **ExcelWorksheet01** by clicking the Minimize button that displays at the right side of the Title bar.

d. Make **ExcelWorksheet03** the active workbook and then minimize it.

e. Minimize **ExcelWorksheet05**.

5. Close all workbooks by holding down the Shift key, clicking File, and then clicking Close All.

Moving, Copying, and Pasting Data

With more than one workbook open, you can move, copy, and/or paste data from one workbook to another. To move, copy, and/or paste data between workbooks, use the cutting and pasting options you learned earlier in this chapter, together with the information about windows in this chapter.

exercise 12

COPYING SELECTED CELLS FROM ONE OPEN WORKSHEET TO ANOTHER

1. Open **ExcelWorksheet35**.
2. If you just completed Exercise 11, click the Maximize button so the worksheet fills the entire worksheet window.
3. Save the worksheet and name it **sec5x12**.
4. With **sec5x12** still open, open **ExcelWorksheet01**.
5. Select and then copy text from **ExcelWorksheet01** to **sec5x12** by completing the following steps:
   a. With **ExcelWorksheet01** the active workbook, select cells A5 through D10.
   b. Click the Copy button on the Standard toolbar.
   c. Click Window and then click *2 sec5x12*.

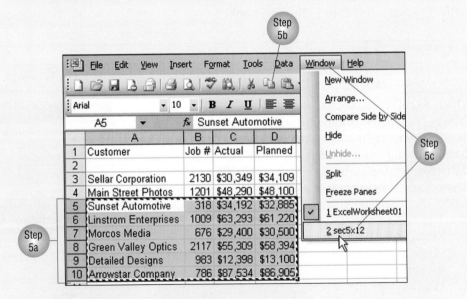

EXCEL

d. Make cell A7 the active cell and then click the Paste button on the Standard toolbar.

6. Select cells A1 through D12 in **sec5x11** and then apply the Colorful 1 autoformat.

7. Print **sec5x12** horizontally and vertically centered on the page.

8. Save the worksheet again with the same name (**sec5x12**).

9. Close **sec5x12**.

10. Close **ExcelWorksheet01**.

Linking Data between Worksheets

In workbooks containing multiple worksheets or between related workbooks, you may want to create a link between worksheets or workbooks with data in cells. When data is linked, a change made in a linked cell is automatically made to the other cells in the link. Links can be made with individual cells or with a range of cells.

Linking cells between worksheets creates what is called a **dynamic link**. Dynamic links are useful in worksheets or workbooks that need to maintain consistency and control over critical data. The worksheet that contains the original data is called the **source** worksheet and the worksheet relying on the source worksheet for the data in the link is called the **dependent** worksheet.

To create a link, make active the cell containing the data to be linked (or select the cells), and then click the Copy button on the Standard toolbar. Make active the worksheet where you want to paste the cell or cells, click Edit, and then click Paste Special. This displays the Paste Special dialog box as shown in Figure 5.9.

QUICK STEPS

Link Data between Worksheets
1. Select cells.
2. Click Copy button.
3. Click desired worksheet tab.
4. Click in desired cell.
5. Click Edit, Paste Special.
6. Click Paste Link button.

FIGURE

5.9 *Paste Special Dialog Box*

HINT

To open the source of a link, open the dependent workbook, click Edit, and then click Links. Click the workbook name in the Source box and then click the Open Source button.

At the Paste Special dialog box, specify what in the cell you want to copy and what operators you want to include, and then click the Paste Link button. When a change is made to the cell or cells in the source worksheet, the change is automatically made to the linked cell or cells in the dependent worksheet.

exercise 13

1. Open **ExcelWorksheet34**.
2. Save the worksheet with Save As and name it **sec5x13**.
3. Make the following changes to the worksheet:
   a. Change the text in cell A1 from *First Quarter* to *FIRST HALF, 2004*.
   b. Insert the formula =**B3-C3** in cell D3.
   c. Copy the formula in cell D3 down to cells D4 through D9.
4. Copy data in the worksheet to *Sheet2* by completing the following steps:
   a. Select cells A1 through D9.
   b. Click the Copy button on the Standard toolbar.
   c. Click the *Sheet2* tab.
   d. With cell A1 the active cell, click the Paste button on the Standard toolbar.
   e. Automatically adjust the widths of the cells.
   f. Select cells C3 through C9 and then delete the cell data.
5. Link cells C3 through C9 from *Sheet1* to *Sheet2* by completing the following steps:
   a. Click the *Sheet1* tab.
   b. Select cells C3 through C9.
   c. Click the Copy button on the Standard toolbar.
   d. Click the *Sheet2* tab.
   e. Make cell C3 active.
   f. Click Edit and then Paste Special.
   g. At the Paste Special dialog box, make sure *All* is selected in the *Paste* section of the dialog box, and then click the Paste Link button.

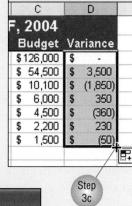

Step 3c

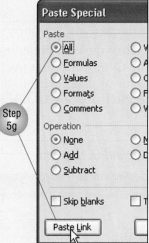

Step 5g

EXCEL

6. With *Sheet2* still the active worksheet, make the following changes to the specified cells:

> A1: Change *FIRST HALF, 2004* to *SECOND HALF, 2004*
> B3: Change *$126,000* to *123,500*
> B4: Change *$58,000* to *53,000*
> B6: Change *$6,350* to *6,125*

7. Make *Sheet1* the active worksheet and then make the following changes to some of the linked cells:

> C3: Change *$126,000* to *128,000*
> C4: Change *$54,500* to *56,000*
> C8: Change *$2,200* to *2,400*

	A	B	C	D
1	**SECOND HALF, 2004**			
2	Expense	Actual	Budget	Variance
3	Salaries	$123,500	$126,000	$ (2,500)
4	Commissions	$ 53,000	$ 54,500	$ (1,500)
5	Media space	$ 8,250	$ 10,100	$ (1,850)
6	Travel expenses	$ 6,125	$ 6,000	$ 125
7	Dealer display	$ 4,140	$ 4,500	$ (360)
8	Payroll taxes	$ 2,430	$ 2,200	$ 230
9	Telephone	$ 1,450	$ 1,500	$ (50)

Step 6

8. Click the *Sheet2* tab and notice that the values in cells C3, C4, and C8 automatically changed (because they are linked to *Sheet1*).
9. Save the worksheet with the same name (**sec5x13**).
10. Print both worksheets in the workbook.
11. Close **sec5x13**.

Linking Worksheets with a 3-D Reference

In multiple worksheet workbooks, you can use a 3-D reference to analyze data in the same cell or range of cells. A 3-D reference includes the cell or range of cells, preceded by a range of worksheet names. For example, you can add all of the values contained in cells in B2 through B5 in worksheets 1 and 2 in a workbook using a 3-D reference. To do this, you would complete these basic steps:

1. Make active the cell where you want to enter the function.
2. Type =SUM(and then click the *Sheet1* tab.
3. Hold down the Shift key and then click the *Sheet2* tab.
4. Select cells B2 through B5 in the worksheet.
5. Type) (this is the closing parenthesis that ends the formula) and then press Enter.

exercise 14

LINKING WORKSHEETS WITH A 3-D REFERENCE

1. Open **ExcelWorksheet33**.
2. Save the workbook with Save As and name it **sec5x14**.
3. Make sure *Sales 2002* is the active worksheet.
4. Select columns B, C, and D and change the width to 14.00.
5. Make the following changes to the *Sales 2002* worksheet:
   a. Make cell B10 active.
   b. Click the Center button and then the Bold button on the Formatting toolbar.

   c. Type January Sales and then press Alt + Enter.

   d. Type 2002-2004 and then press Enter.

6. Link the *Sales 2002*, *Sales 2003*, and *Sales 2004* worksheets with a 3-D reference by completing the following steps:

   a. With cell B11 active, type =SUM(.

   b. Hold down the Shift key, click the *Sales 2004* sheet tab, and then release the Shift key. (This selects all three sheet tabs.)

   c. Select cells B3 through B8.

   d. Type) and then press Enter.

   e. Make cell B11 active.

   f. Click the Currency Style button on the Formatting toolbar and then click twice on the Decrease Decimal button.

DATE	▾ X ✓ *fx* =SUM('Sales 2002:Sales 2004'!B3:B8		
	A	B	C	D
1		FIRST-QUARTER SALES - 2002		
2	Customer	January	February	March
3	Lakeside Trucking	$ 84,231	$ 73,455	$ 97,549
4	Gresham Machines	$ 33,199	$ 40,390	$ 50,112
5	Real Photography	$ 30,891	$ 35,489	$ 36,400
6	Genesis Productions	$ 72,190	$ 75,390	$ 83,219
7	Landower Company	$ 22,188	$ 14,228	$ 38,766
8	Jewell Enterprises	$ 19,764	$ 50,801	$ 32,188
9				
10		January Sales 2002-2004		
11		=SUM('Sales 2002:Sales 2004'!B3:B8		
12		SUM(**number1**, [number2], ...)		

Steps 6a–6c

7. Complete steps similar to those in Step 5 to add *February Sales 2002-2004* (on two lines) in cell C10 and complete steps similar to those in Step 6 to insert the formula with the 3-D reference in cell C11.

8. Complete steps similar to those in Step 5 to add *March Sales 2002-2004* (on two lines) in cell D10 and complete steps similar to those in Step 6 to insert the formula with the 3-D reference in cell D11.

9. Save the workbook again with the same name (**sec5x14**).

10. Print the *Sales 2002* worksheet of the workbook.

11. Close **sec5x14**.

Copying and Pasting a Worksheet between Programs

Microsoft Office is a suite that allows integration, which is the combining of data from two or more programs into one file. Integration can occur by copying and pasting data between programs. The program containing the data to be copied is called the *source* program and the program where the data is pasted is called the *destination* program. For example, you can create a worksheet in Excel and then copy it to a Word document. The steps to copy and paste between programs are basically the same as copying and pasting within the same program.

When copying data between worksheets or from one program to another, you can copy and paste, copy and link, or copy and embed the data. Consider the following when choosing a method for copying data:

- Copy data in the source program and paste it in the destination program when the data will not need to be edited.

- Copy data in the source program and then link it in the destination program when the data is updated regularly in the source program and you want the update reflected in the destination program.

EXCEL

- Copy data in the source program and then embed it in the destination program when the data will be edited in the destination program (with the tools of the source program).

Earlier in this chapter, you copied and pasted cells within and between worksheets and you also copied and linked cells between worksheets. You can also copy and link data between programs. Copy and embed data using options at the Paste Special dialog box. In Exercise 15, you will copy cells in a worksheet and then embed the cells in a Word document. With the worksheet embedded in a Word document, double-click the worksheet and Excel tools display in the document for editing the worksheet.

exercise 15

COPYING AND PASTING A WORKSHEET INTO A WORD DOCUMENT

1. Open the Word program and then open **WordLetter02**.
2. Save the document and name it **seWordc5x15**.
3. With **seWordc5x15** still open, make Excel the active program.
4. Open **ExcelWorksheet03**.
5. Save the worksheet with Save As and name it **sec5x15**.
6. Make the following changes to the worksheet:
   a. Select cells B3 through D8 and then click the Percent Style button on the Formatting toolbar.
   b. Select cells A1 through D8 and then apply the Classic 2 autoformat.
7. Save the worksheet again with the same name (**sec5x15**).
8. Copy the worksheet to the letter in **seWordc5x15** by completing the following steps:
   a. Select cells A1 through D8.
   b. Click the Copy button on the Standard toolbar.
   c. Click the button on the Taskbar representing the Word document **seWordc5x15**.
   d. Position the insertion point a double space below the first paragraph of text in the body of the letter.
   e. Click Edit and then Paste Special.
   f. At the Paste Special dialog box, click *Microsoft Office Excel Worksheet Object* in the *As* list box, and then click OK.

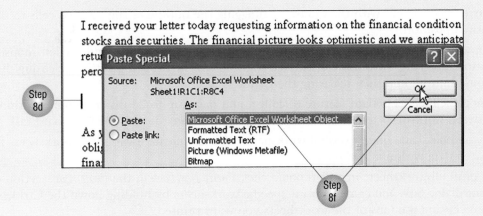

9. Edit a few of the cells in the worksheet by completing the following steps:

   a. Double-click anywhere in the worksheet. (This displays the Excel toolbar for editing.)

   b. Click in each of the following cells and make the change indicated:

> return on investments. The following table displays the actual, percentages.

	A	B	C	D
1	ANALYSIS OF FINANCIAL CONDITION			
2		Actual	Planned	Prior Year
3	Stockholder's equity ratio	62%	60%	57%
4	Bond holder's equity ratio	45%	39%	41%
5	Liability liquidity ratio	122%	115%	120%
6	Fixed obligation security ratio	110%	104%	101%
7	Fixed interest ratio	23%	20%	28%
8	Earnings ratio	7%	6%	6%

Sheet1 / Sheet2 / Sheet3 /

As you can see from the table, the highest increase of percenta

Step 9b

B6: Change *196%* to *110%*
C6: Change *190%* to *104%*
D6: Change *187%* to *101%*

   c. Click outside the worksheet to remove the Excel tools (and deselect the worksheet).

10. Save, print, and then close **seWordc5x15**.
11. Exit Word.
12. With Excel the active program, close **sec5x15**.

CHAPTER summary

➤ Move selected cells and cell contents in and between worksheets using the Cut, Copy, and Paste buttons on the Standard toolbar; dragging with the mouse; or with options from the Edit drop-down menu.

➤ Move selected cells with the mouse by dragging the outline of the selected cells to the desired position.

➤ Copy selected cells with the mouse by holding down the Ctrl key and the left mouse button, dragging the outline of the selected cells to the desired location, releasing the left mouse button, and then releasing the Ctrl key.

➤ Use the Office Clipboard feature to collect and paste up to 24 different items within and between worksheets and workbooks. To use this feature, display the Clipboard task pane.

➤ A workbook can contain several worksheets. You can create a variety of worksheets for related data within a workbook.

➤ To print all worksheets in a workbook, click *Entire workbook* in the *Print what* section of the Print dialog box. You can also print specific worksheets by holding down the Ctrl key and then clicking the tabs of the worksheets you want printed.

➤ Perform maintenance activities, such as deleting and renaming, on worksheets within a workbook by clicking the right mouse button on a sheet tab, and then clicking the desired option at the shortcut menu.

➤ You can use the mouse to move or copy worksheets. To move a worksheet, drag the worksheet tab with the mouse. To copy a worksheet, hold down the Ctrl key, and then drag the worksheet tab with the mouse.

➤ Use the Tab Color option at the worksheet shortcut menu to apply a color to a worksheet tab.

➤ Manage more than one worksheet at a time by first selecting the worksheets. Use the mouse together with the Shift key to select adjacent worksheet tabs and use the mouse together with the Ctrl key to select nonadjacent worksheet tabs.

➤ Hide a worksheet by clicking Format, pointing to Sheet, and then clicking Hide. To unhide a worksheet, click Format, point to Sheet, and then click Unhide. At the Unhide dialog box, double-click the name of the worksheet you want to unhide.

➤ If you want formatting to apply to multiple worksheets in a workbook, select the tabs of the desired worksheets and then apply the formatting.

➤ Split the worksheet window into panes with the Split option from the Window drop-down menu or with the split bars on the horizontal and vertical scroll bars.

➤ Remove the split window by clicking Window and then Remove Split; or drag the split bars.

➤ Freeze window panes by clicking Window and then Freeze Panes. When panes are frozen, only the display of the pane with the active cell changes. Unfreeze window panes by clicking Window and then Unfreeze Panes.

➤ A selected group of cells is referred to as a range. A range can be named and used in a formula. Name a range by typing the name in the Name Box button located to the left of the Formula bar.

➤ To open multiple workbooks that are adjacent, display the Open dialog box, click the first workbook, hold down the Shift key, click the last workbook, and then click the Open button. If workbooks are nonadjacent, click the first workbook, hold down the Ctrl key, click the desired workbooks, and then click the Open button.

➤ Click Window on the Menu bar to see a list of open workbooks.

➤ Close all open workbooks at one time by holding down the Shift key, clicking File and then clicking Close All.

➤ Arrange multiple workbooks in a window with options at the Arrange Windows dialog box.

➤ Click the Maximize button located at the right side of the Title bar of the active workbook to make the workbook fill the entire window area. Click the Minimize button to shrink the active workbook to a button on the Taskbar. Click the Restore button to return the workbook to its previous size.

➤ You can move, copy, and/or paste data between workbooks.

➤ Copy and then link data if you make changes in the source worksheet and you want the changes reflected in the destination worksheet. The worksheet containing the original data is called the source worksheet and the worksheet relying on the source worksheet for data in the link is called the dependent worksheet.

➤ Copy and link data using the Paste Special dialog box.

➤ You can copy data from a document in one program (called the source program) and paste the data into a file in another program (called the destination program).

➤ Use a 3-D reference to analyze data in the same cell or range of cells.

➤ You can copy and then paste, link, or embed data between programs in the Office suite. Integrating is the combining of data from two or more programs in the Office suite.

FEATURES summary

FEATURE	BUTTON	MENU	KEYBOARD
Cut selected cells	✂	Edit, Cut	Ctrl + X
Paste selected cells	📋 ▾	Edit, Paste	Ctrl + V
Copy selected cells	📋	Edit, Copy	Ctrl + C
Clipboard task pane		Edit, Office Clipboard	Ctrl + C, Ctrl + C
Hide worksheet		Format, Sheet, Hide	
Unhide dialog box		Format, Sheet, Unhide	
Split window into panes		Window, Split	
Freeze window panes		Window, Freeze Panes	
Unfreeze window panes		Window, Unfreeze Panes	
Arrange Windows dialog box		Window, Arrange	
Paste Special dialog box		Edit, Paste Special	

CONCEPTS check

Completion: On a blank sheet of paper, indicate the correct term, symbol, or command for each description.

1. To copy selected cells with the mouse, hold down this key while dragging the outline of the selected cells to the desired location.
2. Press Ctrl + C twice and this task pane displays.
3. Click this option at the Print dialog box to print all worksheets in the workbook.
4. Use this option at the worksheet shortcut menu to apply a color to a worksheet tab.
5. To hide a worksheet, click Format, point to this, and then click Hide.
6. To split a window using a split bar, position the mouse pointer on the split bar until the mouse pointer turns into this.
7. Clicking Window and then Split causes the active worksheet to be split into this number of windows.

8. To see what workbooks are currently open, click this option on the Menu bar.
9. To close all open workbooks at the same time, hold down this key while clicking File and then Close All.
10. Arrange all open workbooks with options from this dialog box.
11. Click this button to shrink the active workbook to a button on the Taskbar.
12. Click this button to return the workbook back to its original size.
13. Click this button to make the active workbook fill the entire window area.
14. When copying and pasting data between programs, the program containing the original data is called this.
15. List the steps you would complete to open all of the following workbooks at one time: ExcelWorksheet02, ExcelWorksheet03, and ExcelWorksheet05.
16. List the steps you would complete to copy a range of cells from one workbook to another.

SKILLS check

Assessment 1

1. Open **ExcelWorksheet34**.
2. Save the worksheet with Save As and name it **sec5sc01**.
3. Make the following changes to the worksheet:
   a. Insert a column between columns C and D. (The new column will be column D.)
   b. Move the content of cells B2 through B9 to D2 through D9.
   c. Delete the blank column B.
   d. Insert a formula in cell D3 that subtracts the Actual amount from the Budget amount.
   e. Copy the formula in cell D3 down to cells D4 through D9.
4. Save, print, and then close **sec5sc01**.

Assessment 2

1. Open **ExcelWorksheet05**.
2. Save the worksheet with Save As and name it **sec5sc02**.
3. Make the following changes:
   a. Copy cells A1 through C8 to *Sheet2*.
   b. With *Sheet2* active, make the following changes:

      A1: Change *January* to *February*
      B3: Change *35* to *40*
      B6: Change *24* to *20*
      B7: Change *15* to *20*
      C4: Change *$19.00* to *20.15*
      C6: Change *$16.45* to *17.45*

   c. Automatically adjust the width of column A.
   d. Copy cells A1 through C8 to *Sheet3*.
   e. With *Sheet3* active, make the following changes:

      A1: Change *February* to *March*
      B4: Change *20* to *35*
      B8: Change *15* to *20*

f. Automatically adjust the width of column A.
4. Rename *Sheet1* to *Jan. Payroll*, *Sheet2* to *Feb. Payroll*, and *Sheet3* to *Mar. Payroll*.
5. Change the color of the *Jan. Payroll* sheet tab to green, the color of the *Feb. Payroll* tab to yellow, and the color of the *Mar. Payroll* tab to red.
6. Save the worksheets again and then print all worksheets in the **sec5sc02** workbook.
7. Close **sec5sc02**.

Assessment 3

1. Open **ExcelWorksheet09**.
2. Save the worksheet with Save As and name it **sec5sc03**.
3. Make the following changes to the worksheet:
    a. Split the window.
    b. Drag the intersection of the horizontal and vertical gray lines so that the horizontal gray line is immediately below row 9 and the vertical gray line is immediately to the right of column A.
    c. Freeze the window panes.
    d. Insert a new row 8 and then type the following in the specified cells:

A8	=	Loaned Out
B8	=	10
C8	=	0
D8	=	5
E8	=	0
F8	=	11
G8	=	3
H8	=	16
I8	=	0
J8	=	0
K8	=	5
L8	=	0
M8	=	0

    e. Remove the split.
    f. Select rows 1 through 10 and then change the row height to 18.00.
4. Print the worksheet in landscape orientation (it will print on two pages) so the row titles print on each page.
5. Save and then close **sec5sc03**.

Assessment 4

1. Open **ExcelWorksheet01**.
2. Save the worksheet with Save As and name it **sec5sc04**.
3. Make the following changes to the worksheet:
    a. Type Difference in cell E1.
    b. Insert the formula =*D3-C3* in cell E3 and then copy it down to E4 through E10.
    c. Select cells E3 through E10 and then name the range *Difference*.
    d. Type Max Difference in cell A13.
    e. Insert the formula =*MAX(Difference)* in cell B13.
    f. Type Min Difference in cell A14.
    g. Insert the formula =*MIN(Difference)* in cell B14.
    h. Type Ave Difference in cell A15.
    i. Insert the formula =*AVERAGE(Difference)* in cell B15.

EXCEL

j.   Select cells B13 through B15 and then click the Currency Style button on the Formatting toolbar.
k.   With cells B13 through B15 selected, click twice the Decrease Decimal button.
l.   Automatically adjust the width of column B.
m. Bold and center the text in cells A1 through E1.
4. Save and then print **sec5sc04**.
5. Make the following changes to the worksheet:
a.   Change *63,293* in cell C6 to *55,500*.
b.   Change *12,398* in cell C9 to *13,450*.
c.   Create a custom header that prints *Customer Jobs* centered at the top of the page.
6. Save, print, and then close **sec5sc04**.

Assessment 5

1. Create the worksheet shown in Figure 5.10 (change the width of column A to 21.00).
2. Save the worksheet and name it **sec5sc05**.
3. With **sec5sc05** still open, open **ExcelWorksheet09**.
4. Select and copy the following cells from **ExcelWorksheet09** to **sec5sc05**:
a.   Copy cells A3 through G3 in **ExcelWorksheet09** and paste them into **sec5sc05** beginning with cell A12.
b.   Copy cells A9 through G9 in **ExcelWorksheet09** and paste them into **sec5sc05** beginning with cell A13.
5. With **sec5sc05** the active worksheet, apply an autoformat of your choosing to cells A1 through G13.
6. Print **sec5sc05** in landscape orientation and centered horizontally and vertically on the page.
7. Save and then close **sec5sc05**.
8. Close **ExcelWorksheet09** without saving the changes.

F I G U R E

5.10 *Assessment 5*

	A	B	C	D	E	F	G	H
1		EQUIPMENT USAGE REPORT						
2		January	February	March	April	May	June	
3	Machine #12							
4	Total Hours Available	2,300	2,430	2,530	2,400	2,440	2,240	
5	In Use	2,040	2,105	2,320	2,180	2,050	1,995	
6								
7	Machine #25							
8	Total Hours Available	2,100	2,240	2,450	2,105	2,390	1,950	
9	In Use	1,800	1,935	2,110	1,750	2,215	1,645	
10								
11	Machine #30							
12								

Assessment 6

1. Open **ExcelWorksheet33**.
2. Save the workbook with Save As and name it **sec5sc06**.
3. Change the color of the *Sales 2002* tab to light purple, the color of the *Sales 2003* tab to light blue, and the color of the *Sales 2004* tab to light green.
4. Make the following changes to the workbook:
a.   Make sure the *Sales 2002* worksheet is the active worksheet.

    b.   Select columns B, C, and D and then change the width to 15.00.

    c.   Insert the heading *Average January Sales 2002-2004* (on multiple lines) in cell B10.

    d.   Insert a formula in cell B11 with a 3-D reference that averages the total in cells B3 through B8 in the *Sales 2002*, *Sales 2003*, and *Sales 2004* worksheets.

    e.   Make cell B11 active and then change to the Currency Style with zero decimal places.

    f.   Insert the heading *Average February Sales 2002-2004* (on multiple lines) in cell C10.

    g.   Insert a formula in cell C11 with a 3-D reference that averages the total in cells C3 through C8 in the *Sales 2002*, *Sales 2003*, and *Sales 2004* worksheets.

    h.   Make cell C11 active and then change to the Currency Style with zero decimal places.

    i.   Insert the heading *Average March Sales 2002-2004* (on multiple lines) in cell D10.

    j.   Insert a formula in cell D11 with a 3-D reference that averages the total in cells D3 through D8 in the *Sales 2002*, *Sales 2003*, and *Sales 2004* worksheets.

    k.   Make cell D11 active and then change to the Currency Style with zero decimal places.

5. Save the workbook and then print only the *Sales 2002* worksheet.

6. Close **sec5sc06**.

Assessment 7

1. Use Excel's Help feature to learn about linking data between programs.

2. After locating and reading the information on linking, open the Word program and then open **WordLetter02**.

3. Save the document and name it **seWordc5sc07**.

4. Make Excel the active program and then open **ExcelWorksheet03**.

5. Save the worksheet with Save As and name it **sec5sc07**.

6. Make the following changes to the worksheet:

    a.   Select cells B3 through D8 and then click the Percent Style button on the Formatting toolbar.

    b.   Select cells A1 through D8 and then apply the Colorful 2 autoformat.

7. Save and then print the worksheet.

8. Copy the worksheet and link it to **seWordc5sc07** (between the two paragraphs in the body of the letter).

9. Save and then print **seWordc5sc07**.

10. Click the button on the Taskbar representing the Excel worksheet **sec5sc07** and then make the following changes to data in cells:

    a.   Change the title in cell A1 from *ANALYSIS OF FINANCIAL CONDITION* to *FINANCIAL ANALYSIS*.

    b.   Change the content of cell B3 from *62%* to *80%*.

    c.   Change the content of cell B4 from *45%* to *70%*.

11. Save, print, and then close **sec5sc07**.

12. Make active the Word document **seWordc5sc07** and then close the document.

13. Open **seWordc5sc07** and update the links.

14. Save, print, and then close **seWordc5sc07**.

15. Exit Word.

CHAPTER challenge

You are the sales manager for Campton's Camera Company and have been asked by the regional sales manager to report to him the first quarter sales for the last three years. You decide to provide him with a detailed summary. Create an Excel workbook containing three worksheets (one for each of the three years). In each of the worksheets show first quarter sales for the following camera models: Models A, B, and C. In a fourth worksheet, called *Totals*, link the three worksheets using a 3-D reference. The *Totals* sheet should show the total monthly sales for each of the camera models. Name each of the sheet tabs appropriately. Attractively format all of the worksheets. Save the workbook.

Although naming sheet tabs is very useful in keeping a workbook organized and understandable, you feel that using tab color would be helpful as your regional sales manager interprets the information in the workbook. Use the Help feature to learn about tab color, then apply tab colors to the various sheet tabs in the workbook created in the first part of the Chapter Challenge. Save the workbook again.

The regional sales manager was so impressed with your work that he has asked you to present the information to the Board of Directors. Create a PowerPoint presentation that includes the information created in the first part of the Chapter Challenge. Begin the presentation with a title slide and then include the information from each of the worksheets on a separate slide. The information from the *Totals* sheet should be linked to the presentation. Save the presentation.

6.9

4.5

MAINTAINING WORKBOOKS

PERFORMANCE OBJECTIVES

Upon successful completion of Chapter 6, you will be able to:
- **Create and rename a folder**
- **Delete workbooks and folders**
- **Copy and move workbooks within and between folders**
- **Copy, move, and rename worksheets within a workbook**
- **Save a workbook in a variety of formats**
- **Search for specific workbooks**
- **Maintain consistent formatting with styles**
- **Use comments for review and response**
- **Create financial forms using templates**

Once you have been working with Excel for a period of time you will have accumulated several workbook files. Workbooks should be organized into folders to facilitate fast retrieval of information. Occasionally you should perform file maintenance activities such as copying, moving, renaming, and deleting workbooks to ensure the workbook list in your various folders is manageable.

Maintaining Workbooks

Many workbook management tasks can be completed at the Open and Save As dialog boxes. These tasks can include copying, moving, printing, and renaming workbooks; opening multiple workbooks; and creating and renaming a new folder. Some file maintenance tasks such as creating a folder and deleting files are performed by using buttons on the Open dialog box or Save As dialog box toolbar. Figure 6.1 displays the Open dialog box toolbar buttons.

6.1 *Open Dialog Box Toolbar Buttons*

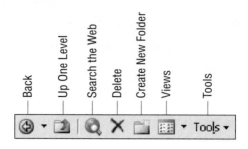

Create a Folder
1. Click File, Open.
2. Click Create New Folder button.
3. Type folder name.
4. Press Enter.

HINT

Change the default folder with the *Default file location* option at the Options dialog box with the General tab selected.

New Folder

Creating a Folder

In Excel, workbooks should be grouped logically and stored in folders. For example, all of the workbooks related to one department could be stored in one folder with the department name being the folder name. A folder can be created within a folder (called a *subfolder*). If you create workbooks for a department by individual, each individual could have a subfolder name within the department folder. The main folder on a disk or drive is called the root folder. Additional folders are created as a branch of this root folder.

At the Open or Save As dialog boxes, workbook file names display in the list box preceded by a workbook icon and a folder name is preceded by a folder icon. Create a new folder by clicking the Create New Folder button located on the dialog box toolbar at the Open dialog box or Save As dialog box. At the New Folder dialog box shown in Figure 6.2, type a name for the folder in the *Name* text box, and then click OK or press Enter. The new folder becomes the active folder.

F I G U R E

6.2 *New Folder Dialog Box*

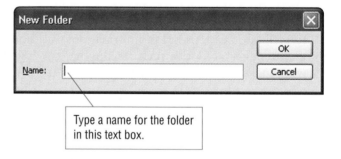

Type a name for the folder in this text box.

If you want to make the previous folder the active folder, click the Up One Level button on the dialog box toolbar. Clicking this button changes to the folder that is up one level from the current folder. After clicking the Up One Level button, the Back button becomes active. Click this button and the previously active folder becomes active again.

A folder name can contain a maximum of 255 characters. Numbers, spaces, and symbols can be used in the folder name, except those symbols explained in Chapter 1 in the "Saving a Workbook" section.

Up One Level   Back

Renaming a Folder

As you organize your files and folders, you may decide to rename a folder. Rename a folder using the Tools button on the Open dialog box toolbar or using a shortcut menu. To rename a folder using the Tools button, display the Open dialog box, click in the list box the folder you want to rename, click the Tools button on the dialog box toolbar, and then click Rename at the drop-down menu. This selects the folder name and inserts a border around the name. Type the new name for the folder and then press Enter. To rename a folder using a shortcut menu, display the Open dialog box, right-click the folder name in the list box, and then click Rename at the shortcut menu. Type a new name for the folder and then press Enter.

QUICK STEPS

Rename a Folder
1. Click File, Open.
2. Right-click folder name.
3. Click Rename.
4. Type new name.
5. Press Enter.

HINT

Display all files in a folder by changing the *Files of type* option at the Open dialog box to *All Files*.

exercise 1

CREATING AND RENAMING A FOLDER

1. Create a folder named *Payroll* on your disk. To begin, display the Open dialog box.
2. Double-click the *ExcelChapter06S* folder name to make it the active folder.
3. Click the Create New Folder button (located on the dialog box toolbar).
4. At the New Folder dialog box, type Payroll.
5. Click OK or press Enter. (The Payroll folder is now the active folder.)
6. Change back to the ExcelChapter06S folder by clicking the Up One Level button on the dialog box toolbar.
7. Rename the Payroll folder to *Finance* by completing the following steps:
   a. Right-click the *Payroll* folder name in the Open dialog box list box.
   b. Click Rename at the shortcut menu.
   c. Type Finance and then press Enter.
8. Click the Cancel button to close the Open dialog box.

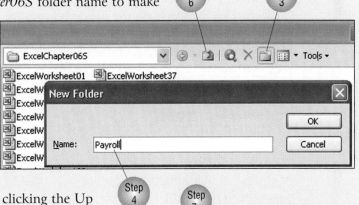

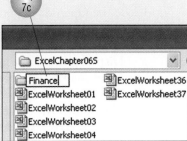

Deleting Workbooks and Folders

At some point, you may want to delete certain workbooks from your data disk or any other disk or folder in which you may be working. If you use Excel on a regular basis, you should establish a periodic system for deleting workbooks that are no longer used. The system you choose depends on the work you are doing and the amount of folder or disk space available. To delete a workbook, display the Open or Save As dialog box, select the workbook, and then click the Delete button on the dialog box toolbar. At the dialog box asking you to confirm the deletion, click Yes.

Delete

Tools

EXCEL

QUICK STEPS

Delete Workbook/ Folder
1. Click File, Open.
2. Click workbook or folder name.
3. Click Delete button.
4. Click Yes.

You can also delete a workbook by displaying the Open dialog box, selecting the workbook to be deleted, clicking the Tools button on the dialog box toolbar, and then clicking Delete at the drop-down menu. Another method for deleting a workbook is to display the Open dialog box, right-click the workbook to be deleted, and then click Delete at the shortcut menu. Delete a folder and all of its contents in the same manner as deleting a workbook or selected workbooks.

exercise 2

DELETING A WORKBOOK AND SELECTED WORKBOOKS

1. Open **ExcelWorksheet05**.
2. Save the worksheet with Save As and name it **sec6x02**.
3. Close **sec6x02**.
4. Delete **sec6x02** by completing the following steps:
   a. Display the Open dialog box with the ExcelChapter06S folder active.
   b. Click *sec6x02* to select it.
   c. Click the Delete button on the dialog box toolbar.

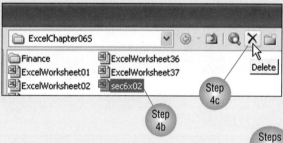

   d. At the question asking if you are sure you want to delete the item, click Yes.
5. Close the Open dialog box.
6. Delete selected workbooks by completing the following steps:
   a. Display the Open dialog box with the ExcelChapter06S folder active.
   b. Click *ExcelWorksheet02*.
   c. Hold down the Shift key and then click *ExcelWorksheet04*.
   d. Position the mouse pointer on one of the selected workbooks and then click the right mouse button.
   e. At the shortcut menu that displays, click Delete.
   f. At the question asking if you are sure you want to delete the items, click Yes.
   g. At the message telling you that **ExcelWorksheet02** is a read-only file and asking if you want to delete it, click the Yes to All button.
7. Close the Open dialog box.

EXCEL

Deleting to the Recycle Bin

Workbooks deleted from your data disk are deleted permanently. (Recovery programs are available, however, that will help you recover deleted text. If you accidentally delete one or more workbooks from a disk, do not do anything more with the disk until you can run a recovery program.) Workbooks deleted from the hard drive are automatically sent to the Windows Recycle Bin. If you accidentally delete a workbook to the Recycle Bin, it can be easily restored. To free space on the drive, empty the Recycle Bin on a periodic basis. Restoring a workbook from or emptying the contents of the Recycle Bin is done at the Windows desktop (not in Excel).

To display the Recycle Bin, minimize the Excel window, and then double-click the *Recycle Bin* icon located on the Windows desktop. At the Recycle Bin, you can restore file(s) and empty the Recycle Bin.

Copying Workbooks

In previous chapters, you opened a workbook from the data disk and saved it with a new name on the same disk. This process makes an exact copy of the workbook, leaving the original on the disk. You copied workbooks and saved the new workbook in the same folder as the original. You can also copy a workbook into another folder and use the workbook's original name or give it a different name, or select workbooks at the Open dialog box and copy them to the same folder or into a different folder. To copy a workbook into another folder, open the workbook, display the Save As dialog box, change to the desired folder, and then click the Save button.

The Open and Save As dialog boxes contain an Up One Level button (located on the dialog box toolbar). Use this button if you want to change to the folder that is up one level from the current folder.

QUICK STEPS

Copy a Workbook
1. Click File, Open.
2. Right-click workbook name.
3. Click Copy.
4. Navigate to desired folder.
5. Right-click white area in list box.
6. Click Paste.

---

exercise **3**

SAVING A COPY OF AN OPEN WORKBOOK

1. Open **ExcelWorksheet10**.
2. Save the workbook with Save As and name it **Quota&Bonus**. (Make sure ExcelChapter06S is the active folder.)
3. Save a copy of the Quota&Bonus workbook in the Finance folder created in Exercise 1 by completing the following steps. (If you did not complete Exercise 1, check with your instructor before continuing.)
   a. With **Quota&Bonus** still open, display the Save As dialog box.
   b. At the Save As dialog box, change to the Finance folder. To do this, double-click *Finance* at the beginning of the list box (folders are listed before workbooks).
   c. Click the Save button located in the lower right corner of the dialog box.
4. Close **Quota&Bonus**.
5. Change back to the ExcelChapter06S folder by completing the following steps:
   a. Display the Open dialog box.
   b. Click the Up One Level button located on the dialog box toolbar.
   c. Close the Open dialog box.

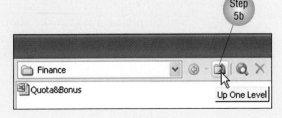

Step 5b

A workbook can be copied to another folder without opening the workbook first. To do this, use the Copy and Paste options from a shortcut menu at the Open (or Save As) dialog box.

exercise 4

COPYING A WORKBOOK AT THE OPEN DIALOG BOX

1. Copy **ExcelWorksheet07** to the Finance folder. To begin, display the Open dialog box with the ExcelChapter06S folder active.
2. Position the arrow pointer on *ExcelWorksheet07*, click the right mouse button, and then click Copy at the shortcut menu.
3. Change to the Finance folder by double-clicking *Finance* at the beginning of the list box.
4. Position the arrow pointer in any white area (not on a workbook name) in the list box, click the right mouse button, and then click Paste at the shortcut menu.
5. Change back to the ExcelChapter06S folder by clicking the Up One Level button located on the dialog box toolbar.
6. Close the Open dialog box.

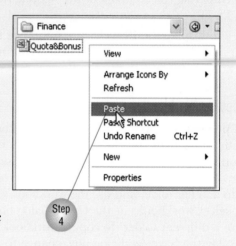

Step 4

A workbook or selected workbooks can be copied into the same folder. When you do this, Excel names the duplicated workbook(s) "Copy of xxx" (where *xxx* is the current workbook name). You can copy one workbook or selected workbooks into the same folder.

exercise 5

COPYING SELECTED WORKBOOKS INTO THE SAME FOLDER

1. Copy workbooks into the same folder. To begin, display the Open dialog box with ExcelChapter06S the active folder.
2. Select *ExcelWorksheet01*, *ExcelWorksheet07*, and *ExcelWorksheet09*. (To do this, hold down the Ctrl key while clicking each workbook name.)
3. Position the arrow pointer on one of the selected workbooks, click the right mouse button, and then click Copy at the shortcut menu.
4. Position the arrow pointer in any white area in the list box, click the right mouse button, and then click Paste at the shortcut menu. (In a few seconds, Excel will redisplay the Open dialog box with the following workbooks added: Copy of ExcelWorksheet01, Copy of ExcelWorksheet07, and Copy of ExcelWorksheet09.)
5. Close the Open dialog box.

EXCEL

exercise 6

1. Copy selected workbooks to the Finance folder. To begin, display the Open dialog box with ExcelChapter06S the active folder.
2. Select *ExcelWorksheet06*, *ExcelWorksheet08*, and *ExcelWorksheet10*.
3. Position the arrow pointer on one of the selected workbooks, click the right mouse button, and then click Copy at the shortcut menu.
4. Double-click the *Finance* folder.
5. Position the arrow pointer in any white area in the list box, click the right mouse button, and then click Paste at the shortcut menu.
6. Click the Up One Level button to change back to the ExcelChapter06S folder.
7. Close the Open dialog box.

Sending Workbooks to a Different Drive or Folder

Copy workbooks to another folder or drive with the Copy and Paste options from the shortcut menu at the Open or Save As dialog box. With the Send To option, you can quickly send a copy of a workbook to another drive or folder. To use this option, position the arrow pointer on the workbook you want copied, click the right mouse button, point to Send To (this causes a side menu to display), and then click the desired drive or folder.

Cutting and Pasting a Workbook

You can remove a workbook from one folder or disk and insert it in another folder or on another disk using the Cut and Paste options from the shortcut menu at the Open dialog box. To do this, display the Open dialog box, position the arrow pointer on the workbook to be removed (cut), click the right mouse button, and then click Cut at the shortcut menu. Change to the desired folder or drive, position the arrow pointer in a white area in the list box, click the right mouse button, and then click Paste at the shortcut menu.

QUICK STEPS

Move a Workbook
1. Click File, Open.
2. Right-click workbook name.
3. Click Cut.
4. Navigate to desired folder.
5. Right-click white area in list box.
6. Click Paste.

exercise 7

1. Move a workbook to a different folder. To begin, display the Open dialog box with the ExcelChapter06S folder active.
2. Position the arrow pointer on *ExcelWorksheet05*, click the right mouse button, and then click Cut at the shortcut menu.
3. Double-click *Finance* to make it the active folder.
4. Position the arrow pointer in the white area in the list box, click the right mouse button, and then click Paste at the shortcut menu.
5. At the Confirm File Move dialog box asking if you are sure you want to move the file, click Yes. (This dialog box usually does not appear when you cut and paste. Since the files you copied from your student CD-ROM are read-only files, this warning message appears.)
6. Click the Up One Level button to make the ExcelChapter06S folder the active folder.
7. Close the Open dialog box.

QUICK STEPS

Rename a Workbook
1. Click File, Open.
2. Right-click workbook name.
3. Click Rename.
4. Type new name.
5. Press Enter.

Renaming Workbooks

At the Open dialog box, use the Rename option from the Tools drop-down menu or the shortcut menu to give a workbook a different name. The Rename option changes the name of the workbook and keeps it in the same folder. To use Rename, display the Open dialog box, click once on the workbook to be renamed, click the Tools button on the dialog box toolbar, and then click Rename. This causes a thin black border to surround the workbook name and the name to be selected. Type the new name and then press Enter.

You can also rename a workbook by right-clicking the workbook name at the Open dialog box and then clicking Rename at the shortcut menu. Type the new name for the workbook and then press the Enter key.

exercise 8

RENAMING A WORKBOOK

Step 4

Step 5

1. Rename a workbook located in the Finance folder. To begin, display the Open dialog box with ExcelChapter06S the active folder.
2. Double-click *Finance* to make it the active folder.
3. Click once on *ExcelWorksheet07* to select it.
4. Click the Tools button on the dialog box toolbar.
5. At the drop-down menu that displays, click Rename.
6. Type Equipment and then press the Enter key.
7. At the message asking if you are sure you want to change the name of the read-only file, click Yes.
8. Complete steps similar to those in Steps 3 through 6 to rename **ExcelWorksheet06** to *TestScores*.
9. Click the Up One Level button.
10. Close the Open dialog box.

Deleting a Folder and Its Contents

As you learned earlier in this chapter, a workbook or selected workbooks can be deleted. In addition to workbooks, a folder (and all of its contents) can be deleted. Delete a folder in the same manner as a workbook is deleted.

exercise 9

DELETING A FOLDER AND ITS CONTENTS

1. Delete the Finance folder and its contents. To begin, display the Open dialog box with the ExcelChapter06S folder active.
2. Right-click on the *Finance* folder.
3. Click Delete at the shortcut menu.
4. At the Confirm Folder Delete dialog box, click Yes.
5. At the Confirm File Delete dialog box, click the Yes to All button.
6. Close the Open dialog box.

Printing Workbooks

Up to this point, you have opened a workbook and then printed it. With the Print option from the Tools drop-down menu or the Print option from the shortcut menu at the Open dialog box, you can print a workbook or several workbooks without opening them.

exercise 10

PRINTING WORKBOOKS

1. Display the Open dialog box with the ExcelChapter06S folder active.
2. Select *ExcelWorksheet01* and *ExcelWorksheet08*.
3. Click the Tools button on the dialog box toolbar.
4. At the drop-down menu that displays, click Print.

Managing Worksheets

Individual worksheets within a workbook can be moved or copied within the same workbook or to another existing workbook. Exercise caution when moving sheets since calculations or charts based on data on a worksheet might become inaccurate if you move the worksheet.

Copying a Worksheet to Another Workbook

To copy a worksheet to another existing workbook, open both the source and the destination workbooks. Activate the sheet you want to copy in the source workbook, click Edit, and then click Move or Copy Sheet, or right-click the sheet tab located at the bottom of the screen just above the Status bar and then click Move or Copy at the shortcut menu. At the Move or Copy dialog box shown in Figure 6.3, select the destination workbook name from the *To book* drop-down list, select the worksheet that you want the copied worksheet placed before in the *Before sheet* list box, click the *Create a copy* check box, and then click OK.

> **HINT**
> Make a duplicate of a worksheet in the same workbook by holding the Ctrl key and then dragging the worksheet tab to the desired position.

FIGURE

| 6.3 | *Move or Copy Dialog Box* |

Insert a check mark in this check box if you want to copy the worksheet.

1. Open **ExcelWorksheet26** and **Copy of ExcelWorksheet09**.
2. Copy the Equipment Usage Report worksheet from the workbook named Copy of ExcelWorksheet09 to the ExcelWorksheet26 workbook by completing the following steps:
   a. Make sure **Copy of ExcelWorksheet09** is the active workbook.
   b. Right-click the *Sheet1* tab located at the bottom left of the screen just above the Status bar, and then click Move or Copy at the shortcut menu.

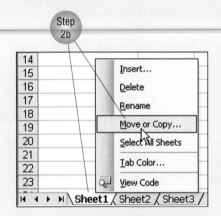

c. Click the down-pointing arrow next to the *To book* option box and then click *ExcelWorksheet26.xls* at the drop-down list.
d. Click *Sheet2* in the *Before sheet* list box.
e. Click the *Create a copy* check box to insert a check mark.
f. Click OK. (Excel switches to the workbook **ExcelWorksheet26** and inserts the copied sheet with the sheet name *Sheet1 (2)*.)

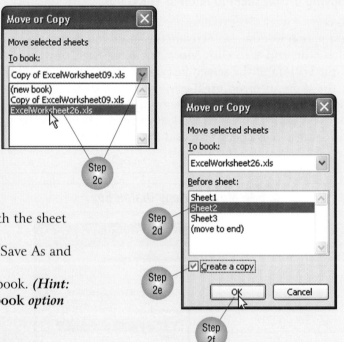

3. Save **ExcelWorksheet26** with Save As and name it **sec6x11**.
4. Print the entire **sec6x11** workbook. *(Hint: Do this with the Entire workbook option at the Print dialog box.)*
5. Close **sec6x11**.
6. Close **Copy of ExcelWorksheet09**.

Moving a Worksheet to Another Workbook

To move a worksheet to another existing workbook, open both the source and the destination workbooks. Make active the sheet you want to move in the source workbook, click Edit, and then Move or Copy Sheet, or right-click the sheet tab located at the bottom of the screen just above the Status bar and click Move or Copy at the shortcut menu. At the Move or Copy dialog box shown in Figure 6.3, select the destination workbook name from the *To book* drop-down list, select the worksheet that you want the worksheet placed before in the *Before sheet* list box, and then click OK.

HINT
To reposition a worksheet tab, drag the tab to the desired position.

Be careful when moving a worksheet to another workbook file. If formulas exist in the workbook that depend on the contents of the cells in the worksheet that is moved, they will no longer calculate properly.

exercise 12

MOVING A WORKSHEET TO ANOTHER WORKBOOK

1. Open **ExcelWorksheet01**.
2. Save the workbook with Save As and name it **sec6x12w01**.
3. Open **ExcelWorksheet10**.
4. Save the workbook with Save As and name it **sec6x12w02**.
5. Move *Sheet1* from **sec6x12w02** to **sec6x12w01** by completing the following steps:
   a. With **sec6x12w02** the active workbook, click Edit on the Menu bar, and then click Move or Copy Sheet at the drop-down menu.
   b. Click the down-pointing arrow next to the *To book* option box and then click *sec6x12w01.xls* at the drop-down list.
   c. Click *Sheet2* in the *Before sheet* list box.
   d. Click OK. (Excel switches to the workbook **sec6x12w01** and inserts the moved sheet with the sheet name *Sheet1 (2)*.)
6. Save the worksheet with the same name (**sec6x12w01**).
7. Print the entire **sec6x12w01** workbook.
8. Close **sec6x12w01**.
9. Close **sec6x12w02** without saving changes.

Step 5c

Step 5d

Searching for Specific Workbooks

Use options at the Basic File Search task pane shown in Figure 6.4 to search for specific workbooks. To display this task pane, click File and then File Search. (If the Advanced File Search task pane displays, scroll down to the end of the task pane and then click the Basic File Search hyperlink.) At the Basic File Search task pane, click in the *Search text* box and then enter one or more words specific to the workbooks for which you are searching. The word or words can be contained in the workbook name, the text of the workbook, keywords assigned to the workbook, or in the workbook properties. After entering the search word or words, click the Go button and workbooks matching the search criteria display in the Search Results task pane.

FIGURE

6.4   *Basic File Search Task Pane*

In this text box, enter one or more words specific to the workbooks for which you are searching.

Use this option to specify the locations to search.

Use this option to specify the types of files to search.

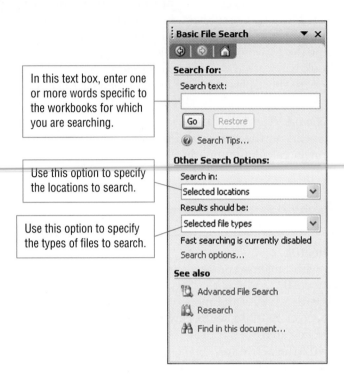

HINT

Click the Advanced File Search hyperlink to display the Advanced File Search task pane containing options for setting limits and conditions on the search.

Specify the locations to search with the *Search in* option. Click the down-pointing arrow at the right side of the *Search in* option box. This displays a drop-down list containing folders and network places. Click the plus symbol preceding a folder name to expand the display to include any subfolders. Insert a check mark in the check boxes next to any folders you want searched. Click a check box once and a check mark is inserted in the box and only that folder is searched. Click a check box a second time to specify that you want the folder and all subfolders searched. When you click the check box a second time, the check box changes to a cascading check box (check boxes overlapping). Click a check box a third time and the folder is deselected but all subfolders remain selected. Click a check box a fourth time and all subfolders are deselected.

Specify the types of files to search with the *Results should be* option. Click the down-pointing arrow at the right side of the *Results should be* option box and then, at the drop-down list that displays, insert a check mark in the check boxes before the types of files you want searched. For example, if you want only Excel files displayed, insert a check mark in the *Excel Files* check box.

exercise 13

1. At a blank Excel worksheet, click File and then File Search. (If the Advanced File Search task pane displays, scroll down to the end of the task pane and then click the Basic File Search hyperlink.)

2. Search for all Excel workbooks on your disk in drive A that contain the company name *Real Photography* by completing the following steps:

    a. Click in the *Search text* box. (If text displays in the text box, select the text and then delete it.)

    b. Type **Real Photography** in the *Search text* box.

    c. Click the down-pointing arrow at the right side of the *Search in* option box.

    d. Click the plus sign that precedes *My Computer*.

    e. Click twice in the *3½ Floppy (A:)* check box to insert a check mark (and cascade the check box). (Make sure that it is the only check box containing a check mark.)

    f. Click in the task pane outside the *Search in* list box to remove the list.

    g. Click the down-pointing arrow at the right side of the *Results should be* option box.

    h. At the drop-down list, click in the *Excel Files* check box to insert a check mark. (Make sure that it is the only check box containing a check mark.)

    i. Click in the task pane outside the *Results should be* list box to remove the list.

    j. Click the Go button. (In a few moments, the Search Results task pane will display with workbook names containing *Real Photography*.)

    k. When the list of workbooks displays in the Search Results task pane, double-click *ExcelWorksheet07* in the task pane. (This opens the **ExcelWorksheet07** workbook.)

    l. Close **ExcelWorksheet07**.

3. Close the Search Results task pane.

Step 2e

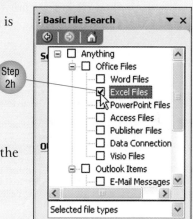

Step 2h

Saving Workbooks in a Variety of Formats

In some situations, you may want to share Excel data with other users who may open the data in an application other than Excel. Excel offers a variety of file formats for saving Excel data allowing for transportability of the data. For example, you can save data in an Excel worksheet as text and then open that text file in Word or save Excel data in XML (Extensible Markup Language), which is a method for putting data in a text file that follows specific standard guidelines that can be read by a variety of applications.

HINT

Formatting rules for XML data are generally organized into style sheets, which format the data appropriately.

Save Workbook in Different Format
1. Click File, Save As.
2. Type name for workbook.
3. Click down-pointing arrow at right of *Save as type* option box.
4. Click desired type in drop-down list.
5. Click Save button.

To save an Excel workbook in a different format, open the workbook, and then display the Save As dialog box. At the Save As dialog box, click the down-pointing arrow at the right side of the *Save as type* option, and then click the desired format at the drop-down list. In Exercise 14, you will save an Excel worksheet as a text file with tab delimiters, as a text file with comma delimiters, and as an XML spreadsheet. You will then open each of the three files in Microsoft Word.

exercise 14

SAVING A WORKSHEET IN A VARIETY OF FORMATS

1. Open **ExcelWorksheet19**.
2. Save the worksheet with Save As and name it **sec6x14**.
3. Save the worksheet in the Text (Tab delimited) format by completing the following steps:
   a. Click File and then Save As.
   b. At the Save As dialog box, type sec6x14tab in the *File name* text box.
   c. Click the down-pointing arrow at the right side of the *Save as type* list box, and then click *Text (Tab delimited)* at the drop-down list.
   d. Click the Save button.

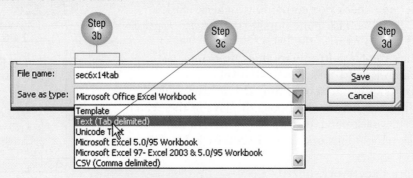

   e. At the message telling you that the selected file type does not support workbooks that contain multiple worksheets, click OK.
   f. At the message telling you that the file may contain features that are not compatible with Text (Tab delimited) and asking if you want to keep the workbook in the format, click Yes.
   g. Close the workbook. (At the message asking if you want to save the changes, click Yes. At the message telling you that the file type does not support workbooks containing multiple worksheets, click OK. At the message asking if you want to keep the workbook in the format, click Yes.)
4. Open **sec6x14** and then save it in the CSV (Comma delimited) format by completing the following steps:
   a. Click File and then Save As.

b. At the Save As dialog box, type sec6x14comma in the *File name* text box.

c. Click the down-pointing arrow at the right side of the *Save as type* list box, and then click *CSV (Comma delimited)* at the drop-down list.

d. Click the Save button.

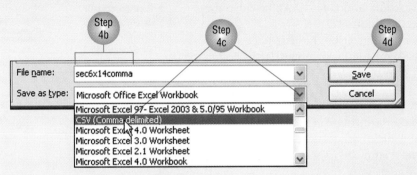

e. At the message telling you that the selected file type does not support workbooks that contain multiple worksheets, click OK.

f. At the message telling you that the file may contain features that are not compatible with CSV (Comma delimited) and asking if you want to keep the workbook in the format, click Yes.

g. Close the workbook. (At the message asking if you want to save the changes, click Yes. At the message telling you that the file type does not support workbooks containing multiple worksheets, click OK. At the message asking if you want to keep the workbook in the format, click Yes.)

5. Open **sec6x14** and then save it in the XML format by completing the following steps:

a. Click File and then Save As.

b. At the Save As dialog box, type sec6x14xml in the *File name* text box.

c. Click the down-pointing arrow at the right side of the *Save as type* list box, and then click *XML Spreadsheet* at the drop-down list.

d. Click the Save button.

e. Close the workbook.

6. Open and then print **sec6x14tab** in Microsoft Word by completing the following steps:

a. Open Microsoft Word.

b. Click the Open button on the Standard toolbar.

c. At the Open dialog box, navigate to the ExcelChapter06S folder on your disk.

d. Click the down-pointing arrow at the right side of the *Files of type* list box and then click *All Files* at the drop-down list.

e. Double-click **sec6x14tab** in the list box.

f. With the file open, click the Print button on the Standard toolbar.

g. Click File and then Close to close the **sec6x14tab** file.

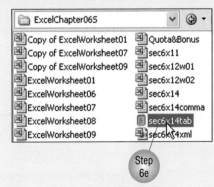

7. Open and then print **sec6x14comma** by completing the following steps:

a. In Microsoft Word, click the Open button on the Standard toolbar.

b. Make sure the ExcelChapter06S folder on your disk in the active folder.

c. Make sure the *Files of type* option is set at *All Files*.

d. Double-click *sec6x14comma* in the list box.

e. With the file open, click the Print button on the Standard toolbar.

f. Click File and then Close to close the **sec6x14comma** file.

8. Open and then print the first page of the **sec6x14xml** file by completing the following steps:

a. In Microsoft Word, click the Open button on the Standard toolbar.

b. Make sure the ExcelChapter06S folder on your disk is the active folder.

c. Make sure the *Files of type* option is set at *All Files*.

d. Double-click *sec6x14xml* in the list box.

e. With the file open, print only the first page by completing the following steps:

1) Click File and then Print.

2) At the Print dialog box, click in the *Pages* text box, and then type 1.

3) Click OK.

f. Click File and then Close to close the **sec6x14xml** file.

g. Close Microsoft Word.

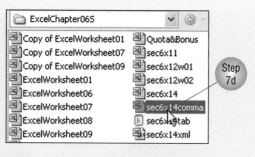

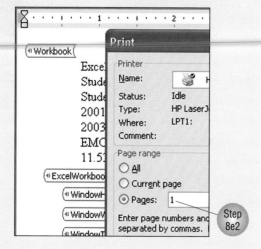

Formatting with Styles

To automate the formatting of cells in a workbook, consider defining and applying a style. A style, which is a predefined set of formatting attributes such as font, font size, alignment, borders, shading, and so forth, is particularly useful in large workbooks with data requiring a considerable amount of formatting.

Using a style to apply formatting has several advantages. A style helps to ensure consistent formatting from one worksheet to another. Once you define all attributes for a particular style, you do not have to define them again. If you need to change the formatting, change the style, and all cells formatted with that style automatically reflect the change.

Defining a Style

Excel contains some common number styles you can apply with buttons on the Formatting toolbar. For example, clicking the Currency Style button on the Formatting toolbar applies currency formatting to the cell or selected cells. The Percent Style and Comma Style buttons also apply styles to cells.

Two basic methods are available for defining your own style. You can define a style with formats already applied to a cell or you can display the Style dialog box, click the Modify button, and then choose formatting options at the Format Cells dialog box. Styles you create are only available in the workbook in which they are created. To define a style with existing formatting, you would complete these steps:

1. Select the cell or cells containing the desired formatting.
2. Click Format and then Style.
3. At the Style dialog box, shown in Figure 6.5, type a name for the new style in the *Style name* text box.
4. Click OK to close the dialog box.

6.5 *Style Dialog Box*

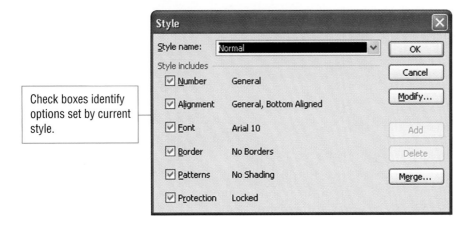

Check boxes identify options set by current style.

To define a new style without first applying the formatting, you would complete the following steps:

1. Click Format and then Style.
2. At the Style dialog box, type a name for the new style in the *Style name* text box.
3. Click the Modify button.
4. At the Format Cells dialog box, select the formats you want included in the style.
5. Click OK to close the Format Cells dialog box.
6. At the Style dialog box, remove the check mark from any formats that you do not want included in the style.
7. Click OK to define and apply the style to the selected cell. To define the style without applying it to the selected cell, click the Add button, and then click the Close button.

Applying a Style

To apply a style, select the cells you want to format, and then display the Style dialog box. At the Style dialog box, click the down-pointing arrow at the right side of the *Style name* text box, and then click the desired style name. Click OK to close the dialog box and apply the style.

1. Open **ExcelWorksheet36**.
2. Save the worksheet with Save As and name it **sec6x15**.
3. Format a cell and then define a style with the formatting by completing the following steps:
   a. Make sure cell A1 is active.
   b. Change the font and apply a bottom border by completing the following steps:
      1) Click Format and then Cells.
      2) At the Format Cells dialog box, click the Font tab.
      3) At the Font tab, change the font to *Tahoma*, the font style to *Bold*, the size to *12*, and the color to *Indigo*. (Indigo is the second color from the right in the top row.)
      4) Click the Border tab.
      5) At the Format Cells dialog box with the Border tab selected, click the sixth *Line Style* option from the top in the second column.
      6) Click the down-pointing arrow at the right side of the *Color* option and then click the Violet color at the color palette (seventh color from the left in the third row from the top).
      7) Click the bottom border of the preview cell in the dialog box.

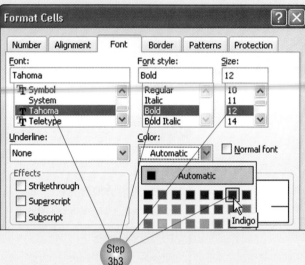

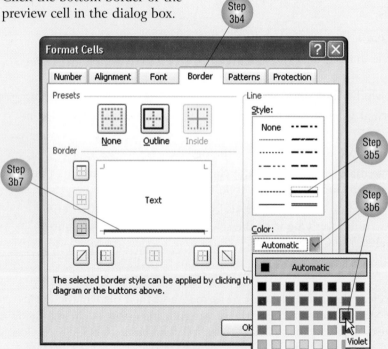

8) Click OK to close the Format Cells dialog box.

c. With cell A1 still the active cell, define a style named Title with the formatting you just applied by completing the following steps:
   1) Click Format and then Style.
   2) At the Style dialog box, type **Title** in the *Style name* text box.
   3) Click the Add button.
   4) Click the Close button.

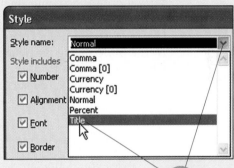

Step 3c2

Step 3c3

4. Apply the Title style to cell A1 by completing the following steps:
   a. Make sure cell A1 is the active cell. (Even though cell A1 is already formatted, the style has not been applied to it. Later, you will modify the style and the style must be applied to the cell for the change to affect it.)
   b. Click Format and then Style.
   c. At the Style dialog box, click the down-pointing arrow at the right side of the *Style name* text box, and then click *Title* at the drop-down list.
   d. Click OK to close the Style dialog box.

Step 4c

5. Apply the Title style to other cells by completing the following steps:
   a. Select cells A2 through D2.
   b. Click Format and then Style.
   c. At the Style dialog box, click the down-pointing arrow at the right side of the *Style name* text box, and then click *Title* at the drop-down list.
   d. Click OK to close the Style dialog box.

6. Define a new style named Font without first applying the formatting by completing the following steps:
   a. Click in any empty cell.
   b. Click Format and then Style.
   c. At the Style dialog box, type **Font** in the *Style name* text box.
   d. Click the Modify button.
   e. At the Format Cells dialog box, click the Font tab.
   f. At the Format Cells dialog box with the Font tab selected, change the font to *Tahoma*, the size to *12*, and the color to *Indigo*.
   g. Click the Patterns tab.
   h. At the Format Cells dialog box with the Patterns tab selected, click a light blue color of your choosing in the color palette.
   i. Click OK to close the Format Cells dialog box.
   j. At the Style dialog box, click the Add button.
   k. Click the Close button. (Do not click the OK button.)

7. Apply the Font style by completing the following steps:
   a. Select cells A3 through D9.
   b. Click Format and then Style.
   c. At the Style dialog box, click the down-pointing arrow at the right side of the *Style name* text box, and then click *Font* at the drop-down list.
   d. Click OK to close the Style dialog box.

8. Make the following changes to the worksheet:
   a. Select cells B3 through D9.
   b. Click the Currency Style button on the Formatting toolbar.
   c. Click twice on the Decrease Decimal button on the Formatting toolbar.
   d. Automatically adjust columns A through D.
9. Save and then print **sec6x15**.
10. With **sec6x15** still open, modify the Title style by completing the following steps:
    a. Click in any empty cell.
    b. Display the Style dialog box.
    c. Click the down-pointing arrow at the right side of the *Style name* text box and then click *Title* at the drop-down list.
    d. Click the Modify button.
    e. At the Format Cells dialog box, click the Alignment tab.
    f. At the Format Cells dialog box with the Alignment tab selected, click the down-pointing arrow to the right of the *Vertical* option box, and then click *Center* at the drop-down list.
    g. Click OK to close the Format Cells dialog box.
    h. At the Style dialog box, click the Add button.
    i. Click the Close button to close the Style dialog box.
11. Save, print, and then close **sec6x15**.

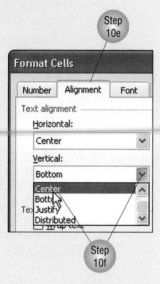

Step 10e

Step 10f

Copying Styles to Another Workbook

 HINT

The Undo command will not reverse the effects of the Merge Style dialog box.

Styles you define are saved with the workbook in which they are created. You can, however, copy styles from one workbook to another. To do this, you would complete the following steps:

1. Open the workbook containing the styles you want to copy.
2. Open the workbook into which you want to copy the styles.
3. Display the Style dialog box.
4. At the Style dialog box, click the Merge button.
5. At the Merge Styles dialog box shown in Figure 6.6, double-click the name of the workbook that contains the styles you want to copy.
6. Click OK to close the Style dialog box.

FIGURE

| 6.6 | *Merge Styles Dialog Box* |

Removing a Style

If you apply a style to text and then decide you do not want the formatting applied, remove the style. To do this, select the cells formatted with the style you want to remove and then display the Style dialog box. At the Style dialog box, click the down-pointing arrow at the right side of the *Style name* text box, and then click *Normal* at the drop-down list.

Deleting a Style

Delete a style at the Style dialog box. To do this, display the Style dialog box, click the down-pointing arrow at the right side of the *Style name* text box. At the drop-down list that displays, click the style you want deleted, and then click the Delete button.

exercise 16

1. Open **sec6x15**.
2. Open **ExcelWorksheet13**.
3. Save the workbook with Save As and name it **sec6x16**.
4. Delete column H.
5. Copy the styles in **sec6x15** into **sec6x16** by completing the following steps:
   a. Display the Style dialog box.
   b. At the Style dialog box, click the Merge button.
   c. At the Merge Styles dialog box, double-click **sec6x15.xls** in the *Merge styles from* list box.
   d. Click OK to close the Style dialog box.

Step 5c

6. Modify the Font style by completing the following steps:
   a. Click in any empty cell.
   b. Display the Style dialog box.
   c. At the Style dialog box, click the down-pointing arrow at the right side of the *Style name* text box, and then click *Font*.
   d. Click the Modify button.
   e. At the Format Cells dialog box, click the Font tab.
   f. Change the font to *Arial* and the size to *10*.
   g. Click OK to close the Format Cells dialog box.
   h. At the Style dialog box, click the Add button.
   i. Click the Close button to close the Style dialog box.
7. Apply the following styles:
   a. Select cells A1 through G2 and then apply the Title style.
   b. Select cells A3 through G8 and then apply the Font style.
8. Remove the Font style from cells B3 through B8 by completing the following steps:
   a. Select cells B3 through B8.
   b. Display the Style dialog box.
   c. At the Style dialog box, click the down-pointing arrow at the right side of the *Style name* text box, and then click *Normal*.

Step 8c

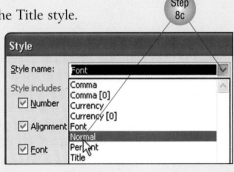

        d.   Click OK to close the dialog box.
    9.   Select cells D3 through D8 and then press F4. (This repeats the last action, which was changing the style to *Normal*.)
   10.   Select cells F3 through F8 and then press F4.
   11.   Make the following changes to the workbook:
        a.   Change the width of columns B through G to 11.00.
        b.   Select cells B3 through G8, click the Currency button on the Formatting toolbar, and then click twice on the Decrease Decimal button.
   12.   Save, print, and then close **sec6x16**.
   13.   Close **sec6x15**.

Inserting Comments

Insert a Comment
1. Click Insert, Comment.
2. Type comment.
    OR
1. Display Reviewing toolbar.
2. Click New Comment button.
3. Type comment.

If you want to make comments in a worksheet, or if a reviewer wants to make comments in a worksheet prepared by someone else, insert a comment. A comment is useful for providing specific instructions, identifying critical information, or for multiple individuals reviewing the same worksheet to insert comments. Some employees in a company may be part of a ***workgroup***, which is a networked collection of computers sharing files, printers, and other resources. In a workgroup, you may collaborate with coworkers on a specific workbook. Comments provide a method for reviewing the workbook and responding to others in the workgroup.

Insert a comment by clicking Insert and then Comment or by clicking the New Comment button on the Reviewing toolbar. The Reviewing toolbar contains buttons for inserting and managing comments. Display this toolbar, shown in Figure 6.7, by clicking View, pointing to Toolbars, and then clicking Reviewing.

FIGURE

   6.7   **Reviewing Toolbar Buttons**

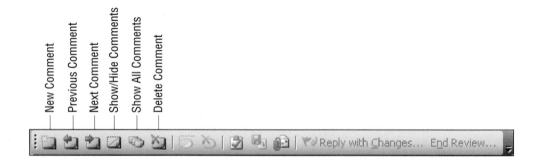

Inserting a Comment

New Comment

Insert a comment by clicking Insert and then Comment or by clicking the New Comment button on the Reviewing toolbar. This displays a yellow pop-up comment box with the user's name. Type the desired information or comment in this comment box. Click outside the comment box and the box is removed. A small, red triangle appears in the upper right corner of a cell containing a comment. You can also insert a comment by right-clicking a cell and then clicking Insert Comment at the shortcut menu.

Displaying a Comment

Hover the mouse over a cell containing a comment and the comment box displays. Turn on the display of all comments by clicking the Show All Comments button on the Reviewing toolbar. Turn on the display of an individual comment by making the cell active and then clicking the Show/Hide Comments button on the Reviewing toolbar. Hide the display of an individual comment by making the cell active and then clicking the Hide Comment button on the Reviewing toolbar. (The Show/Hide Comments button becomes the Hide Comment button if the comment in the active cell is visible.) Move to comments in a worksheet by clicking the Next Comment or Previous Comment buttons on the Reviewing toolbar.

Show All   Show/
Comments   Hide
Comments

Next   Previous
Comment   Comment

HINT

You can also display all comments by clicking View and then Comments.

Printing a Comment

By default, comments do not print. If you want comments to print, display the Page Setup dialog box with the Sheet tab selected and then click the down-pointing arrow at the right side of the *Comments* option box. At the drop-down menu that displays, choose *At end of sheet* to print comments on the page after cell contents, or choose the *As displayed on sheet* option to print the comments in the comment box in the worksheet.

 **17**

INSERTING, DISPLAYING, AND PRINTING COMMENTS

1. Open **ExcelWorksheet26**.
2. Save the worksheet with Save As and name it **sec6x17**.
3. Turn on the display of the Reviewing toolbar by clicking View, pointing to Toolbars, and then clicking Reviewing. (Skip this step if the Reviewing toolbar is already displayed.)
4. Insert a comment by completing the following steps:
   a. Click cell F3 to make it active.
   b. Click the New Comment button on the Reviewing toolbar.
   c. In the comment box, type **Bill Lakeside Trucking for only 7 hours for the backhoe and front loader on May 1.**
   d. Click outside the comment box.
5. Insert another comment by completing the following steps:
   a. Click cell C6 to make it active.
   b. Click the New Comment button on the Reviewing toolbar.
   c. In the comment box, type **I think Country Electrical has changed their name to Northwest Electrical.**
   d. Click outside the comment box.

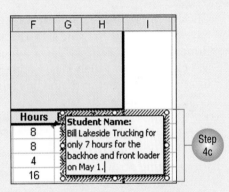

6. Assume that more than one person is reviewing and commenting on this worksheet. Change the user name and then insert additional comments by completing the following steps:

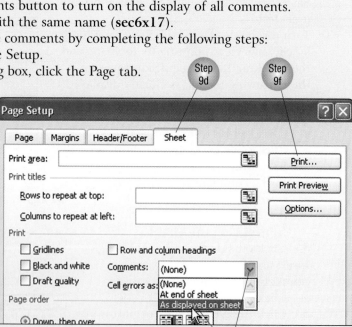

Step 6c

a. Click Tools and then Options.
b. At the Options dialog box, click the General tab.
c. Select the current name in the *User name* text box (remember the name you are selecting) and then type Jean Coen.
d. Click OK to close the dialog box.
e. Click cell D11 to make it active.
f. Click the New Comment button on the Reviewing toolbar.
g. In the comment box, type This rental should be credited to *Monahan* instead of *Leuke*.
h. Click outside the comment box.
i. Click cell G11 to make it active.
j. Click the New Comment button on the Reviewing toolbar.
k. In the comment box, type The hourly rental for the pressure sprayer is $25.
l. Click outside the comment box.
m. Complete steps similar to those in Steps 6a through 6d to return the user name back to the original name (the name that displayed before you changed it to *Jean Coen*).

7. Click the Show All Comments button to turn on the display of all comments.
8. Save the worksheet again with the same name (**sec6x17**).
9. Print the worksheet and the comments by completing the following steps:
a. Click File and then Page Setup.
b. At the Page Setup dialog box, click the Page tab.
c. Click *Landscape* in the *Orientation* section.
d. Click the Sheet tab.
e. Click the down-pointing arrow at the right side of the *Comments* option and then click *As displayed on sheet*.
f. Click the Print button that displays toward the upper right corner of the dialog box.
g. At the Print dialog box, click OK.

Step 9d   Step 9f

Step 9e

10. Click the Hide All Comments button (previously the Show All Comments button) to turn off the display of comments.
11. Save and then close **sec6x17**.

Editing a Comment

To edit a comment, click the cell containing the comment, and then click the Edit Comment button on the Reviewing toolbar. (The New Comment button changes to the Edit Comment button when the active cell contains a comment.) You can also edit a comment by right-clicking the cell containing the comment and then clicking Edit Comment at the shortcut menu.

Edit Comment

Deleting a Comment

Cell comments exist in addition to data in a cell. Deleting data in a cell does not delete the comment. To delete a comment, click the cell containing the comment, and then click the Delete Comment button on the Reviewing toolbar. You can also delete a comment by clicking Edit, pointing to Clear, and then clicking Comments.

Delete Comment

exercise 18

EDITING, DELETING, AND RESPONDING TO COMMENTS

1. Open **sec6x17**.
2. Save the worksheet with Save As and name it **sec6x18**.
3. Make sure the Reviewing toolbar is displayed.
4. Display comments by completing the following steps:
   a. Click cell A3 to make it the active cell.
   b. Click the Next Comment button on the Reviewing toolbar.
   c. Read the comment and then click the Next Comment button.
   d. Continue clicking the Next Comment button until a message displays telling you that Microsoft Excel has reached the end of the workbook and asking if you want to continue reviewing from the beginning of the workbook. At this message, click the Cancel button.
   e. Click outside the comment box.
5. Edit a comment by completing the following steps:
   a. Click cell D11 to make it active.
   b. Click the Edit Comment button.
   c. Edit the comment so it displays as This rental should be credited to *Steele* instead of *Leuke*.
6. Delete a comment by completing the following steps:
   a. Click cell C6 to make it active.
   b. Click the Delete Comment button on the Reviewing toolbar.
7. Respond to the comments by making the following changes:
   a. Change the contents of F3 from *8* to *7*.
   b. Change the contents of F4 from *8* to *7*.
   c. Change the contents of D11 from *Leuke* to *Steele*.
   d. Change the contents of G11 from *$20* to *$25*.

Step 4b

Step 4a

Step 5c

Date	Hours	Rate	Total
5/1/2003	8	$75	$ 600
5/1/2003	8	$65	$ 520
5/1/2003	4	$45	$ 180
5/1/2003	16	$75	$1,200
5/2/2003	5	$55	$ 275
5/2/2003	5	$25	$ 125
5/2/2003	10	$70	$ 700
			$ 200
			$ 160
			$ 120
			$ 160
			$ 650
5/3/2003	10	$55	$ 550

Jean Coen:
This rental should be credited to *Steele* instead of *Leuke*.

8. Save the worksheet again with the same name (**sec6x18**).
9. Print the worksheet and the comments by completing the following steps:
   a. Click File and then Page Setup.
   b. At the Page Setup dialog box, click the Sheet tab.
   c. Click the down-pointing arrow at the right side of the *Comments* option and then click *At end of sheet*.
   d. Click the Print button that displays toward the upper right corner of the dialog box.
   e. At the Print dialog box, click OK. (The worksheet will print on one page and the comments will print on a second page.)
10. Close **sec6x18**.

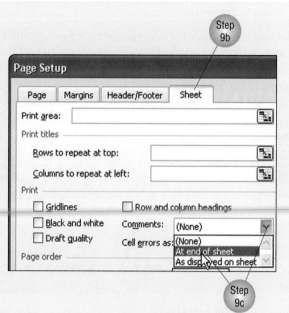

Using Excel Templates

Excel has included a number of *template* worksheet forms formatted for specific uses. For example, Excel has provided template forms for a balance sheet, expense statement, loan amortization, sales invoice, and timecard. To view the templates available with Excel, click File and then New to display the New Workbook task pane. At the task pane, click the <u>On my computer</u> hyperlink. At the Templates dialog box, click the Spreadsheet Solutions tab and the template forms display as shown in Figure 6.8.

F I G U R E

6.8 *Templates Dialog Box with Spreadsheet Solutions Tab Selected*

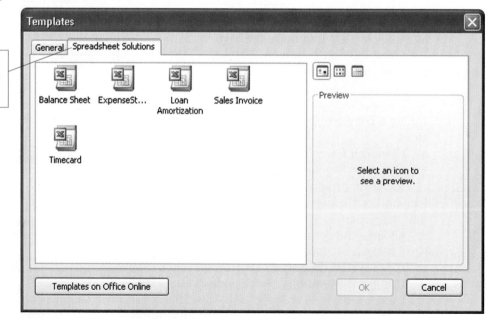

Click the Spreadsheet Solutions tab to display available templates.

CONCEPTS check

Completion: On a blank sheet of paper, indicate the correct term, symbol, or command for each description.

1. File management tasks such as copying, moving, or deleting workbooks can be performed at the Open dialog box or this dialog box.
2. Click this button on the Open dialog box toolbar to display the folder that is up a level from the current folder.
3. Workbooks and/or folders deleted from the hard drive can be restored by opening this feature in Windows.
4. Click the down-pointing arrow at the right side of this option at the Save As dialog box to display a list of available workbook formats.
5. Search for specific workbooks with options at this task pane.
6. Click this button at the Style dialog box to display the Format Cells dialog box.
7. In a cell containing a comment, this displays in the upper right corner of the cell.
8. Print comments by choosing the desired printing location with the *Comments* option at the Page Setup dialog box with this tab selected.
9. Click this button on the Reviewing toolbar to display all comments in the worksheet.
10. Click this hyperlink in the New Workbook task pane to display the Templates dialog box.

SKILLS check

Assessment 1

1. Display the Open dialog box with ExcelChapter06S the active folder.
2. Create a new folder named *Sales* in the ExcelChapter06S folder.
3. Copy **ExcelWorksheet01** and **ExcelWorksheet10** to the Sales folder.
4. Rename **ExcelWorksheet01** to **SalesByJob** in the Sales folder. (At the message asking if you are sure you want to rename the read-only file, click Yes.)
5. Rename **ExcelWorksheet10** to **SalesbySalesperson** in the Sales folder. (At the message asking if you are sure you want to rename the read-only file, click Yes.)
6. Change the active folder back to ExcelChapter06S.
7. Close the Open dialog box.

Assessment 2

1. Display the Open dialog box.
2. Delete all of the workbooks in the ExcelChapter06S folder that begin with *Copy of*.
3. Move **ExcelWorksheet07** and **ExcelWorksheet29** to the *Sales* folder.
4. Change the active folder back to ExcelChapter06S.
5. Close the Open dialog box.

Assessment 3

1. Display the Open dialog box and make Sales the active folder.
2. Open **ExcelWorksheet07** and **ExcelWorksheet29**.
3. Make **ExcelWorksheet07** the active workbook and then copy *Sheet1* from **ExcelWorksheet07** and position it before Sheet2 in **ExcelWorksheet29**.
4. With **ExcelWorksheet29** the active workbook, rename *Sheet1* to *Accounts*.
5. With **ExcelWorksheet29** the active workbook, rename *Sheet1 (2)* to *Depreciation*.
6. Save **ExcelWorksheet29** with Save As and name it **sec6sc03**.
7. Print the entire workbook and then close **sec6sc03**.
8. Close **ExcelWorksheet07**.

Assessment 4

1. Use the Basic File Search task pane to search for all workbooks on your disk containing the word *Equipment*.
2. Search for all workbooks on your disk containing the words *Lakeside Trucking*.

Assessment 5

1. At a clear worksheet, define a style named *Heading* that contains the following formatting:
   a. 14-point Times New Roman bold in Blue-Gray color
   b. Horizontal alignment of Center
   c. Double-line top and bottom border in Dark Red color
   d. Light purple shading
2. Define a style named *Column01* that contains the following formatting:
   a. 12-point Times New Roman in Blue-Gray color
   b. Light purple shading
3. Define a style named *Column02* that contains 12-point Times New Roman in Blue-Gray color.
4. Save the worksheet and name it **sec6style01**.
5. With **sec6style01** open, open **ExcelWorksheet09**.
6. Save the worksheet with Save As and name it **sec6sc05**.
7. Copy the styles from **sec6style01** into **sec6sc05**. *(Hint: Do this through the Style dialog box.)*
8. Select cells A1 through M1 and then click the Merge and Center button on the Formatting toolbar.
9. Apply the following styles:
   a. Select cells A1 through M2 and then apply the Heading style.
   b. Select cells A3 through A9 and then apply the Column01 style.
   c. Select cells B3 through G9 and then apply the Column02 style.
   d. Select cells H3 through M9 and then apply the Column01 style.
10. Automatically adjust the widths of columns A through M.
11. Save the worksheet again and then print **sec6sc05** on one page in landscape orientation. (Make sure you choose the *Fit to* option at the Page Setup dialog box.)
12. With **sec6sc05** still open, modify the following styles:
    a. Modify the Heading style so it changes the font color to Plum (instead of Blue-Gray) and inserts a solid, thick top and bottom border in Plum (instead of a double-line top and bottom border in Dark Red).
    b. Modify the Column02 style so it adds a font style of Bold Italic (leave all of the other formatting attributes).
13. Automatically adjust the widths of columns A through M.

EXCEL

14. Save the worksheet again and then print **sec6sc05** on one page and in landscape orientation.
15. Close **sec6sc05**.
16. Close **sec6style01**.

Assessment 6

1. Open **ExcelWorksheet37**.
2. Save the worksheet with Save As and name it **sec6sc06**.
3. Insert the following comments in the specified cells:

    B7   =   Should we include Sun Valley, Idaho, as a destination?
    B12   =   Please include the current exchange rate.
    G8   =   What other airlines fly into Aspen, Colorado?

4. Save **sec6sc06**.
5. Turn on the display of all comments.
6. Print the worksheet in landscape orientation with the comments as displayed on the worksheet.
7. Turn off the display of all comments.
8. Delete the comment in cell B12.
9. Print the worksheet again with the comments printed at the end of the worksheet. (The comments will print on a separate page from the worksheet.)
10. Save and then close **sec6sc06**.

Assessment 7

1. In this chapter, you learned about the styles feature, which automates formatting in a workbook. Another formatting feature is Conditional Formatting. Use Excel's Help feature to learn about Conditional Formatting.
2. Open **ExcelWorksheet06**.
3. Save the worksheet with Save As and name it **sec6sc07**.
4. Select cells B3 through M20 and then use Conditional Formatting to display all percentages between 95% and 100% in red and with a red border.
5. Save, print in landscape orientation, and then close **sec6sc07**.

CHAPTER challenge

Case study

You have recently opened a new business called Sit and Soak Spas. You decide to create a financial form based on Excel's Timecard template. Use the Timecard template to create an Excel workbook called Employee Time Card. Save the workbook in a new folder named Financial Forms. Since each of the employees will complete the time card on the computer, you decide providing additional information might be helpful. Insert comments in at least three different areas that would benefit the employees when they are completing the time card. Also, create and apply a new style (containing formats of your choice) to the bolded headings. Do not apply the style to the main title of the form, "TIMECARD". Save the workbook again.

Although Excel has several templates from which to choose, you may have a need for a variety of other templates. Use the Help feature to learn how to obtain additional templates. Access the World Wide Web and locate a template (not already located on your computer) that would be helpful in your new business. Download the template to your computer. Complete the template with information of your own and save it as an Excel workbook in the folder Financial Forms.

To give customers more exposure to your new business and to help them in the decision-making process of buying a spa, you decide to make the template downloaded in the second part of the Chapter Challenge available on the Web. If the template is not appropriate, choose another one or use the Loan Amortization template located under the Spreadsheets Solutions tab. Save the template as a Web page in the Financial Forms folder.

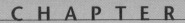

CREATING A CHART IN EXCEL

PERFORMANCE OBJECTIVES

Upon successful completion of Chapter 7, you will be able to:
- **Create a chart with data in an Excel worksheet**
- **Create a chart in a separate worksheet**
- **Print a selected chart and print a worksheet containing a chart**
- **Size, move, and delete a chart**
- **Change the type of chart**
- **Choose a custom chart type**
- **Change data in a chart**
- **Add, delete, and customize elements in a chart**

In the previous Excel chapters, you learned to create data in worksheets. While a worksheet does an adequate job of representing data, you can present some data more visually by charting the data. A chart is sometimes referred to as a **graph** and is a picture of numeric data. In this chapter, you will learn to create and customize charts in Excel.

Creating a Chart

Chart
Wizard

**QUICK
STEPS**

Create a Chart
1. Select cells.
2. Click Chart Wizard button.
3. Complete the four steps of the wizard.

In Excel, create a chart by selecting cells containing the data you want to chart, and then clicking the Chart Wizard button on the Standard toolbar. Four steps are involved in creating a chart with the Chart Wizard. Suppose you wanted to create a chart with the worksheet shown in Figure 7.1. To create the chart with the Chart Wizard, you would complete the following steps:

1. Select the cells containing data (in the worksheet in Figure 7.1, this would be cells A1 through C4).
2. Click the Chart Wizard button on the Standard toolbar.
3. At the Chart Wizard - Step 1 of 4 - Chart Type dialog box shown in Figure 7.2, choose the desired chart type and chart sub-type, and then click the Next button.

4. At the Chart Wizard - Step 2 of 4 - Chart Source Data dialog box shown in Figure 7.3, make sure the data range displays correctly (for the chart in Figure 7.1, the range will display as =Sheet1!$A$1:$C$4), and then click the Next button.

5. At the Chart Wizard - Step 3 of 4 - Chart Options dialog box shown in Figure 7.4, make any changes to the chart, and then click the Next button.

6. At the Chart Wizard - Step 4 of 4 - Chart Location dialog box shown in Figure 7.5, specify where you want the chart inserted, and then click the Finish button.

If the chart was created with all of the default settings at the Chart Wizard dialog boxes, the chart would display below the cells containing data as shown in Figure 7.6.

FIGURE

7.1 *Excel Worksheet*

	A	B	C	D
1	**Salesperson**	**June**	**July**	
2	Chaney	$34,239	$39,224	
3	Ferraro	$23,240	$28,985	
4	Jimenez	$56,892	$58,450	
5				

FIGURE

7.2 *Chart Wizard - Step 1 of 4 - Chart Type Dialog Box*

Choose a chart from this list.

Choose a chart sub-type from these examples.

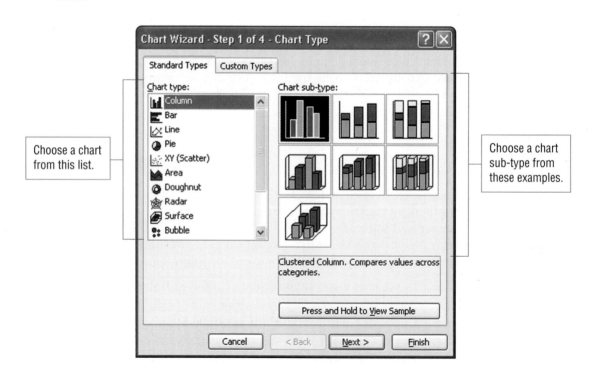

7.3 Chart Wizard - Step 2 of 4 - Chart Source Data Dialog Box

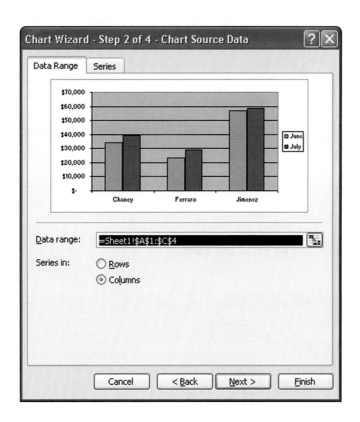

7.4 Chart Wizard - Step 3 of 4 - Chart Options Dialog Box

Add and/or format chart elements with options from this dialog box with various tabs selected.

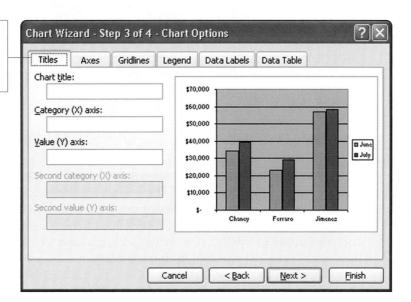

7.5 Chart Wizard - Step 4 of 4 - Chart Location Dialog Box

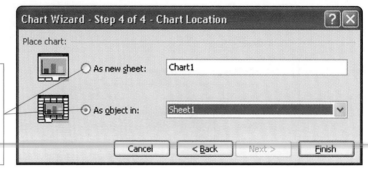

To insert a chart in the active window, leave this at the default setting of *As object in*. Choose the *As new sheet* option to create the chart in a separate sheet.

7.6 Chart Based on Excel Worksheet

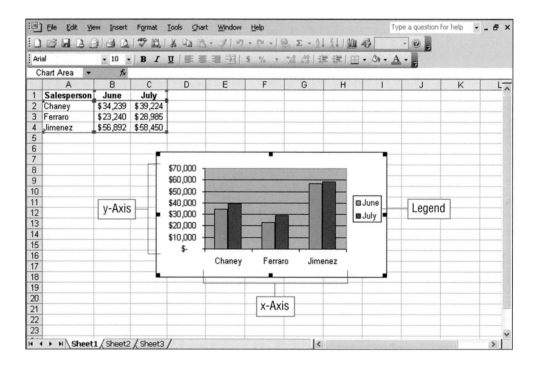

In the chart created in Excel shown in Figure 7.6, the left vertical side of the chart is referred to as the y-axis. The y-axis contains tick marks with amounts displaying the value at that particular point on the axis. The values in the chart in Figure 7.6 are broken into tick marks by ten thousands beginning with zero and continuing to 70,000. The values for the y-axis will vary depending on the data in the table. The names in the first column are used for the x-axis, which runs along the bottom of the chart.

1. Open **ExcelWorksheet15**.
2. Save the worksheet with Save As and name it **sec7x01**.
3. Create a chart using the Chart Wizard by completing the following steps:
   a. Select cells A1 through E5.
   b. Click the Chart Wizard button on the Standard toolbar.

Step
3b

	A	B	C	D	E	F	G	H	I	J
1	Region	1st Qtr.	2nd Qtr.	3rd Qtr.	4th Qtr.					
2	Northwest	300,560	320,250	287,460	360,745					
3	Southwest	579,290	620,485	490,125	635,340					
4	Northeast	890,355	845,380	795,460	890,425					
5	Southeast	290,450	320,765	270,450	300,455					

Step
3a

   c. At the Chart Wizard - Step 1 of 4 - Chart Type dialog box, click the Next button.
   d. At the Chart Wizard - Step 2 of 4 - Chart Source Data dialog box, make sure the data range displays as *=Sheet1!$A$1:$E$5* and then click the Next button.
   e. At the Chart Wizard - Step 3 of 4 - Chart Options dialog box, click the Next button.
   f. At the Chart Wizard - Step 4 of 4 - Chart Location dialog box, make sure the *As object in* option is selected and that *Sheet1* displays in the text box, and then click the Finish button.
   g. Click outside the chart to deselect the chart.
4. Print **sec7x01** in landscape orientation.
5. Save and then close **sec7x01**.

Printing Only the Chart

In a worksheet containing data in cells as well as a chart, you can print only the chart. To do this, click the chart to select it and then display the Print dialog box. At the Print dialog box, *Selected Chart* will automatically be selected in the *Print what* section. Click OK to print only the selected chart.

Previewing a Chart

Preview a chart by clicking the Print Preview button on the Standard toolbar or by clicking File and then Print Preview. This displays the worksheet containing the chart in Print Preview. After previewing the chart, click the Close button, or print the worksheet by clicking the Print button on the Print Preview toolbar and then clicking OK at the Print dialog box.

exercise 2

1. Open **sec7x01**.
2. Preview the chart by completing the following steps:
   a. Click the Print Preview button on the Standard toolbar.
   b. In Print Preview, click the Zoom button to make the display of the worksheet bigger.
   c. Click the Zoom button again to return to the full-page view.
   d. Click the Close button to close Print Preview.
3. Print only the chart by completing the following steps:
   a. Click the chart to select it.
   b. Click File and then Print.
   c. At the Print dialog box, make sure *Selected Chart* is selected in the *Print what* section of the dialog box and then click OK.
4. Close **sec7x01**.

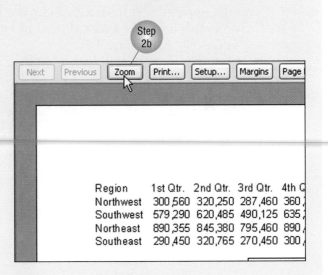

Step 2b

Region	1st Qtr.	2nd Qtr.	3rd Qtr.	4th Q
Northwest	300,560	320,250	287,460	360,
Southwest	579,290	620,485	490,125	635,
Northeast	890,355	845,380	795,460	890,
Southeast	290,450	320,765	270,450	300,

Creating a Chart in a Separate Worksheet

The chart you created in Excel in Exercise 1 was inserted in the same worksheet as the cells containing data. You should not delete the data (displaying only the chart) because the data in the chart will also be deleted. If you want to create a chart in a worksheet by itself, click the *As new sheet* option at the Chart Wizard - Step 4 of 4 - Chart Location dialog box. When the chart is completed, it displays in a separate sheet and fills most of the page. The sheet containing the chart is labeled *Chart1*. This sheet label displays on a tab located toward the bottom of the screen. The worksheet containing the data is located in *Sheet 1*. You can move between the chart and the worksheet by clicking the desired tab.

exercise 3

1. Open **ExcelWorksheet15**.
2. Save the worksheet with Save As and name it **sec7x03**.
3. Create a chart as a separate sheet using the Chart Wizard by completing the following steps:
   a. Select cells A1 through E5.
   b. Click the Chart Wizard button on the Standard toolbar.
   c. At the Chart Wizard - Step 1 of 4 - Chart Type dialog box, click the Next button.

EXCEL

d.	At the Chart Wizard - Step 2 of 4 - Chart Source Data dialog box, make sure the data range displays as =*Sheet1!$A$1:$E$5*, and then click the Next button.

e.	At the Chart Wizard - Step 3 of 4 - Chart Options dialog box, click the Next button.

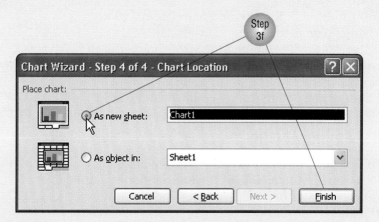

f.	At the Chart Wizard - Step 4 of 4 - Chart Location dialog box, click *As new sheet*, and then click the Finish button.

4.	Save the workbook (two sheets) again and then print only the sheet containing the chart. (To do this, make sure the sheet containing the chart displays, and then click the Print button on the Standard toolbar.)

5.	Close **sec7x03**.

Deleting a Chart

Delete a chart created in Excel by clicking once in the chart to select it and then pressing the Delete key. If a chart created in a new worksheet is deleted, the chart is deleted but the worksheet is not. To delete the chart as well as the worksheet, position the mouse pointer on the *Chart1* tab, click the *right* mouse button, and then click Delete at the shortcut menu. At the message box telling you that selected sheets will be permanently deleted, click OK.

Sizing and Moving a Chart

You can change the size of a chart created in Excel in the same worksheet as the data containing cells. To do this, click the chart once to select it (this inserts black square sizing handles around the chart), and then drag the sizing handles in the desired direction.

A chart created with data in a worksheet can be moved by selecting the chart and then dragging it with the mouse. To move a chart, click once inside the chart to select it. Position the arrow pointer inside the chart, hold down the left mouse button, drag the outline of the chart to the desired location, and then release the button.

1. Open **sec7x01**.
2. Save the worksheet with Save As and name it **sec7x04**.
3. Size the chart by completing the following steps:
   a. Select the chart by positioning the arrow pointer in the white portion of the chart just inside the chart border until a yellow box with the words *Chart Area* displays next to the arrow pointer (takes approximately one second) and then clicking the left mouse button. (Do not click on a chart element. This selects the element, not the entire chart.)

   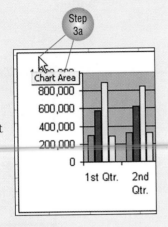
   Step 3a

   b. Position the arrow pointer on the black, square sizing handle located in the middle of the bottom border until the arrow pointer turns into a double-headed arrow pointing up and down.
   c. Hold down the left mouse button, drag the outline of the bottom border of the chart down approximately five rows, and then release the mouse button.

   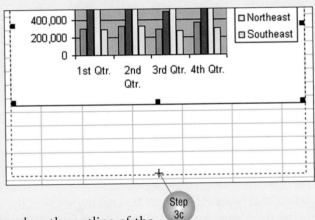
   Step 3c

   d. Position the arrow pointer on the black square sizing handle located in the middle of the right border until the arrow pointer turns into a double-headed arrow pointing left and right.
   e. Hold down the left mouse button, drag the outline of the border to the right approximately two columns, and then release the mouse button.
   f. Deselect the chart. (To do this, click in an empty cell somewhere in the worksheet.)
4. Change the page orientation to landscape and then print **sec7x04**.
5. Save the worksheet again with the same name (**sec7x04**).
6. Close **sec7x04**.

Changing the Chart Type

In Exercises 1 and 3, you created a column chart, which is the default. The Chart Wizard offers 14 basic chart types along with built-in autoformats you can apply to save time to get the desired look for the chart. Table 7.1 shows an illustration and explanation of the 14 chart types.

EXCEL

	Area	An Area chart emphasizes the magnitude of change, rather than time and the rate of change. It also shows the relationship of parts to a whole by displaying the sum of the plotted values.
	Bar	A Bar chart shows individual figures at a specific time, or shows variations between components but not in relationship to the whole.
	Bubble	A Bubble chart compares sets of three values in a manner similar to a scatter chart, with the third value displayed as the size of the bubble marker.
	Column	A Column chart compares separate (noncontinuous) items as they vary over time.
	Cone	A Cone chart displays columns with a conical shape.
	Cylinder	A Cylinder chart displays columns with a cylindrical shape.
	Doughnut	A Doughnut chart shows the relationship of parts of the whole.
	Line	A Line chart shows trends and change over time at even intervals. It emphasizes the rate of change over time rather than the magnitude of change.
	Pie	A Pie chart shows proportions and relationships of parts to the whole.
	Pyramid	A Pyramid chart displays columns with a pyramid shape.
	Radar	A Radar chart emphasizes differences and amounts of change over time and variations and trends. Each category has its own value axis radiating from the center point. Lines connect all values in the same series.
	Stock	A Stock chart shows four values for a stock—open, high, low, and close.
	Surface	A Surface chart shows trends in values across two dimensions in a continuous curve.
	XY (Scatter)	A Scatter chart either shows the relationships among numeric values in several data series or plots the interception points between *x* and *y* values. It shows uneven intervals of data and is commonly used in scientific data.

You can choose a chart type in Step 1 of the Chart Wizard steps or change the chart type for an existing chart. When creating a chart with the Chart Wizard, choose the desired chart type and sub-type at the first Chart Wizard dialog box. To change the chart type for an existing chart, make sure the chart is active, click Chart, and then click Chart Type. This displays the Chart Type dialog box. Choose the desired chart type and chart sub-type at this dialog box and then click the OK button.

You can also change the chart type in an existing chart with a shortcut menu. To do this, position the arrow pointer in a white portion of the chart (inside the chart but outside any chart element), and then click the *right* mouse button. At the shortcut menu that displays, click Chart Type. This displays the Chart Type dialog box that contains the same options as the Chart Wizard - Step 1 of 4 - Chart Type dialog box.

exercise 5

CHANGING CHART TYPE IN EXCEL

1. Open **sec7x03**.
2. Save the workbook with Save As and name it **sec7x05**.
3. Make sure the chart is displayed. If not, click the *Chart1* tab located at the bottom of the worksheet window.
4. Change the chart type to a Line chart by completing the following steps:
   a. Click Chart and then Chart Type.
   b. At the Chart Type dialog box, click *Line* in the *Chart type* list box.
   c. Change the chart sub-type by clicking the first chart in the second row in the *Chart sub-type* list box.

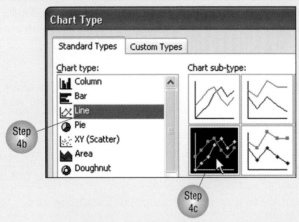

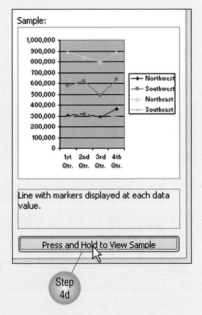

   d. View a sample of how this sub-type chart will display by positioning the arrow pointer on the Press and Hold to View Sample button and then holding down the left mouse button. After viewing a sample of the selected Line chart, release the mouse button.
   e. Click OK to close the dialog box.
5. Save the workbook again and then print only the sheet containing the chart. (To do this, make sure the sheet containing the chart is displayed, and then click the Print button on the Standard toolbar.)

EXCEL

6. With **sec7x05** still open, change the chart type to *Bar* by completing the following steps:
   a. Click Chart and then Chart Type.
   b. At the Chart Type dialog box, click *Bar* in the *Chart type* list box.
   c. Change the chart sub-type by clicking the first chart in the second row in the *Chart sub-type* list box.

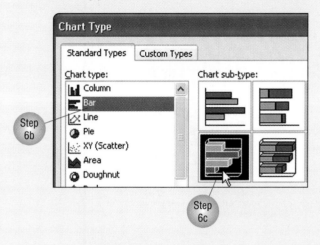

Step 6b

Step 6c

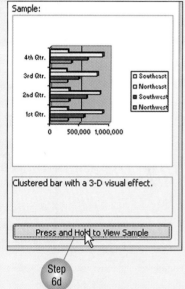

   d. View a sample of how this sub-type chart will display by positioning the arrow pointer on the Press and Hold to View Sample button and then holding down the left mouse button. After viewing a sample of the selected Bar chart, release the mouse button.

Step 6d

   e. Click OK to close the dialog box.
7. Save the workbook again and then print only the sheet containing the chart. (To do this, make sure the sheet containing the chart displays, and then click the Print button on the Standard toolbar.)
8. Close **sec7x05**.

Choosing a Custom Chart Type

The chart feature offers a variety of preformatted custom charts. A custom chart can be chosen in Step 1 of the Chart Wizard steps or a custom chart type can be chosen for an existing chart. To choose a custom chart type while creating a chart, click the Custom Types tab at the Chart Wizard - Step 1 of 4 - Chart Type dialog box.

You can also choose a custom chart for an existing chart. To do this, click Chart and then Chart Type. At the Chart Type dialog box, click the Custom Types tab. This displays the Chart Type dialog box as shown in Figure 7.7. You can also display the Chart Type dialog box by positioning the arrow pointer in the chart, clicking the *right* mouse button, and then clicking Chart Type at the shortcut menu. At the Chart Type dialog box with the Custom Types tab selected, click the desired custom chart type in the *Chart type* list box.

HINT

Preformatted custom charts are available. Use one of these custom charts if the formatting is appropriate.

7.7 **Chart Type Dialog Box with Custom Types Tab Selected**

Choose a custom chart type from this list box and preview it at the right in the *Sample* box.

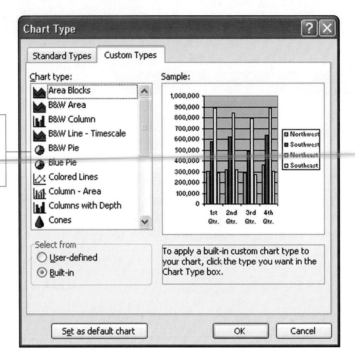

exercise 6

1. Open **sec7x03**.
2. Save the workbook with Save As and name it **sec7x06**.
3. Choose a custom chart type by completing the following steps:
   a. Click Chart and then Chart Type.
   b. At the Chart Type dialog box, click the Custom Types tab.
   c. At the Chart Type dialog box with the Custom Types tab selected, click *Columns with Depth* in the *Chart type* list box.
   d. Click OK to close the Chart Type dialog box.
4. Save the workbook again and then print only the sheet containing the chart.
5. Close **sec7x06**.

Step 3b

Step 3c

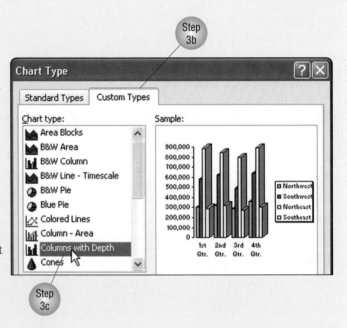

EXCEL

Changing Data in Cells

The Excel chart feature uses data in cells to create a chart. This data can be changed and the chart will reflect the changes. When a change is made to data in a worksheet, the change is also made to any chart created with the cells in the worksheet. The change is reflected in a chart whether it is located in the same worksheet as the changed cells or in a new sheet.

HINT

The chart is linked to the selected cells. If data is changed in a selected cell, the chart is automatically updated.

exercise 7

CHANGING NUMBERS IN AN EXCEL WORKSHEET

1. Open **sec7x03**.
2. Save the workbook with Save As and name it **sec7x07**.
3. Make sure the worksheet containing the cells (not the chart) is active. If not, click the *Sheet1* tab located at the bottom of the worksheet window.
4. Make the following changes to the specified cells:

    C2: Change *320,250* to *295,785*
    D3: Change *490,125* to *550,350*
    C5: Change *320,765* to *298,460*
    E5: Change *300,455* to *275,490*

5. Display the worksheet containing the chart *(Chart1)*.
6. Save the workbook again and then print only the sheet containing the chart.
7. Close **sec7x07**.

Changing the Data Series

When a chart is created, the Chart Wizard uses the data in the first column (except the first cell) to create the x-axis (the information along the bottom of the chart) and uses the data in the first row (except the first cell) to create the legend. For example, in the chart in Figure 7.6, the names (Chaney, Ferraro, and Jimenez) were used for the x-axis (along the bottom of the chart) and the months (June and July) were used for the legend.

When a chart is created, the option *Columns* is selected by default at the Chart Wizard - Step 2 of 4 - Chart Source Data dialog box. Change this to *Rows* and the data in the first row (except the first cell) will be used to create the x-axis and the data in the first column will be used to create the legend.

Change the data series in an existing chart by making the chart active, clicking Chart, and then clicking Source Data. This displays the Source Data dialog box shown in Figure 7.8. Another method for displaying the Source Data dialog box is to position the arrow pointer in a white portion of the chart (inside the chart but outside any chart element) and then click the *right* mouse button. At the shortcut menu that displays, click Source Data. The Source Data dialog box contains the same options as the Chart Wizard - Step 2 of 4 - Chart Source Data dialog box.

HINT

A data series is information represented on the chart by bars, lines, columns, pie slices, and so on.

QUICK STEPS

Change Chart Data Series
1. Make the chart active.
2. Click Chart, Source Data.
3. Click the desired tab and options.
4. Click OK.

Source Data Dialog Box

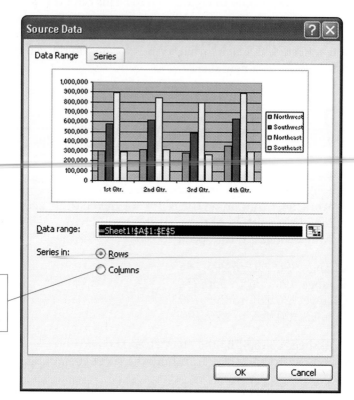

Choose the *Columns* option to reverse the x-axis and the legend.

exercise 8

CHANGING DATA SERIES IN AN EXCEL CHART

1. Open **sec7x01**.
2. Save the workbook with Save As and name it **sec7x08**.
3. Change the data series by completing the following steps:
   a. Position the arrow pointer in a white portion of the chart (inside the chart but outside any chart element) and then click the *right* mouse button.
   b. At the shortcut menu that displays, click Source Data.
   c. At the Source Data dialog box, click the *Columns* option.
   d. Click OK to close the Source Data dialog box.
   e. Click outside the chart to deselect it.
4. Save, print in landscape orientation, and then close **sec7x08**.

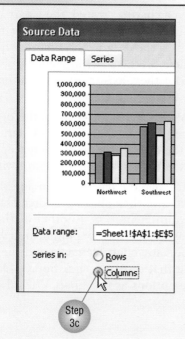

Step 3c

EXCEL

1. Open **ExcelWorksheet16**.
2. Save the worksheet with Save As and name it **sec7x09**.
3. Create a pie chart by completing the following steps:
    a. Select cells A4 through B10.
    b. Click the Chart Wizard button on the Standard toolbar.
    c. At the Chart Wizard - Step 1 of 4 - Chart Type dialog box, click *Pie* in the *Chart type* list box, and then click the Next button.
    d. At the Chart Wizard - Step 2 of 4 - Chart Source Data dialog box, make sure the data range displays as *=Sheet1!$A$4:$B$10*. Click the *Rows* option to see what happens to the pie when the data series is changed, click *Columns* to return the data series back, and then click the Next button.
    e. At the Chart Wizard - Step 3 of 4 - Chart Options dialog box, click the Data Labels tab.
    f. At the dialog box with the Data Labels tab selected, click *Percentage*.
    g. Click the Next button.
    h. At the Chart Wizard - Step 4 of 4 - Chart Location dialog box, click *As new sheet* and then click the Finish button.
4. Save the workbook again and then print only the sheet containing the chart.
5. Close **sec7x09**.

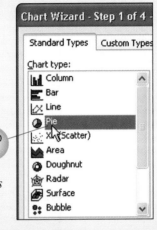

Step 3c

Step 3f

Adding Chart Elements

Certain chart elements are automatically inserted in a chart created by the Chart Wizard including a chart legend and labels for the x-axis and y-axis. Add other chart elements such as a chart title and data labels at the Chart Wizard - Step 3 of 4 - Chart Options dialog box. Add chart elements to an existing chart by making the chart active, clicking Chart, and then clicking Chart Options. This displays the Chart Options dialog box shown in Figure 7.9. Another method for displaying this dialog box is to position the arrow pointer in a white portion of the chart (inside the chart but outside any chart element), click the *right* mouse button, and then click Chart Options. The Chart Options dialog box contains the same options as the Chart Wizard - Step 3 of 4 - Chart Options dialog box.

HINT
The legend identifies which data series is represented by which data marker.

Add a Chart Element
1. Make the chart active.
2. Click Chart, Chart Options.
3. Click the desired tab and options.
4. Click OK.

7.9 *Chart Options Dialog Box with Titles Tab Selected*

Customize a chart with options at this dialog box with the various tabs selected.

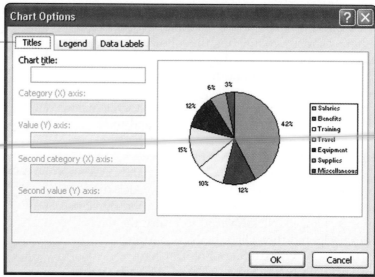

exercise 10

ADDING A TITLE TO A CHART AND CHANGING THE LEGEND LOCATION

1. Open **sec7x09**.
2. Save the workbook with Save As and name it **sec7x10**.
3. Add a title and data labels to the chart and change the location of the chart legend by completing the following steps:
   a. Make sure the sheet *(Chart1)* containing the pie chart displays.
   b. Click Chart and then Chart Options.
   c. At the Chart Options dialog box, click the Titles tab. (Skip this step if the Titles tab is already selected.)
   d. Click inside the *Chart title* text box and then type DEPARTMENT EXPENSES BY PERCENTAGE.

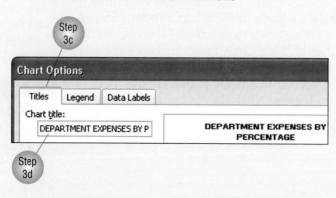

   e. Click the Data Labels tab.
   f. Click the *Legend key* option to insert a check mark.

g. Click the Legend tab.
h. At the Chart Options dialog box with
    the Legend tab selected, click *Left*.
i. Click the OK button to close the
    dialog box.
4. Save the workbook again and then print
    only the sheet containing the pie chart.
5. Close **sec7x10**.

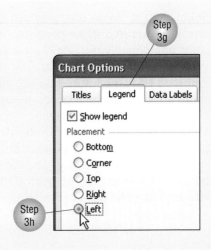

Moving/Sizing Chart Elements

When additional elements are added to a chart, the chart can become quite full
and elements may overlap. If elements in a chart overlap, an element can be
selected and then moved. To select an element, position the arrow pointer on a
portion of the element, and then click the left mouse button. This causes sizing
handles to display around the element. Position the mouse pointer toward the
edge of the selected element until it turns into an arrow pointer, hold down the
left mouse button, drag the element to the desired location, and then release the
mouse button. To change the size of an element, drag the sizing handles in the
desired direction.

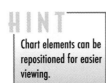

HINT
Chart elements can be repositioned for easier viewing.

Deleting/Removing Chart Elements

Chart elements can be selected by clicking the desired element. Once an element
is selected, it can be moved and it can also be deleted. To delete a selected
element, press the Delete key. If you delete a chart element in a chart and then
decide you want it redisplayed in the chart, immediately click the Undo button
on the Standard toolbar.

exercise 11

MOVING/SIZING/ADDING CHART ELEMENTS

1. Open **sec7x10**.
2. Save the workbook with Save As and name it **sec7x11**.
3. Move the legend to the right side of the chart by completing the following steps:
    a. Click the legend to select it.
    b. With the arrow pointer positioned in the legend, hold down the left mouse button,
        drag the outline of the legend to the right side of the chart, and then release the
        mouse button.
4. Move the pie to the left by completing the following steps:

a. Select the pie. To do this, position the arrow pointer in a white portion of the chart immediately outside the pie (a yellow box displays with *Plot Area* inside) and then click the left mouse button. (This should insert a square border around the pie. If not, try selecting the pie again.)

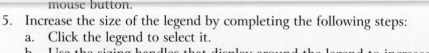

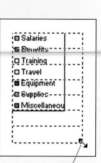

b. With the pie selected (square border around the pie), position the arrow pointer inside the square border that displays around the pie (not inside the pie), hold down the left mouse button, drag the outline of the pie to the left until it looks balanced with the legend, and then release the mouse button.

5. Increase the size of the legend by completing the following steps:
   a. Click the legend to select it.
   b. Use the sizing handles that display around the legend to increase the size. (You determine the direction to drag the sizing handles and the final size of the legend. Make sure the pie and legend are balanced.)

6. Save the workbook again and then print only the sheet containing the pie chart.
7. With **sec7x11** still open, delete the legend by completing the following steps:
   a. Click the legend to select it.
   b. Press the Delete key.
8. Change the data labels by completing the following steps:
   a. Position the arrow pointer in a white portion of the chart (outside any chart element) and then click the *right* mouse button.
   b. At the shortcut menu that displays, click Chart Options.
   c. At the Chart Options dialog box, click the Data Labels tab.
   d. At the Chart Options dialog box with the Data Labels tab selected, click the *Category name* option to insert a check mark. (Make sure the *Percentage* option still contains a check mark.)
   e. Click OK to close the Chart Options dialog box.
9. Move the pie by completing the following steps:
   a. Make sure the pie is selected. (If the pie is not selected, select it by positioning the arrow pointer in a white portion of the chart outside but immediately left or right at the top or bottom of the pie [a yellow box displays with *Plot Area* inside] and then clicking the left mouse button.)
   b. With the pie selected (square border around the pie), position the arrow pointer inside the square border that displays around the pie (not inside the pie), hold down the left mouse button, drag the outline of the pie until it looks centered between the left and right sides of the chart, and then release the mouse button.
10. Save the workbook again and then print only the sheet containing the pie chart.
11. Close **sec7x11**.

Adding Gridlines

Gridlines can be added to a chart for the category, series, and value. Depending on the chart, some but not all of these options may be available. To add gridlines, display the Chart Options dialog box and then click the Gridlines tab. This displays

EXCEL

the Chart Options dialog box with the Gridlines tab selected as shown in Figure 7.10. At this dialog box, insert a check mark in those options for which you want gridlines.

F I G U R E

7.10 *Chart Options Dialog Box with Gridlines Tab Selected*

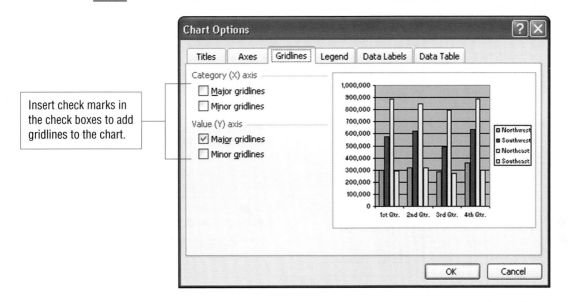

Insert check marks in the check boxes to add gridlines to the chart.

exercise 12

ADDING GRIDLINES TO A CHART

1. Open **sec7x03**.
2. Save the workbook with Save As and name it **sec7x12**.
3. Add gridlines to the chart by completing the following steps:
   a. Make sure the sheet containing the chart is displayed. (If not, click the *Chart1* tab located toward the bottom of the screen.)
   b. Click Chart and then Chart Options.
   c. At the Chart Options dialog box, click the Gridlines tab.
   d. At the Chart Options dialog box with the Gridlines tab selected, insert a check mark in the two options in the *Category (X) axis* section and also the two options in the *Value (Y) axis* section.
   e. Click OK to close the Chart Options dialog box.
4. Save the workbook again and then print only the sheet containing the chart.
5. Close **sec7x12**.

Step 3c

Step 3d

Chart Options

Titles | Axes | Gridlines

Category (X) axis
☑ Major gridlines
☑ Minor gridlines

Value (Y) axis
☑ Major gridlines
☑ Minor gridlines

Formatting Chart Elements

A variety of formatting options is available for a chart or chart elements. Formatting can include adding a pattern, changing background and foreground colors of the selected element or chart, changing the font, and changing the alignment or placement. To customize a chart, double-click in the chart area (outside any chart element). This displays the Format Chart Area dialog box with the Patterns tab selected as shown in Figure 7.11. You can also display this dialog box by clicking once in the chart area, clicking Format, and then clicking Selected Chart Area.

7.11 *Format Chart Area Dialog Box with Patterns Tab Selected*

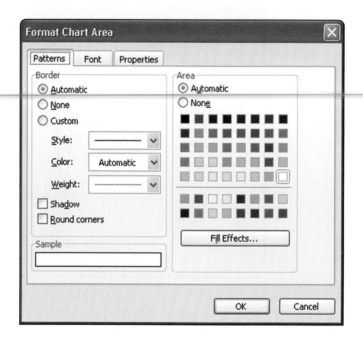

Customize the chart area by adding a pattern and/or fill color and background at the Format Chart Area dialog box with the Patterns tab selected. Click the Font tab and options for changing the typeface, type style, and type size display.

The font and pattern of chart elements can also be customized along with additional formatting for specific elements. For example, if you double-click a chart title, the Format Chart Title dialog box displays. (You can also display this dialog box by clicking once on the title, clicking Format, and then clicking Selected Chart Title.) This dialog box contains three tabs—Patterns, Font, and Alignment. Clicking the Patterns or the Font tab displays the same options as those available at the Format Chart Area dialog box. Click the Alignment tab and options for changing the text alignment (horizontal or vertical) display along with options for the title orientation.

Double-click a chart legend and the Format Legend dialog box displays with three tabs—Patterns, Font, and Placement. (You can also display this dialog box by clicking once on the legend, clicking Format, and then clicking Selected Legend.) Clicking the Patterns or the Font tab displays the same options as those available at the Format Chart Area dialog box. Click the Placement tab to display options for specifying the location of the legend in relation to the chart.

Each chart element contains a formatting dialog box. To display this dialog box, double-click the desired chart element. For example, double-click text in either the x-axis or the y-axis and the Format Axis dialog box displays.

1. Open **ExcelWorksheet25**.
2. Save the worksheet with Save As and name it **sec7x13**.
3. Create a Column chart with the data in the worksheet by completing the following steps:
   a. Select cells A4 through C7.
   b. Click the Chart Wizard button on the Standard toolbar.
   c. At the Chart Wizard - Step 1 of 4 - Chart Type dialog box, click the Next button.
   d. At the Chart Wizard - Step 2 of 4 - Chart Source Data dialog box, make sure the data range displays as *=Sheet1!$A$4:$C$7* and then click the Next button.
   e. At the Chart Wizard - Step 3 of 4 - Chart Options dialog box, make the following changes:
      1) Click the Titles tab.
      2) Click inside the *Chart title* text box and then type NORTHWEST REGION.
      3) Click the Next button.

Step 3e1

Step 3e2

   f. At the Chart Wizard - Step 4 of 4 - Chart Location dialog box, click the *As new sheet* option, and then click the Finish button.

4. Change the font for the title and legend and add a border and shading by completing the following steps:
   a. Double-click the title *NORTHWEST REGION*.
   b. At the Format Chart Title dialog box, click the Font tab, and then change the font to 24-point Century bold (or a similar serif typeface).
   c. Click the Patterns tab.
   d. Click the white circle before *Custom* in the *Border* section of the dialog box.
   e. Click the down-pointing arrow to the right of the *Weight* text box. From the drop-down list that displays, click the third option.
   f. Click the check box before the *Shadow* option.
   g. Add the Light Green color by clicking the fourth color from the left in the fifth row.
   h. Click OK to close the Format Chart Title dialog box.

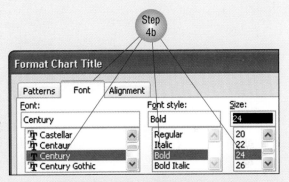

Step 4b

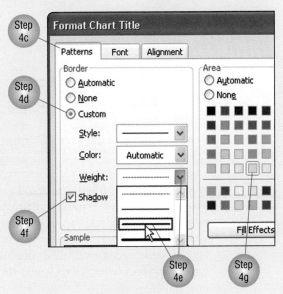

Step 4c

Step 4d

Step 4f

Step 4e

Step 4g

5. Format the legend with the same options as the title (complete steps similar to those in Step 4, except change the font to 10-point Century bold instead of 24-point).
6. With the legend still selected, increase the width by dragging the left middle sizing handle to the left so the legend slightly overlaps the chart. (Make sure *# of Computers* is completely visible in the legend.)
7. Save the workbook again and then print only the sheet containing the chart.
8. Close **sec7x13**.

Changing Element Colors

Fill Color

A fill color can be added to a chart or a chart element with the Fill Color button on the Formatting toolbar. To add a fill color, select the chart or the chart element, and then click the down-pointing arrow at the right side of the Fill Color button on the Formatting toolbar. This displays a palette of color choices as shown in Figure 7.12. Click the desired color on the palette.

FIGURE

7.12 **Fill Color Button Palette**

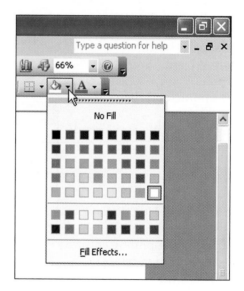

exercise 14

CHANGING ELEMENT COLORS IN A CHART

1. Open **sec7x09**.
2. Save the workbook with Save As and name it **sec7x14**.
3. Change the color of the piece of pie representing *Salaries* to red by completing the following steps:
   a. Position the arrow pointer on the *Salaries* piece of pie and then click the left mouse button. (Make sure the sizing handles surround only the *Salaries* piece of pie. You may need to experiment a few times to select the piece correctly.)

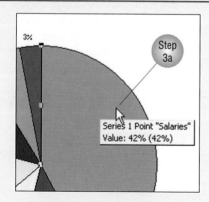

b. Click the down-pointing arrow at the right of the Fill Color button on the Formatting toolbar.

c. At the color palette, click the Red color (first color in the third row).

4. Change the color of the *Miscellaneous* piece of pie to green by completing steps similar to those in Step 3. (You determine the shade of green.)

5. Change the color of the *Supplies* piece of pie to yellow by completing steps similar to those in Step 3. (You determine the shade of yellow.)

6. Change the color of the *Equipment* piece of pie to blue by completing steps similar to those in Step 3. (You determine the shade of blue.)

7. Change the color of the *Travel* piece of pie to violet by completing steps similar to those in Step 3.

8. Change the color of the *Training* piece of pie to light turquoise by completing steps similar to those in Step 3.

9. Change the color of the *Benefits* piece of pie to a color you have not used on the other pieces of pie by completing steps similar to those in Step 3.

10. Add a background color to the chart by completing the following steps:

a. Select the entire chart. (To do this, position the arrow pointer inside the chart window but outside the chart, and then click the left mouse button.)

b. Click the down-pointing arrow at the right of the Fill Color button on the Formatting toolbar.

c. From the color palette that displays, click a light blue color of your choosing.

11. Save the workbook again and then print only the sheet containing the pie chart.

12. Close **sec7x14**.

Step 3b

Step 3c

No Fill

Red

Fill Effects...

Training

CHAPTER summary

➤ Create a chart with data in an Excel worksheet. A chart is a visual presentation of data.

➤ Create a chart by selecting the cells containing the data to be charted and then clicking the Chart Wizard button on the Standard toolbar. Complete the four steps in the Chart Wizard.

➤ Insert a chart in the same worksheet as the cells containing data or in a separate sheet. If a chart is created in a separate sheet, the sheet is named *Chart1*.

➤ The left vertical side of a chart is referred to as the y-axis, and the bottom of the chart is referred to as the x-axis.

➤ In a worksheet containing cells of data as well as a chart, the chart can be printed (rather than all data in the worksheet) by selecting the chart first and then displaying the Print dialog box.

➤ To delete a chart in a worksheet, click the chart to select it, and then press the Delete key. To delete a chart created in a separate sheet, position the mouse pointer on the chart tab, click the right mouse button, and then click Delete.

- Change the size of a chart in an Excel worksheet by clicking the chart and then dragging the sizing handles in the desired direction. To move a chart, select the chart, position the arrow pointer inside the chart, hold down the left mouse button, drag the outline of the chart to the desired location, and then release the mouse button.

- Fourteen basic chart types are available and include Area, Bar, Bubble, Column, Cone, Cylinder, Doughnut, Line, Pie, Pyramid, Radar, Stock, Surface, and XY (scatter).

- The default chart type is a Column chart. Change this default type at the first Chart Wizard dialog box or at the Chart Type dialog box.

- A variety of custom charts are available at the Chart Type dialog box with the Custom Types tab selected.

- Change data in a cell used to create a chart and the data in the chart reflects the change.

- Add chart elements to a chart at the Step 3 Chart Wizard dialog box or at the Chart Options dialog box.

- Move a chart element by selecting the element and then dragging the element to the desired location.

- Size a chart element by selecting the chart element and then dragging a sizing handle to the desired size.

- Delete a chart element by selecting the element and then pressing the Delete key.

- Customize the formatting of a chart element by double-clicking the element. This causes a formatting dialog box to display. The options at the dialog box will vary depending on the chart element.

- Add fill color to a chart or a chart element by selecting the chart or element and then clicking the Fill Color button on the Formatting toolbar. Click the desired color at the palette of color choices that displays.

FEATURES summary

FEATURE	BUTTON	MENU	KEYBOARD
Create default chart			F11
Begin Chart Wizard		Insert, Chart	
Chart Type dialog box		Chart, Chart Type	
Chart Source Data dialog box		Chart, Source Data	
Chart Options dialog box		Chart, Chart Options	
Format Chart Area dialog box		Format, Selected Chart Area	Ctrl + 1

EXCEL

ENHANCING THE DISPLAY OF WORKBOOKS

PERFORMANCE OBJECTIVES

Upon successful completion of Chapter 8, you will be able to:

- Save a workbook as a Web page
- Preview a Web page using Web Page Preview
- Create and modify a hyperlink
- Search for and request specific information from online sources
- Add a background image to a worksheet
- Insert, size, move, and format a clip art image
- Insert and customize a diagram
- Create, size, move, and customize WordArt
- Draw and customize shapes, lines, and autoshapes using buttons on the Drawing toolbar

Chapter08S

EXCEL

You can save an Excel workbook as a Web page and then view it in Web Page Preview and in a Web browser. You can also insert hyperlinks in a workbook that connect to a Web site or to another workbook and use options at the Research task pane to search for and request information from online sources. Microsoft Excel contains a variety of features that help you enhance the visual appeal of a workbook. Some methods for adding visual appeal that you will learn in this chapter include inserting and modifying images, inserting and customizing a diagram, creating and customizing WordArt text, and drawing and aligning shapes.

Creating and Viewing a Web Page

You can save an Excel workbook as a Web page. The Web page can be viewed in the default Web browser software, and hyperlinks can be inserted in the Web page to jump to other workbooks or sites on the Internet with additional information pertaining to the workbook content. In an organization, an Excel workbook can be saved as a Web page and posted on the company intranet as a timely method of distributing the workbook to the company employees.

Saving a Workbook as a Web Page

If you want to make a workbook available on the Internet, save the workbook as a Web page. You can save a workbook as a Web page as a folder with an HTML file and all supporting files or you can save a workbook as a Web page as a single file with all supporting files. *HTML* is an acronym for Hypertext Markup Language, which is the programming language used to code pages to display graphically on the World Wide Web. HTML is a collection of instructions that include *tags* applied to text and graphics to instruct the Web browser software how to properly display the page. If you save your workbook as a Web page, the file is saved as an HTML file with the *.htm* file extension. If you save a workbook as a single file, the file is saved as a MHTML file with the *.mht* file extension. (The *m* refers to *MIME*, which is a list of standards for conveying multimedia objects via the Internet and identifies all of the workbook elements in the single file.)

When you save a workbook as a Web page, you can choose to save the workbook as interactive or noninteractive. If you save the workbook as an interactive Web page, users are able to interact with the workbook in a variety of ways, such as applying formatting, manipulating data, changing formulas, and switching between worksheets. If you save the workbook as noninteractive, users cannot change or interact with the data in the Web browser.

Save a workbook as a Web page by opening the workbook, clicking File, and then clicking Save as Web Page. At the Save As dialog box shown in Figure 8.1, specify which part of the workbook you want published, whether the worksheet is to be interactive or not, and if you want to add an HTML title to the Web page. Click the Publish button and the Publish as Web Page dialog box appears as shown in figure 8.2. This dialog box contains advanced options for publishing a Web page.

By default, a Web page is saved as a static page (cannot be modified). You can save a workbook as an interactive Web page (can be modified) by inserting a check mark in the *Add interactivity* check box at the Save As dialog box.

FIGURE

8.1 *Save As Dialog Box*

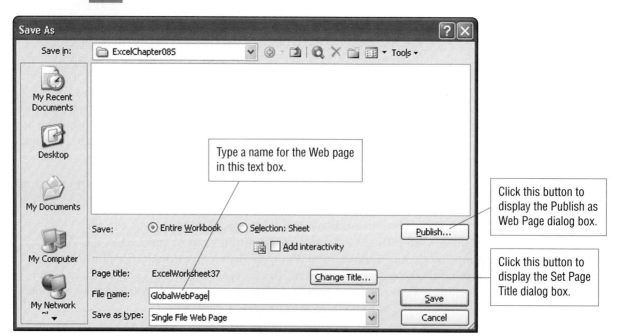

8.2 *Publish as Web Page Dialog Box*

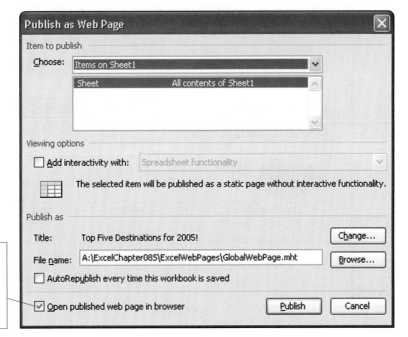

Publish as Web Page

Item to publish

Choose: Items on Sheet1

| Sheet | All contents of Sheet1 |

Viewing options

☐ Add interactivity with: Spreadsheet functionality

The selected item will be published as a static page without interactive functionality.

Publish as

Title: Top Five Destinations for 2005! [Change...]

File name: A:\ExcelChapter08S\ExcelWebPages\GlobalWebPage.mht [Browse...]

☐ AutoRepublish every time this workbook is saved

☑ Open published web page in browser [Publish] [Cancel]

Insert a check mark in this check box if you want the worksheet to automatically display in the default Web browser.

Previewing a Workbook in Web Page Preview

When creating a Web page, you may want to preview it in your default Web browser. Depending on the browser you are using, some of the formatting in a workbook may not display in the browser. To preview a workbook in your default Web browser, click File and then click Web Page Preview. This displays the currently open worksheet in the default Web browser and displays formatting supported by the browser. Close the Web browser window when you are finished previewing the page to return to Microsoft Excel. Figure 8.3 displays the GlobalWebPage file in Web Page Preview.

QUICK STEPS

Preview Workbook in Web Page Preview
1. Click File, Web Page Preview.
2. Click File, Close to close browser.

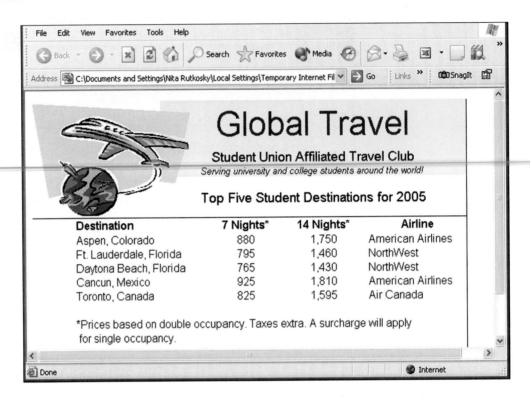

Creating Hyperlinks

Create a Hyperlink
1. Click desired cell.
2. Click Insert Hyperlink button on Standard toolbar.
3. Type Web address or file name.
4. Click OK.

Insert Hyperlink

A hyperlink is text or an object that you click to go to a different file, an HTML page on the Internet, or an HTML page on an intranet. Create a hyperlink in an Excel worksheet by typing the address of an existing Web page such as www.emcp.com. By default, the automatic formatting of hyperlinks is turned on and the Web address is formatted as a hyperlink (text is underlined and the color changes to blue). (You can turn off the automatic formatting of hyperlinks. To do this, display the AutoCorrect dialog box by clicking Tools and then AutoCorrect Options. At the AutoCorrect dialog box, click the AutoFormat As You Type tab, and then remove the check mark from the *Internet and network paths with hyperlinks* check box.)

You can also create a customized hyperlink by clicking the desired cell in a workbook and then clicking the Insert Hyperlink button on the Standard toolbar. At the Insert Hyperlink dialog box shown in Figure 8.4, type the file name or Web site address in the *Address* text box, and then click OK. You can also use the *Look in* option to browse to the desired folder and file and then double-click the file name. To link to the specified file or Web page, position the mouse pointer on the hyperlink, and then click the left mouse button.

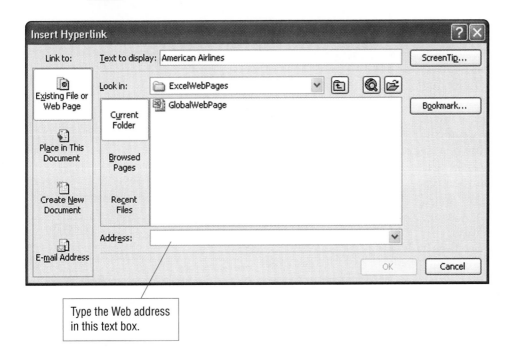

8.4 *Insert Hyperlink Dialog Box*

Type the Web address
in this text box.

Adding a Background Image to a Worksheet

Add visual interest to a worksheet by adding a background image. To insert a
background image in a workbook, click Format, point to Sheet, and then click
Background. This displays the Sheet Background dialog box with the contents of the
My Pictures folder. (This default may vary.) Navigate to the folder containing the
image you want to insert in the worksheet and then double-click the desired image.

A background image inserted in a worksheet does not print and is not retained
in individual worksheets saved as Web pages. If you want to retain the worksheet
background image, publish the entire workbook as a Web page.

**Add a Background
Image to Worksheet**
1. Click Format, Sheet,
   Background.
2. Navigate to desired
   folder.
3. Double-click desired
   image.

exercise 1

SAVING A WORKBOOK AS A WEB PAGE, PREVIEWING THE WEB PAGE,
AND CREATING HYPERLINKS

1. Create a folder named *ExcelWebPages* within the ExcelChapter08S folder on your disk.
2. Open **ExcelWorksheet37**.
3. Save the workbook with Save As and name it **sec8x01**.
4. Save the worksheet as a single Web page in the ExcelWebPages folder by completing
   the following steps:
   a. Click File and then Save as Web Page.
   b. At the Save As dialog box, double-click *ExcelWebPages* in the list box.

c. Make sure the *Save as type* option is set at *Single File Web Page*. (If it is not, click the down-pointing arrow at the right of the *Save as type* option and then click *Single File Web Page* at the drop-down menu.)

d. Select the text in the *File name* text box and then type **GlobalWebPage**.

e. Click the Change Title button.

f. At the Set Page Title dialog box, type **Top Five Destinations for 2005!** in the *Page title* text box, and then click OK.

g. At the Save As dialog box, click the Publish button.

h. At the Publish as Web Page dialog box, click the *Open published web page in browser* option to insert a check mark.

i. Click the Publish button. (This automatically displays the worksheet in your default Web browser.)

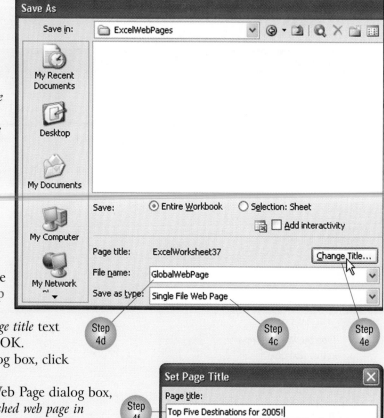

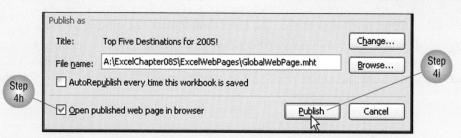

j. After viewing your Web page, close the Web page browser.

k. Save and then close **sec8x01**.

5. Preview the workbook in Web Page Preview by completing the following steps:

a. Display the Open dialog box and then open the **GlobalWebPage** file.

b. Click File and then click Web Page Preview.

c. If the viewing area in the browser is limited, click the Maximize button located in the upper right corner of the browser window.

d. After viewing the worksheet in the Web browser, click File and then Close.

6. Create a hyperlink so that clicking *American Airlines* displays the American Airlines Web page by completing the following steps:

a. Click cell G10 (this is the cell containing *American Airlines*).

b. Click the Insert Hyperlink button on the Standard toolbar.

c. At the Insert Hyperlink dialog box, type **www.aa.com** in the *Address* text box. (The *http://* is automatically inserted in the address.)

d. Click OK. (This changes the color of the *American Airlines* text and also adds underlining to the text.)

e. Repeat Steps 6b through 6d in cell G13.

7. Complete steps similar to those in Step 6 to create a hyperlink from *Northwest Airlines* to the URL www.nwa.com in cells G11 and G12.

8. Complete steps similar to those in Step 6 to create a hyperlink from *Air Canada* to the URL www.aircanada.ca in cell G14.

9. Click the Save button on the Standard toolbar to save the Web page with the hyperlinks added.

Step 6c

10. Jump to the hyperlinked sites by completing the following steps:

    a. Make sure you are connected to the Internet.
    b. Click one of the <u>American Airlines</u> hyperlinks.
    c. When the American Airlines Web page displays, scroll through the page, and then click a hyperlink that interests you.
    d. After looking at this next page, click File and then Close.
    e. At the **GlobalWebPage** workbook, click the <u>Air Canada</u> hyperlink.
    f. At the Air Canada Web page, click the hyperlink to see their site displayed in English.
    g. After viewing the Air Canada page, click File and then Close.
    h. At the **GlobalWebPage** workbook, click one of the <u>Northwest</u> hyperlinks.
    i. At the Northwest Airlines Web page, click a link that interests you.
    j. After viewing the Northwest Airlines page, click File and then Close.

11. Save and then print **GlobalWebPage**.

12. Add a background image to the worksheet by completing the following steps:

    a. With **GlobalWebPage** open, click Format, point to Sheet, and then click Background.
    b. At the Sheet Background dialog box, navigate to the Background folder on the CD that accompanies this text. (The Background folder is located in the Excel2003Specialist folder.)
    c. Double-click the ***Beach*** file that displays in the list box.
    d. View the worksheet in Web Page Preview by clicking File and then Web Page Preview.
    e. After viewing the worksheet in the Web browser, click File and then Close.

13. Close **GlobalWebPage** without saving the changes.

In Exercise 1, you created hyperlinks from an Excel workbook to sites on the Web. You can also insert hyperlinks in a workbook that link to other Excel workbooks or files in other programs in the Office suite. In Exercise 2, you will create a hyperlink that, when clicked, displays another Excel workbook.

You can modify or change hyperlink text or the hyperlink destination. To do this, right-click the hyperlink, and then click Edit Hyperlink. At the Edit Hyperlink dialog box, make any desired changes, and then close the dialog box. The Edit Hyperlink dialog box contains the same options as the Insert Hyperlink dialog box.

HINT

Deactivate a hyperlink by right-clicking the hyperlink and then clicking *Remove Hyperlink* at the shortcut menu.

exercise 2

1. Open **ExcelWorksheet33**.
2. Save the workbook with Save As and name it **sec8x02**.
3. Create a hyperlink that will display **ExcelWorksheet28** by completing the following steps:
   a. Make cell A10 active.
   b. Type Semiannual Sales and then press Enter.
   c. Click cell A10 to make it the active cell.
   d. Click the Insert Hyperlink button on the Standard toolbar.
   e. At the Insert Hyperlink dialog box, click the down-pointing arrow at the right side of the *Look in* option and then navigate to the ExcelChapter08S folder on your disk.
   f. Double-click *ExcelWorksheet28* in the ExcelChapter08S folder on your disk. (This closes the Insert Hyperlink dialog box and displays the *Semiannual Sales* text as a hyperlink in the workbook.)
4. Display **ExcelWorksheet28** by clicking the Semiannual Sales hyperlink.
5. Close **ExcelWorksheet28**.
6. Print **sec8x02**.
7. Modify the hyperlink text in **sec8x02** by completing the following steps:
   a. Position the mouse pointer on the Semiannual Sales hyperlink, click the *right* mouse button, and then click Edit Hyperlink.
   b. At the Edit Hyperlink dialog box, select the text *Semiannual Sales* in the *Text to display* text box and then type Customer Sales Analysis.
   c. Click OK.
8. Click the Customer Sales Analysis hyperlink.
9. Close **ExcelWorksheet28**.
10. Save, print, and then close **sec8x02**.

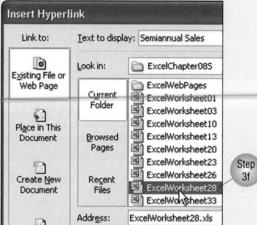

Insert Hyperlink

Link to:	Text to display:	Semiannual Sales

Existing File or Web Page — Look in: ExcelChapter08S

- Current Folder
- Browsed Pages
- Recent Files

ExcelWebPages
ExcelWorksheet01
ExcelWorksheet03
ExcelWorksheet10
ExcelWorksheet13
ExcelWorksheet20
ExcelWorksheet23
ExcelWorksheet26
ExcelWorksheet28 — Step 3f
ExcelWorksheet33

Place in This Document

Create New Document

Address: ExcelWorksheet28.xls

	A	B	C
1	**FIRST-QUARTER SALES - 2002**		
2	**Customer**	**January**	**February**
3	Lakeside Trucking	$84,231	$ 73,455
4	Gresham Machines	$33,199	$ 40,390
5	Real Photography	$30,891	$ 35,489
6	Genesis Productions	$72,190	$ 75,390
7	Landower Company	$22,188	$ 14,228
8	Jewell Enterprises	$19,764	$ 50,801
9			
10	Semiannual Sales		
11			
12	file:///A:\ExcelChapter08S\		
13	ExcelWorksheet28.xls - Click once to follow. Click and hold to select this cell.		

Step 4

Step 7b

Edit Hyperlink

Link to:	Text to display:	Customer Sales Analysis

Existing File or Web Page — Look in: ExcelChapter08S

- Current Folder

ExcelWebPages
ExcelWorksheet01
ExcelWorksheet03

EXCEL

Researching and Requesting Information

Research and Request Information
1. Click Research button on Standard toolbar.
2. Type desired word or topic in the *Search for* text box.
3. Click the down-pointing arrow at right of resources list box and then click desired resource.

Use options at the Research task pane to search for and request specific information from online sources and to translate words from and to a variety of languages. The online resources available to you depend on the locale to which your system is set, authorization information indicating that you are allowed to download the information, and your Internet service provider.

Display the Research task pane by clicking the Research button on the Standard toolbar or clicking Tools and then Research. This displays the Research pane similar to what you see in Figure 8.5. You can also display the Research task pane by holding down the Alt key and clicking a specific word or selected words in a document.

FIGURE

8.5 *Research Task Pane*

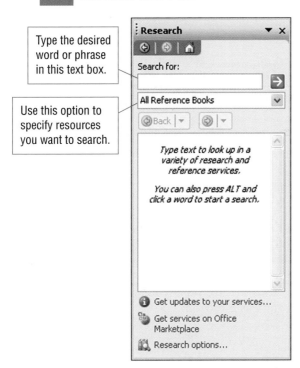

Determine the resources available by clicking the down-pointing arrow at the right of the resources list box (the list box located below the *Search for* text box). The drop-down list contains lists of reference books, research sites, business and financial sites, and other services. If you want to use a specific reference in your search click the desired reference at the drop-down list, type the desired word or topic in the *Search for* text box, and then press Enter. Items matching your word or topic display in the task pane list box. Depending on the item, the list box may contain hyperlinks you can click to access additional information on the Internet.

You can control the available research options by clicking the Research options hyperlink located at the bottom of the Research task pane. This displays the Research Options dialog box shown in Figure 8.6. At this dialog box, insert a check mark before those items you want available and remove the check mark from those items you do not want available.

8.6 *Research Options Dialog Box*

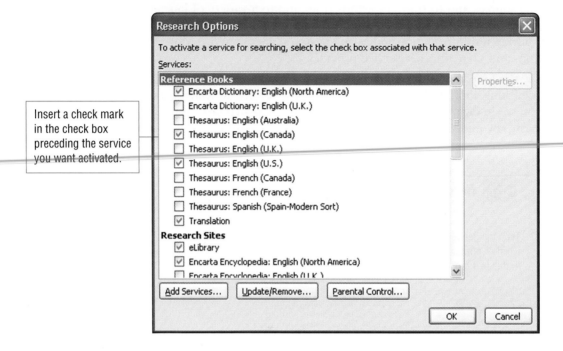

Insert a check mark in the check box preceding the service you want activated.

Inserting Research Information

You can insert into your worksheet some of the information that displays in the Research task pane and other information you can copy and paste into your worksheet. If you look up stock prices, an *Insert Stock Price* option is available for inserting the stock information in your worksheet. If information displays in your browser, select the desired information, click Edit on the Browser's menu bar and then click Copy at the drop-down menu. Make your worksheet active, click Edit, and then click Paste or click the Paste button.

exercise 3

RESEARCHING AND REQUESTING INFORMATION

(Note: Your computer must be connected to the Internet to complete this exercise.)

1. At a clear document screen, display the Research task pane by clicking the Research button on the Standard toolbar.
2. Search for information in a dictionary on Venn diagrams (one of the diagrams you can create with the Diagram feature) by completing the following steps:

a. Click in the *Search for* text box or select any text that displays in the text box and then type Venn.

b. Click the down-pointing arrow to the right of the resources list box (the down-pointing arrow immediately below the Start searching button).

c. At the drop-down list of resources, click *Encarta Dictionary: English (North America)*. If this reference is not available, click any other dictionary that is available to you.

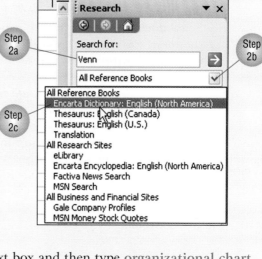

3. Search for information on organizational charts in an encyclopedia by completing the following steps:

a. Select the text *Venn* in the *Search for* text box and then type organizational chart.

b. Click the down-pointing arrow at the right of the resources list box and then click an encyclopedia listed in the *All Research Sites* section of the list box.

c. Look at the information that displays in the task pane list box and then click a hyperlink that interests you.

d. After reading the information that displays in your Web browser, close the browser window.

4. Search for stock information and then insert the information in a worksheet by completing the following steps:

a. Open **ExcelWorksheet44**.

b. Save the worksheet with Save As and name it **sec8x03**.

c. Make sure cell B4 is the active cell.

d. Select the text *organizational chart* in the *Search for* text box and then type IBM.

e. Click the down-pointing arrow at the right of the resources list box and then click *MSN Money Stock Quotes*.

f. Scroll down the Research task pane and then click the Insert Price button.

g. Make cell B5 active.

h. Select *IBM* in the *Search for* text box, type MSFT, and then press Enter. (This will display the stock information for Microsoft.)

i. Scroll down the Research task pane and then click the Insert Price button.

j. Make cell B6 active.

k. Select *Microsoft* in the *Search for* text box, type Dell, and then press Enter.

l. Scroll down the Research task pane and then click the Insert Price button.

5. Save, print, and then close **sec8x03**.

6. Open a blank worksheet.

7. Insert Microsoft stock information in the worksheet by completing the following steps:

a. Make sure cell A1 is the active cell and that the Research task pane is displayed.

b. Make sure *MSN Money Stock Quotes* displays in the resources list box.

c. Select *Dell* that displays in the *Search for* text box, type **MSFT**, and then press Enter.
d. Scroll down the Research task pane until the Insert Price button is visible.
e. Click the down-pointing arrow at the right side of the Insert Price button.
f. Click *Insert Refreshable Stock Data* in the drop-down list. (This inserts stock data into the worksheet.) (If this option does not display, go to the Internet Resource Center for this book at www.emcp.com and click <u>Text Updates</u>.)

8. Save the worksheet and name it **sec8Stocks**.
9. Print the worksheet in landscape orientation and scale it to fit on one page.
10. Close **sec8Stocks**.

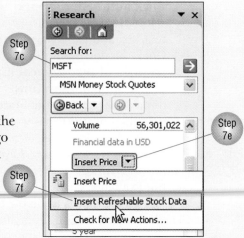

Step 7c

Step 7e

Step 7f

Inserting Images in a Workbook

Insert Clip Art

Drawing

Microsoft Office includes a gallery of media images you can insert in a workbook such as clip art, photographs, and movie images, as well as sound clips. To insert an image in a workbook, click Insert, point to Picture, and then click Clip Art. This displays the Clip Art task pane at the right side of the screen as shown in Figure 8.7. You can also display the Clip Art task pane by clicking the Insert Clip Art button on the Drawing toolbar. (Display the Drawing toolbar by clicking the Drawing button on the Standard toolbar.)

FIGURE

8.7 *Clip Art Task Pane*

Type in this text box the word or topic for which you are searching.

Use these options to specify where to search and the media type.

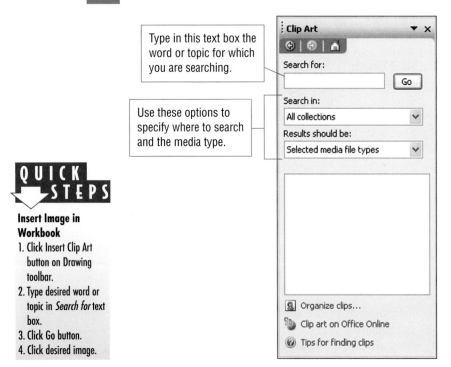

QUICK STEPS

Insert Image in Workbook
1. Click Insert Clip Art button on Drawing toolbar.
2. Type desired word or topic in *Search for* text box.
3. Click Go button.
4. Click desired image.

To view all picture, sound, and motion files, make sure no text displays in the *Search for* text box at the Clip Art task pane, and then click the Go button. Display the desired image and then click the image to insert it in the worksheet.

Narrowing a Search

By default (unless it has been customized), the Clip Art task pane looks for all media images and sound clips found in all locations. You can narrow the search to specific locations and to specific images. The *Search in* option at the Clip Art task pane has a default setting of *All collections*. You can change this to *My Collections*, *Office Collections*, and *Web Collections*. The *Results should be* option has a default setting of *All media file types*. Click the down-pointing arrow at the right side of this option to display media types. To search for a specific media type, remove the check mark before all options at the drop-down list but the desired type. For example, if you are searching only for clip art images, remove the check mark before *Photographs*, *Movies*, and *Sound*.

If you are searching for specific images, click in the *Search for* text box, type the desired word, and then click the Go button. For example, if you want to find images related to computers, click in the *Search for* text box, type computer, and then click the Go button. Clip art images related to *computer* display in the viewing area of the task pane.

Sizing an Image

Size an image in a workbook using the sizing handles that display around a selected image. To change the size of an image, click in the image to select it, and then position the mouse pointer on a sizing handle until the pointer turns into a double-headed arrow. Hold down the left mouse button, drag the sizing handle in or out to decrease or increase the size of the image, and then release the mouse button.

Use the middle sizing handles at the left or right side of the image to make the image wider or thinner. Use the middle sizing handles at the top or bottom of the image to make the image taller or shorter. Use the sizing handles at the corners of the image to change both the width and height at the same time. When sizing an image, consider using the horizontal and vertical rulers that display in the Print Layout view. To deselect an image, click anywhere in the workbook outside the image.

HINT
Drag one of the corner sizing handles to maintain the original proportions of the image.

Moving and Deleting an Image

To move an image, select the image, and then position the mouse pointer inside the image until the pointer turns into a four-headed arrow. Hold down the left mouse button, drag the image to the desired position, and then release the mouse button. Rotate an image by positioning the mouse pointer on the green, round rotation handle until the pointer displays as a circular arrow. Hold down the left mouse button, drag in the desired direction, and then release the mouse button. Delete a clip art image by selecting the image and then pressing the Delete key.

HINT
You can use arrow keys on the keyboard to move a selected object.

exercise 4

1. Open **ExcelWorksheet03**.
2. Save the worksheet with Save As and name it **sec8x04**.
3. Select the first four rows of the worksheet, click Insert and then click Rows. (This inserts four new rows at the beginning of the worksheet.)
4. Click in cell A2, type MYLAN COMPUTERS, and then press Enter.
5. Select cells A1 through D12 and then apply the Accounting 1 autoformat.
6. Select cells B7 through D12 and then click the Percent Style button on the Formatting toolbar.
7. Insert an image in the worksheet by completing the following steps:
   a. Make cell C1 active.
   b. Click Insert, point to Picture, and then click Clip Art.
   c. At the Clip Art task pane, click in the *Search for* text box.
   d. Type computer and then click the Go button.
   e. Click the computer image shown in the figure at the right. (If this computer clip art image is not available, click another image that interests you.)
   f. Close the Clip Art task pane.
   g. With the computer image selected (white sizing handles display around the image), position the mouse pointer on the bottom right sizing handle until it turns into a diagonally pointing two-headed arrow.
   h. Hold down the left mouse button, drag into the image to decrease the size until the image is approximately the size shown at the right, and then release the mouse button.

   i. If necessary, move the image so it is positioned as shown at the right.
   j. Click outside the image to deselect it.
8. Print the worksheet horizontally and vertically centered on the page.
9. Save and then close **sec8x04**.

Formatting Images with Buttons on the Picture Toolbar

You can format images in a variety of ways. Formatting might include adding fill color and border lines, increasing or decreasing the brightness or contrast, choosing a wrapping style, and cropping the image. Format an image with buttons on the Picture toolbar or options at the Format Picture dialog box. Display the Picture toolbar by clicking an image or by right-clicking an image and then clicking Show Picture Toolbar at the shortcut menu. Table 8.1 identifies the buttons on the Picture toolbar.

TABLE

8.1 *Picture Toolbar Buttons*

Button	Name	Function
	Insert Picture From File	Displays the Insert Picture dialog box with a list of subfolders containing additional images.
	Color	Displays a drop-down list with options for controlling how the image displays. Options include *Automatic, Grayscale, Black & White*, and *Washout*.
	More Contrast	Increases contrast of the image.
	Less Contrast	Decreases contrast of the image.
	More Brightness	Increases brightness of the image.
	Less Brightness	Decreases brightness of the image.
	Crop	Crops image so only a specific portion of the image is visible.
	Rotate Left 90°	Rotates the image 90 degrees to the left.
	Line Style	Inserts a border around the image and specifies the border line style.
	Compress Pictures	Reduces resolution or discards extra information to save room on the hard drive or to reduce download time.

Continued on next page

	Format Picture	Displays Format Picture dialog box with options for formatting the image. Tabs in the dialog box include Colors and Lines, Size, Position, Wrapping, and Picture.
	Set Transparent Color	This button is not active. (When an image contains a transparent area, the background color or texture of the page shows through the image. Set transparent color in Microsoft Photo Editor.)
	Reset Picture	Resets image to its original size, position, and color.

exercise 5

1. Open **ExcelWorksheet13**.
2. Save the worksheet with Save As and name it **sec8x05**.
3. Delete column H.
4. Insert a row at the beginning of the worksheet.
5. Change the height of the new row to 99.00.
6. Select cells A1 through G1 and then click the Merge and Center button on the Formatting toolbar.
7. With cell A1 the active cell, make the following changes:
   a. Display the Format Cells dialog box. (To do this, click Format and then Cells.)
   b. At the Format Cells dialog box, click the Alignment tab.
   c. At the Format Cells dialog box with the Alignment tab selected, change the *Horizontal* option to *Right (Indent)* and the *Vertical* option to *Center*.
   d. Click the Font tab.
   e. At the Format Cells dialog box with the Font tab selected, change the font to 32-point Arial bold.
   f. Click OK to close the dialog box.
8. Type Global Transport.
9. Click outside cell A1 and then click cell A1 again.
10. Display the Clip Art task pane by clicking Insert, pointing to Picture, and then clicking Clip Art.
11. Select the text in the *Search for* text box and then type maps.
12. Click the Go button.
13. Click the image shown at the right. (If this image is not available, choose another image related to maps.)
14. Close the Clip Art task pane.

15. Change the size of the image by completing the following steps:

    a. With the clip art image selected, click the Format Picture button on the Picture toolbar. (If the Picture toolbar is not visible, click View, point to Toolbars, and then click Picture.)

    b. At the Format Picture dialog box, click the Size tab.

    c. Select the current measurement in the *Height* text box (in the *Size and rotate* section) and then type 1.5.

    d. Click OK to close the dialog box.

16. Click twice on the More Contrast button on the Picture toolbar.

17. Print the worksheet centered horizontally and vertically on the page.

18. Save and then close **sec8x05**.

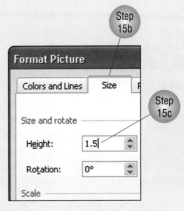

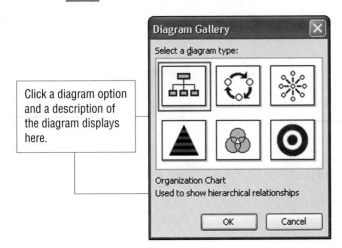

Creating Diagrams and Organizational Charts

Use the Diagram Gallery to create organizational charts or other types of diagrams. Display the Diagram Gallery dialog box, shown in Figure 8.8, by clicking the Insert Diagram or Organization Chart button on the Drawing toolbar or by clicking Insert and then Diagram.

F I G U R E

8.8 *Diagram Gallery Dialog Box*

Click a diagram option and a description of the diagram displays here.

At the Diagram Gallery dialog box, click the desired option in the *Select a diagram type* list box and then click OK. If you click an organizational chart option, chart boxes appear in the worksheet and the Organization Chart toolbar displays. Use buttons on this toolbar to create additional boxes in the chart, specify the layout of the chart, expand or scale the chart, select specific elements in the chart, apply an autoformat to the chart, or specify a text wrapping option.

Insert Diagram in Workbook
1. Click Insert, Diagram.
2. Double-click desired diagram.

If you click a diagram option at the Diagram Gallery dialog box, the diagram is inserted in the worksheet and the Diagram toolbar displays. Use buttons on this toolbar to insert additional shapes; move shapes backward or forward or reverse the diagram; expand, scale, or fit the contents of the diagram; apply an autoformat to the diagram; or change the type of diagram (choices include Cycle, Radial, Pyramid, Venn, and Target).

exercise 6

CREATING AND CUSTOMIZING A DIAGRAM

1. Open **ExcelWorksheet43**.
2. Save the worksheet with Save As and name it **sec8x06**.
3. Insert a Pyramid diagram in cell A1 and modify the diagram by completing the following steps:
   a. Click Insert and then Diagram.
   b. At the Diagram Gallery, double-click the Pyramid diagram (first diagram from the left in the second row).
   c. Click the AutoFormat button on the Diagram toolbar.
   d. At the Diagram Style Gallery, double-click the *Square Shadows* option in the *Select a Diagram Style* list box.
   e. Scroll down the screen until the bottom right sizing handle (small, white circle) displays.
   f. Using the bottom right sizing handle, decrease the size of the Pyramid diagram so it is approximately two columns wide and eight rows high (the approximate size shown in Figure 8.9).
   g. Click the text *Click to add text* that displays towards the bottom of the pyramid and then press the spacebar once. (This removes the text and replaces it with a space, which does not show in the pyramid.)

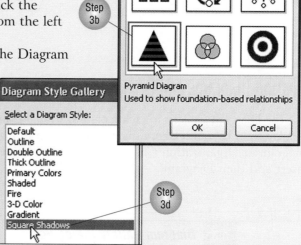

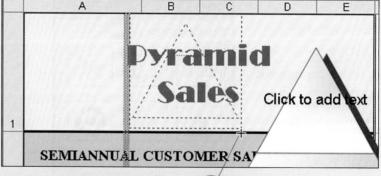

h. Click the text *Click to add text* that displays towards the middle of the pyramid and then press the spacebar.

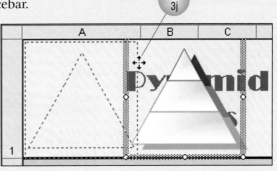

Step 3j

i. Click the text *Click to add text* that displays towards the top of the pyramid and then press the spacebar.

j. Drag the Pyramid diagram so it displays at the left side of cell A1 as shown in Figure 8.9.

k. Copy the pyramid (hold down the Ctrl key while dragging the pyramid) to the right side of cell A1 as shown in Figure 8.9.

4. Save and then print **sec8x06**.

FIGURE

8.9 *Exercise 6*

	A	B	C	D	E	F
1		Pyramid Sales				
2	SEMIANNUAL CUSTOMER SALES ANALYSIS					
3	Customer	October	November	December	Average	
4	Lakeside Trucking	$ 84,231	$ 73,455	$ 97,549	$ 85,078	
5	Gresham Machines	$ 33,199	$ 40,390	$ 50,112	$ 41,234	
6	Real Photography	$ 30,891	$ 35,489	$ 36,400	$ 34,260	
7	Genesis Productions	$ 72,190	$ 75,390	$ 83,219	$ 76,933	
8	Landower Company	$ 22,188	$ 14,228	$ 38,766	$ 25,061	
9	Jewell Enterprises	$ 19,764	$ 50,801	$ 32,188	$ 34,251	
10						

Creating WordArt

With the WordArt application, you can distort or modify text to conform to a variety of shapes. This is useful for creating company logos and headings. With WordArt, you can change the font, style, and alignment of text. You can also use different fill patterns and colors, customize border lines, and add shadow and three-dimensional effects.

To insert WordArt in an Excel workbook click Insert, point to Picture, and then click WordArt. This displays the WordArt Gallery shown in Figure 8.10. You

QUICK STEPS

Create WordArt
1. Click Insert WordArt button on Drawing toolbar.
2. Double-click desired option at WordArt Gallery.
3. Type desired text at Edit WordArt Text box.
4. Click OK.

Insert WordArt

can also display the WordArt Gallery by clicking the Insert WordArt button on the WordArt toolbar or the Drawing toolbar. Display the WordArt or Drawing toolbar by right-clicking a visible toolbar, and then clicking Drawing or WordArt at the drop-down menu.

FIGURE

8.10 *WordArt Gallery*

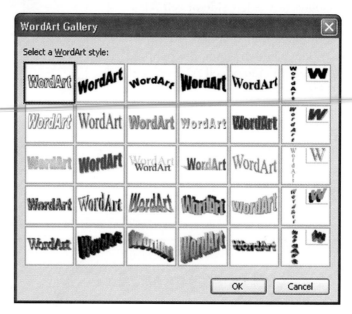

Entering Text

Double-click a WordArt choice at the WordArt Gallery and the Edit WordArt Text dialog box displays as shown in Figure 8.11. At the Edit WordArt Text dialog box, type the WordArt text and then click the OK button. At the Edit WordArt Text dialog box, you can change the font and/or size of text and also apply bold or italic formatting.

FIGURE

8.11 *Edit WordArt Text Dialog Box*

Type WordArt text in this text box.

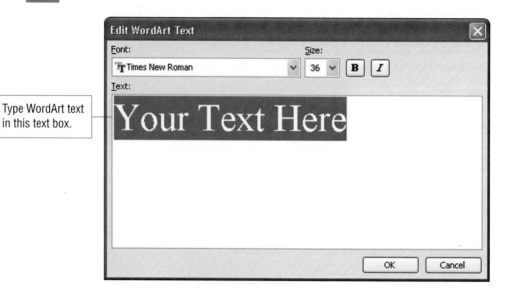

Drawing Lines

To draw a line in a worksheet, click the Line button on the Drawing toolbar. Position the crosshairs where you want to begin the line, hold down the left mouse button, drag the line to the location where you want the line to end, and then release the mouse button. Customize a line by changing the line color, line style, or by applying an arrow style.

exercise 10

1. Open **ExcelWorksheet10**.
2. Save the worksheet with Save As and name it **sec8x10**.
3. Delete column D (contains the heading *Bonus*).
4. Click in cell E1, turn on bold, type Top Sales, and then press Enter.
5. Click in cell A8.
6. Draw and customize two lines as shown in Figure 8.19 by completing the following steps:

    a. Click the Arrow button on the Drawing toolbar.

    b. Position the crosshairs at the left side of the text *Top Sales* (located in cell E1).

    c. Hold down the left mouse button, drag down and to the left until the crosshairs are positioned near the contents of cell C4 (refer to Figure 8.20), and then release the mouse button.

    d. With the line selected, click the down-pointing arrow at the right side of the Line Color button, and then click the Red color (first color from the left in the third row).

    e. Click the Arrow button on the Drawing toolbar and then draw another arrow as shown in Figure 8.19.

    f. With the second arrow selected, click the Line Color button. (This changes the line to red since that was the last color selected.)

7. Save, print, and then close **sec8x10**.

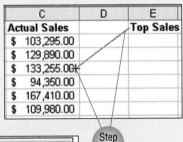

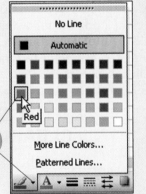

8.19 *Exercise 10*

	A	B	C	D	E	F
1	**Salesperson**	**Quota**	**Actual Sales**		**Top Sales**	
2	Allejandro	$ 95,500.00	$ 103,295.00			
3	Crispin	$ 137,000.00	$ 129,890.00			
4	Frankel	$ 124,000.00	$ 133,255.00			
5	Hiesmann	$ 85,500.00	$ 94,350.00			
6	Jarvis	$ 159,000.00	$ 167,410.00			
7	Littleman	$ 110,500.00	$ 109,980.00			
8						

Creating Autoshapes

Draw a variety of shapes with options from the AutoShapes button. Click the AutoShapes button, point to the desired menu option, and then click the desired shape. When you choose an autoshape, the mouse pointer turns into crosshairs. Position the crosshairs in the workbook, hold down the left mouse button, drag to create the shape, and then release the button.

Flipping and Rotating an Object

A selected object, such as a shape or line, can be rotated and flipped horizontally or vertically. To rotate or flip an object, select the object, click the Draw button on the Drawing toolbar, point to Rotate or Flip, and then click the desired rotation or flip option at the side menu that displays.

Choose an autoshape and then click in the worksheet and Excel will insert a standard-sized autoshape object. Display the AutoShapes toolbar by clicking Insert, pointing to Picture, and then clicking AutoShapes.

exercise 11

DRAWING AND ROTATING AN AUTOSHAPE

1. Open **ExcelWorksheet23**.
2. Save the worksheet with Save As and name it **sec8x11**.
3. Increase the height of row 2 to 60.00.
4. Insert the autoshapes in cell B2 (refer to Figure 8.20) by completing the following steps:
   a. Click the AutoShapes button on the Drawing toolbar, point to Block Arrows, and then click Striped Right Arrow (first shape from the left in the fifth row).

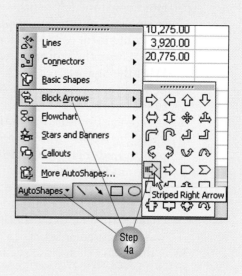

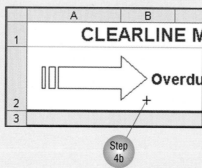

   b. Position the crosshairs at the left side of the text *Overdue Accounts*, hold down the Shift key, and then draw an arrow approximately the size of the arrow in Figure 8.20.
   c. With the arrow selected, click the down-pointing arrow at the right side of the Fill Color button, and then click the Light Turquoise color (fifth color from the left in the bottom row).

Assessment 5

1. Open **ExcelWorksheet34**.
2. Save the worksheet with Save As and name it **sec8sc05**.
3. Insert a new row at the beginning of the worksheet.
4. Select cells A1 through D1 and then click the Merge and Center button.
5. Increase the height of row 1 to 90.00.
6. Insert a formula in cell D4 that subtracts the Actual amount from the Budget amount.
7. Copy the formula in cell D4 down to cells D5 through D10.
8. Insert the text *EZ Sports* as WordArt in cell A1. You determine the formatting and shape of the WordArt. Move and size the WordArt so it fits in cell A1.
9. Save, print, and then close **sec8sc05**.

Assessment 6

1. Open **ExcelWorksheet33**.
2. Save the worksheet with Save As and name it **sec8sc06**.
3. Make sure *Sales 2002* is the active tab. (This workbook contains three worksheets.)
4. Insert a new row at the beginning of the worksheet.
5. Select cells A1 through D1 and then click the Merge and Center button.
6. Increase the height of row 1 to 75.00.
7. In cell A1, type Mountain, press Alt + Enter, and then type Systems.
8. Select *Mountain Systems* and then change the font to 18-point Arial bold.
9. Change the horizontal alignment to *Left (Indent)* and the vertical alignment to *Center*.
10. Click outside cell A1.
11. Use the Isosceles Triangle shape (to find it click AutoShapes, point to Basic Shapes, and then click Isosceles Triangle) to draw a triangle as shown in Figure 8.22.
12. Copy the triangle three times, add fill to the triangles, and position the triangles as shown in Figure 8.22.
13. Print only the *Sales 2002* worksheet.
14. Save and then close **sec8sc06**.

FIGURE

8.22 *Assessment 6*

Assessment 7

1. The Drawing toolbar contains buttons for applying shadow effects and 3-D effects to shapes. Use the Help feature to learn how to apply a shadow style to a shape and then apply shadow formatting by following these basic steps:
   a. Open **sec8x11**.
   b. Save the worksheet with Save As and name it **sec8sc07A**.
   c. Select the left arrow autoshape and apply a shadow style of your choosing.
   d. Select the right arrow autoshape and apply a shadow style of your choosing. (Choose a shadow style that complements the shadow style you applied to the left arrow.)
   e. Save, print, and then close **sec8sc07A**.

2. Use the Help feature to learn how to apply a 3-D effect to a shape and then apply 3-D formatting by following these basic steps:
   a. Open **ExcelWorksheet26**.
   b. Save the worksheet with Save As and name it **sec8sc07B**.
   c. Select all of the triangle shapes in cell A1 and then apply the 3-D Style 7 formatting.
   d. Save, print, and then close **sec8sc07B**.

CHAPTER challenge

 Allen's Auto Sales has hired you to maintain the inventory of vehicles on its lot. Ultimately, this information will be placed on the Web. To begin the task, create a worksheet that contains at least five different types (brand name) of vehicles. Also include the price of the vehicle, destination charges, rebate (if applicable), and final price (use a formula to calculate). Format the worksheet appropriately, using at least three different formatting tools learned in this chapter. Since the worksheet will ultimately be placed on the Web to be used by potential customers, save the workbook as a Web Page. To provide further information for the customer, include two hyperlinks in the Web page. One hyperlink should be to a recommended financial institution Web site, where customers can learn more about financing their vehicle. The second hyperlink should be to a Web site that provides additional information about buying a new or used car. Save the file again.

 After you show the workbook (created in the first part of the Chapter Challenge) to the owner, he suggests sorting the list in a different order. Use the Help feature to learn how to perform single and multiple sorts. After reading about ways to sort, provide the owner with various types of sorts. First, sort the list in descending order by final price. Print the workbook. Then sort the list in ascending order by type of vehicle and then by price (ascending order.) Save the workbook again.

 After working at Allen's Auto Sales for six months, you decide that maintaining the inventory of vehicles could be managed better in a database application. Use Microsoft Access to create a database named **Cars**. Using the workbook created in the first part of the Chapter Challenge, import the section of the worksheet that includes the vehicle type, price, destination charges, rebate, and final price as a table into the **Cars** database. Add one more record to the table. Save the table.

WORKPLACE Ready

Maintaining and Enhancing Workbooks

ASSESSING proficiency

In this unit, you have learned to create, save, print, edit, and format Excel In this unit, you have learned how to work with multiple windows; move, copy, link and paste data between workbooks and applications; create and customize charts with data in a worksheet; save a workbook as a Web page; insert hyperlinks; and insert and customize clip art images, diagrams, WordArt, and drawn objects.

Assessment 1

1. Open **ExcelWorksheet19**.
2. Save the worksheet with Save As and name it **seu2pa01**.
3. Make the following changes to the worksheet:
   a. Type **Ave.** in cell D2.
   b. Apply the same top and bottom border to cell D2 that is applied to cells A2 through C2.
   c. Merge and center cells A1 through D1.
   d. Delete row 14 (the row for Kwieciak, Kathleen).
   e. Insert a formula in cell D3 that averages the percentages in cells B3 and C3.
   f. Copy the formula in cell D3 down to cells D4 through D19.
   g. Make cell A21 active, turn on bold, and then type **Highest Averages**.
   h. Display the Clipboard task pane. (Make sure the Clipboard task pane is empty.)
   i. Select and then copy each of the following rows (individually): row 6, 9, 13, 15, and 17.
   j. Make cell A22 active and then paste row 13 (the row for Jewett, Troy).
   k. Make cell A23 active and then paste row 6 (the row for Cumpston, Kurt).
   l. Make cell A24 active and then paste row 9 (the row for Fisher-Edwards, Teri).
   m. Make cell A25 active and then paste row 15 (the row for Markovits, Claude).
   n. Make cell A26 active and then paste row 17 (the row for Nyegaard, Curtis).
   o. Click the Clear All button in the Clipboard task pane and then close the task pane.
4. Save, print, and then close **seu2pa01**.

Assessment 2

1. Open **ExcelWorksheet17**.
2. Save the worksheet with Save As and name it **seu2pa02**.
3. Select cells A1 through C11 and then copy the cells to *Sheet2*.
4. With *Sheet2* displayed, make the following changes:
   a. Automatically adjust the width of columns A, B, and C.
   b. Delete the contents of cell B2.
   c. Change the contents of the following cells:

      A6: Change *January* to *July*
      A7: Change *February* to *August*
      A8: Change *March* to *September*
      A9: Change *April* to *October*
      A10: Change *May* to *November*
      A11: Change *June* to *December*
      B6: Change *8.30%* to *8.10%*
      B8: Change *9.30%* to *8.70%*

5. Make *Sheet1* active and then copy cell B2 and paste link it to cell B2 in *Sheet2*.
6. Make *Sheet1* active and then determine the effect on projected monthly earnings if the projected yearly income is increased by 10% by changing the number in cell B2 to *$1,480,380*.
7. Save the workbook (two worksheets) again and then print both worksheets of the workbook so they are horizontally and vertically centered on each page.
8. Determine the effect on projected monthly earnings if the projected yearly income is increased by 20% by changing the number in cell B2 to *$1,614,960*.
9. Save the workbook again and then print both worksheets of the workbook so they are horizontally and vertically centered on each page.
10. Save and then close **seu2pa02**.

Assessment 3

1. Open **ExcelWorksheet41**.
2. Save the workbook with Save As and name it **seu2pa03**.
3. Make the following changes to the workbook:
   a. Insert the heading *Average Sales 2003-2005* (on multiple lines) in cell A13.
   b. Insert a formula in cell B13 with a 3-D reference that averages the total in cells B4 through B11 in *Sheet1*, *Sheet2*, and *Sheet3*.
   c. Make cell B13 active and then change to the Currency Style with zero decimal places.
   d. Insert a formula in cell C13 with a 3-D reference that averages the total in cells C4 through C11 in *Sheet1*, *Sheet2*, and *Sheet3*.
   e. Make cell C13 active and then change to the Currency Style with zero decimal places.
4. Rename *Sheet1* to *2003 Sales*, rename *Sheet2* to *2004 Sales*, and rename *Sheet3* to *2005 Sales*.
5. Save the workbook and then print the entire workbook.
6. Close **seu2pa03**.

Assessment 4

1. Open Excel and then type the following information in a worksheet (The text *Country* and *Total Sales* should be set in bold.):

Country	Total Sales
Denmark	$85,345
Finland	$71,450
Norway	$135,230
Sweden	$118,895

2. Using the data just entered in the worksheet, create a column chart as a separate sheet.
3. Save the workbook (worksheet plus chart sheet) and name it **seu2pa04**.
4. Print only the sheet containing the chart.
5. Change the column chart to a line chart of your choosing.
6. Print only the sheet containing the chart.
7. Save and then close **seu2pa04**.

Assessment 5

1. Open **ExcelWorksheet42**.
2. Save the worksheet with Save As and name it **seu2pa05**.
3. Create a pie chart as a separate sheet with the data in cells A3 through B10. You determine the type of pie. Include an appropriate title for the chart and include percentage labels.
4. Print only the sheet containing the chart.
5. Save and then close **seu2pa05**.

Assessment 6

1. Create a new folder named *TravelWebPages* in the ExcelUnit02S folder on your disk.
2. Open **ExcelWorksheet40**.
3. Save the worksheet as a Single File Web Page in the TravelWebPages folder with the following specifications:
   a. Name the Web page **TravelAdvantageWebPage**.
   b. Change the title to *Winter Getaway Destinations!*
4. Preview the Web page in the default browser.
5. Make sure you are connected to the Internet and then search for sites that might be of interest to tourists for each of the cities in the TravelAdvantageWebPage. Write down the URL for the best Web page you find for each city.
6. Create a hyperlink in TravelAdvantageWebPage for each city to jump to the URL you wrote down in Step 5.
7. Test the hyperlinks to make sure you entered the URLs correctly by clicking each hyperlink and then closing the Web browser.
8. Save, print, and then close **TravelAdvantageWebPage**.

Assessment 7

1. Open **ExcelWorksheet14**.
2. Save the worksheet with Save As and name it **seu2pa07**.
3. Make the following changes to the worksheet:
   a. Insert a formula in cell C3 using an absolute reference to determine the projected quotas at 10% of the current quotas.

b. Copy the formula in cell C3 down to cells C4 through C12.
c. Increase the height of row 1 (you determine the height) and then insert a clip art image in row 1 related to *money*. You determine the size and position of the clip art image.
4. Save, print, and then close **seu2pa07**.

Assessment 8

1. Open **ExcelWorksheet33**.
2. Save the worksheet with Save As and name it **seu2pa08**.
3. Make the following changes to the worksheet:
   a. Insert a new row at the beginning of the worksheet.
   b. Select and then merge cells A1 through D1.
   c. Increase the height of row 1 to approximately 100.00.
   d. Insert the text Custom Interiors as WordArt in cell A1. You determine the formatting and shape of the WordArt. Move and size the WordArt so it fits in cell A1.
   e. Insert the following comments in the specified cells:

      D4 = Increase amount to $100,000.
      A5 = Change the name to Gresham Technology.
      A9 = Decrease amounts for this company by 5%.

4. Turn on the display of all comments.
5. Print the worksheet with the comments as displayed on the worksheet.
6. Turn off the display of all comments.
7. Delete the comment in A5.
8. Print the worksheet again with the comments printed at the end of the worksheet. (The comments will print on a separate page from the worksheet.)
9. Save and then close **seu2pa08**.

Assessment 9

1. Open **ExcelWorksheet03**.
2. Save the worksheet with Save As and name it **seu2pa09**.
3. Make the following changes to the worksheet so it displays as shown in figure U2.1:
   a. Insert a new row at the beginning of the worksheet.
   b. Select and then merge cells A1 through D1.
   c. Select cells A2 through D9 and then apply the List 2 autoformat.
   d. Select cells B4 through D9 and then click the Percent Style button.
   e. Increase the height of row 1 to the approximate size shown in figure U2.1.
   f. Insert the text SOLAR ENTERPRISES in cell A1 centered horizontally and vertically and set the text in 18-point Arial bold.
   g. Insert and fill the shapes using the AutoShapes button on the Drawing toolbar. (To find the Sun shape, click Draw, point to Basic Shapes, and then click Sun.)
4. Save, print, and then close **seu2pa09**.

	A	B	C	D	E
1	SOLAR ENTERPRISES				
2	ANALYSIS OF FINANCIAL CONDITION				
3		Actual	Planned	Prior Year	
4	Stockholder's equity ratio	62%	60%	57%	
5	Bond holder's equity ratio	45%	39%	41%	
6	Liability liquidity ratio	122%	115%	120%	
7	Fixed obligation security ratio	196%	190%	187%	
8	Fixed interest ratio	23%	20%	28%	
9	Earnings ratio	7%	6%	6%	
10					

FIGURE U2.1 • Assessment 9

WRITING activities

The following activities give you the opportunity to practice your writing skills along with demonstrating an understanding of some of the important Excel features you have mastered in this unit. Use correct grammar, appropriate word choices, and clear sentence constructions.

Activity 1

Suppose that you are the accounting assistant in the financial department of McCormack Funds and you have been asked to prepare a yearly proposed department budget. The total amount for the department is $1,450,000. You are given the percentages for the proposed budget items, which are: Salaries, 45%; Benefits, 12%; Training, 14%; Administrative Costs, 10%; Equipment, 11%; and Supplies, 8%. Create a worksheet with this information that shows the projected yearly budget, the budget items in the department, the percentage of the budget, and the amount for each item. After the worksheet is completed, save it and name it **seu2act01**. Print and then close **seu2act01**.

Activity 2

Prepare a worksheet in Excel for Carefree Travels that includes the following information (the text *Scandinavian Tours, Country* and *Tours Booked* should be set in bold):

Scandinavian Tours	
Country	Tours Booked
Norway	52
Sweden	62
Finland	29
Denmark	38

Use the information in the worksheet to create a bar chart as a separate worksheet. Save the workbook (worksheet and chart) and name it **seu2act02**. Print only the sheet containing the chart and then close **seu2act02**.

Activity 3

Prepare a worksheet for Carefree Travels that advertises a snow skiing trip. Include the following information in the announcement:

- At the beginning of the worksheet, create a company logo that includes the company name *Carefree Travels* and a clip art image related to travel.

- Include the heading *Whistler Ski Vacation Package* in the worksheet.

- Include the following below the heading:
  - Round-trip air transportation: $395
  - Hotel accommodations for seven nights: $1,550
  - Four all-day ski passes: $425
  - Compact rental car with unlimited mileage: $250
  - Total price of the ski package: (calculate the total price)

- Include the following information somewhere in the worksheet:
  - Book your vacation today at special discount prices
  - Two-for-one discount at many of the local ski resorts

Save the completed worksheet and name it **seu2act03**. Print and then close **seu2act03**.

INTERNET project

Make sure you are connected to the Internet. Using a search engine of your choosing, locate two companies on the Internet that sell new books. At the first new book company site, locate three books on Microsoft Excel. Record the title, author, and price for each book. At the second new book company site, locate the same three books and record the prices. Create an Excel worksheet that includes the following information:

- Name of each new book company
- Title and author of the three books
- Prices for each book from the two book company sites

Create a hyperlink for each book company to the URL on the Internet. Save the completed worksheet and name it **seu2intact**. Print and then close **seu2intact**.

JOB study

Create an invoice form in Excel for the customers of your lawn business from the Unit 1 Job Study. Using the drawing tools, design a logo that will go at the top left corner. Use borders and shading to separate various sections. You can use the Invoice template found within Excel as a sample. Save your template file as **LawnTemplate**. Print one copy. Be sure to copy your template file to the Microsoft

EXCEL

template files folder found on your computer's hard drive. Print out a picture of the directory containing your new **LawnTemplate** file and the other Excel templates.

Open the file *LawnBusiness* you created in the Unit 1 Job Study and create three different chart types for the expenses section and three different chart types for the income section. You determine the options for each chart. Print each chart on a separate worksheet tab. Rename the worksheet tabs accordingly. You will incorporate these six charts into a presentation about your expansion project for the following year that you will give to a potential lender. Save your file as **LawnCharts**.